WOMEN AND EMPOWERMENT

WOMEN AND WORLD DEVELOPMENT SERIES

This series has been developed by the **UN/NGO Group on Women and Development** and makes available the most recent information, debate and action being taken on world development issues, and the impact on women. Each volume is fully illustrated and attractively presented. Each outlines its particular subject, as well as including an introduction to resources and guidance on how to use the books in workshops and seminars. The aim of each title is to bring women's concerns more directly and effectively into the development process, and to achieve an improvement in women's status in our rapidly changing world.

The Group was established in 1980 to organize the production and distribution of UN/NGO development education materials. It was the first time that United Nations agencies and non-governmental organizations had collaborated in this way, and the Group remains a unique example of co-operation between international and non-governmental institutions.

SERIES TITLES – in order of scheduled publication

- **WOMEN AND THE WORLD ECONOMIC CRISIS** PREPARED BY JEANNE VICKERS
- **WOMEN AND DISABILITY** PREPARED BY ESTHER R. BOYLAN
- **WOMEN AND HEALTH** PREPARED BY PATRICIA SMYKE
- **WOMEN AND THE ENVIRONMENT** PREPARED BY ANNABEL RODDA
- **REFUGEE WOMEN** PREPARED BY SUSAN FORBES MARTIN
- **WOMEN AND LITERACY** PREPARED BY MARCELA BALLARA
- **WOMEN AND HUMAN RIGHTS** PREPARED BY KATARINA TOMAŠEVSKI
- **WOMEN AND THE FAMILY** PREPARED BY HELEN O'CONNELL
- **WOMEN AND WORK** PREPARED BY SUSAN BULLOCK
- **WOMEN AND EMPOWERMENT: Participation and Decision Making** PREPARED BY MARILEE KARL

For full details, as well as order forms, please write to:
ZED BOOKS LTD, 7 CYNTHIA STREET, LONDON N1 9JF, U.K. and 165 First Avenue, Atlantic Highlands, New Jersey 07716, U.S.A.

WOMEN AND EMPOWERMENT

PARTICIPATION AND DECISION MAKING

PREPARED BY MARILEE KARL

Zed Books Ltd · London & New Jersey

Women and Empowerment: Participation and Decision Making was first published by Zed Books Ltd, 7 Cynthia Street, London N1 9JF, United Kingdom and 165 First Avenue, Atlantic Highlands, New Jersey 07716, United States of America, in 1995.

The views in this publication do not necessarily reflect the views of the United Nations or the donor agencies.

Cover and book design by Lee Robinson
Cover Photo: M. Eugenie Jelincic
Typeset by Action Typesetting Limited, Gloucester
Printed and bound in the United Kingdom at The Bath Press, Avon.

British Library Cataloguing in Publication Data

A catalogue record for this book is available from the British Library

ISBN 1 85649 191 9
ISBN 1 85649 192 7

Library of Congress Cataloging-in-Publication Data

A catalog record for this book is available from the US Library of Congress

Table 5.1 is taken from Caroline Moser, *Gender Planning and Development: Theory, Practice and Training* (1993) and is reprinted by kind permission of Routledge Publishers, London.

CONTENTS

ACKNOWLEDGEMENTS

Financial contributions:

- Canadian International Development Agency (CIDA)
- Lutheran World Federation (LWF)
- United Nations Development Fund for Women (UNIFEM)
- United States Agency for International Development (USAID)

Editorial panel members:

- Baha'i International Community
- International Council of Jewish Women (ICJW)
- International Council of Women (ICW)
- International Council on Social Welfare (ICSW)
- International Federation of Home Economists (IFHE)
- International Federation of University Women (IFUW)
- International Organization of Consumers Unions (IOCU)
- Inter-Parliamentary Union (IPU)
- Isis–WICCE
- La Leche League International
- Lutheran World Federation (LWF)
- Soroptimist International
- United Nations Centre for Human Rights
- United Nations Children's Fund (UNICEF)
- United Nations Development Programme (UNDP)
- United Nations Economic Commission for Europe (ECE)
- United Nations Economic Commission for Latin America and the Caribbean (ECLAC)
- United Nations Food and Agriculture Organization (FAO)
- United Nations Research Institute for Social Development (UNRISD)
- United Nations University/World Institute for Development and Economic Research (UNU/WIDER)
- United Nations Volunteers (UNV)
- Women's International League for Peace and Freedom (WILPF)
- Young Women's Christian Association (YWCA)
- Zonta International

Special thanks for contribution of articles, research material and illustrations:

- Baha'i International Community
- Center for Women's Global Leadership
- Committee for Asian Women, Hong Kong
- GABRIELA
- International Labour Office (ILO)
- International Women's Tribune Centre
- Inter-Parliamentary Union
- Isis International
- Irina Shupick, researcher and activist in Ukraine
- Sister Namibia, Namibia
- Speak Magazine, South Africa
- UNICEF
- Women's Feature Service, India
- Yeshica Weerasekera and Amie Diop of the African Network for Integrated Development, Senegal

INTRODUCTION

THIS BOOK is the tenth and concluding title in the Women and World Development Series. The series, prepared by the UN-NGO Group on Women and Development, a project co-ordinated since 1989 by the United Nations Non-Governmental Liaison Service (NGLS), Geneva, is the outcome of an interactive, collaborative process of work of United Nations agencies and non-governmental organizations (NGOs).

Altogether over one hundred organizations from all five continents participated in the different stages of the production of the series. Their participation provided a basic element of the unique UN-NGO co-operation that is part of the global process of women's mobilization for empowerment.

Special appreciation is due to the United Nations Non-Governmental Liaison Service and the Finnish International Development Agency (FINNIDA) for providing two programme co-ordinators, Yvonne Backholm (1990–91) and Kirsti Floor (1992–94), for the production of the Women and World Development series. The titles in the series are listed at the beginning of this book.

This last book in the series focuses on how women are mobilizing around the world to participate in the life of their communities and in society. Participation is understood as part of a process of empowerment that leads to greater decision-making power and the transformation of society through the inclusion of women's priorities and perspectives.

Chapter 1 gives an overview of the extensiveness of gender discrimination and the low status of women in society, and its consequences. It looks at factors affecting women's participation and at the concept of empowerment.

Chapters 2 and 3 review the history of women's participation and look at different strategies and achievements of non-governmental organizations and movements for the promotion of women.

Chapter 4 is concerned with women in electoral politics and public life as well as with mechanisms and strategies for increasing women's participation in this sphere.

Chapter 5 is devoted to women and development. It reviews the evolution in thinking on women's participation in development, and discusses interlinkages between women's empowerment and development.

Chapter 6 traces how international mechanisms can be used to increase women's participation and empowerment and the ways women are working in and around the United Nations to address their concerns and advance their status.

The annexes give further information on some of the mechanisms and strategies women use for their empowerment.

1 OBSTACLES AND OPPORTUNITIES

People's participation is becoming the central issue of our time... People today have an urge – an impatient urge – to participate in the events and processes that shape their lives.[1]

WOMEN ARE A MAJOR FORCE behind people's participation in the life of society today: not only do they comprise the majority of those excluded from participation, but they play a leading role in the emergence of groups, organizations and movements worldwide, and are becoming increasingly active in their communities, governments and the international arena.

Why is women's participation so important? In the first place, there can be no true democracy, no true people's participation in governance and development without the equal participation of women and men in all spheres of life and levels of decision making. Second, the goals of development cannot be attained without women's full participation not only in the development process, but also in shaping its goals. And third, women's participation is changing the world in which we live by bringing new priorities and perspectives to the political process and the organization of society. In focusing attention on the most neglected portion of humanity today, women and girls, women's participation will make society more responsive to the needs of all people. In bringing new insights and contributions to all issues, it will enrich and shift the focus and content of discourse in politics and society to include a wider range of views. In raising the status of women and girl children, it will improve the economic and social development of countries. In changing the unequal balance of decision-making power and control in the relations of men and women – in the household, in the workplace, in communities, in government and in the international arena – it will lead to women's empowerment.

Participation has two dimensions: quantitative and qualitative. The tendency in the past has been to focus mainly on the quantitative aspects of people's participation and to measure it principally in terms of numbers of people, irrespective of the quality of their participation or their involvement in decision-making processes. For instance, development agencies often considered people's participation mainly in terms of the numbers involved in development programmes and projects. In this sense, women's participation was measured by how many women were affected by a project even if they were simply passive recipients of development aid, without any voice in the design, implementation or monitoring and evaluation of the project. Similarly, in workers', political and social change organizations and movements, women often make up the majority of the rank and file, but comprise a minority of the leadership and decision makers. There is, of course, a relationship between the quantitative and qualitative aspects of participation: the larger the numbers of participants, the more possibilities exist to make a difference. It generally takes a critical mass of women to effect change. Other factors, however, such as universal gender discrimination, present obstacles not only to the number of women participants but also to their access to leadership and decision making.

Today the focus is changing from the quantitative to the qualitative aspects and participation is conceptualized in broader terms. According to the *Human Development Report 1993*, prepared by the United Nations Development Programme (UNDP):

PHOTO: OLGA YOLANDA LOPEZ/ISIS INTERNATIONAL

Women are increasingly making their voices heard in the political arena

Participation means that people are closely involved in the economic, social, cultural and political processes that affect their lives. People may, in some cases, have complete and direct control over these processes – in other cases, the control may be partial or indirect. The important thing is that people have constant access to decision-making and power. Participation in this sense is an essential element of human development.[2]

FORMS OF PARTICIPATION ☐ The UNDP *Human Development Report* identifies four basic forms of participation:

- household participation
- economic participation
- social and cultural participation
- political participation.

These forms of participation are interrelated and cannot be viewed in isolation. As the *Human Development Report 1993* states:

Since participation can take place in the economic, social and political arenas, each person necessarily participates in many ways, at many levels. In economic life as a producer or a consumer, an entrepreneur or an employee. In social life as a member of a family, or of a community organization or ethnic group. And in political life as a voter, or as a member of a political party or perhaps a pressure group. All these roles overlap and interact, forming patterns of participation that interconnect with — and often reinforce — each other.[3]

HOUSEHOLD PARTICIPATION The household is often the main – and sometimes the only – place where women participate. Women are almost universally responsible for caring for children and other members of the household and for all the domestic work that their caring roles entail. They often have primary responsibility for their families' health and for the provision of food, water and fuel, and their work is not only unpaid, but largely unrecognized as well. Their major responsibilities for the household's well-being do not always mean decision-making power within the family. In many cases, women do not have equal control over the management and allocation of family income, especially if the income has been earned by the men in the family. This fact has only recently been recognized by development agencies, which in the past usually looked at the household as a unit in which an increase in men's income would benefit the whole household equally. Studies have shown, however, that men and women generally spend their incomes in different ways: women use their income to meet the basic needs of their families, such as food, education, health care and clothing, while men devote a greater percentage of their income to non-essential personal goods. Thus women's ability to participate in household decision making has an effect on the well-being of the entire family.

Women's status in the household also affects their ability to participate outside the home. While women can often assert influence over public life through the males of their household, women's secondary status in the family frequently prevents or limits them from taking a direct part in the outside world. Moreover, since women carry the major burden of child care and domestic work, they often face severe time constraints on their participation outside the home. Democratization and redressing the gender imbalance in the home are therefore crucial to women's wider participation and entail not only increasing women's control in the household, but also a more equal partnership of men and women in sharing household responsibilities. Whilst democracy begins in the home, a frequent result of women's increasing involvement in society is their greater decision-making power in the home as well.

ECONOMIC PARTICIPATION Women's economic participation has, on the whole, been increasing. Great inequalities remain, however, between men and women in employment opportunities and rights, remuneration, and recognition of women's economic participation. As the UNDP *Human Development Report 1993* says:

The nature of economic participation can vary widely, from forms of drudgery to creative, productive and independent economic activity. Societies also vary greatly in the value they place on forms of work, ranging from the association of manual work with servitude to a respect for manual labour in more egalitarian societies. And closely related to this range of social attitudes is the nature of the work environment itself, which can be more or less participatory.[4]

Overall, women have far fewer job opportunities than men and are disproportionately found in lower paid and less prestigious occupations. They earn far less even when performing the same work as men. Women hold only a small proportion of management positions and are seldom in the leadership of trade unions, which may explain, at least in part, women's weak position in regard to rights such as maternity leave and job security, and the provision of social services such as child care. Women who work outside the home are still responsible for the domestic work of the household and thus bear a double work burden, which is an obstacle both to better employment opportunities and to social and political participation.

PHOTO: ANNE MARIE GAUDRAS/UNICEF

Women's participation is greatest in community organizations

Women's unpaid household work is usually not valued or considered a contribution to the economy. Lack of income, or lower income, also reduces women's decision-making power in the household and their ability to participate in social and political activities. The inequalities women face in economic participation have an adverse effect on women's self-esteem and their status in society:

Participation in economic life also affords people a basis for self-respect and social dignity, attributes that are integral to participating in all dimensions of life.[5]

SOCIAL AND CULTURAL PARTICIPATION Women participate in the life of society through community associations, religious groups, and a wide variety of other groups and organizations, in which they often comprise the majority of members. A great many factors affect women's social participation, including their household and economic status and traditional customs and attitudes which may either promote or inhibit their activities. In societies with conservative attitudes towards women's participation outside the home or where strong discrimination against women exists, women's social roles may be limited. In many societies, women play a significant part in the cultural life of their communities as the members of the community who preserve the traditional culture in song, dance, storytelling, art and ritual.

POLITICAL PARTICIPATION Women's political participation takes many forms: it includes not only voting and holding public office, but also collective action in associations and organizations. In the sphere of electoral politics, women have made great strides forward in obtaining the vote and the right to be elected to political office in nearly every country, yet today they comprise only 10 per cent of the members of parliaments worldwide and hold only a fraction of other leadership positions nationally and internationally. In the national and international civil services, which are playing an increasingly powerful role in politics and public life today, women occupy only a small portion of the management positions, although many are to be found at the lower levels.

The major sphere of women's political participation is that of community groups, and of women's and other non-governmental organizations (NGOs) on the local, national and international levels. This type of political participation is no less important than participation in government. As Arvonne Fraser, former director of the International Women's Rights Action Watch (IWRAW), states:

Non-governmental organizations are the conscience of the body politic, whether they are providing social welfare services or advocating for changes in public policies. Civil societies cannot exist long without them because NGOs are a check on the power of governments. Every government needs to be held accountable by its citizens, and citizens acting together in non-governmental associations are far more powerful than individuals acting separately. NGOs also have the freedom to generate, test out and promote the adoption of new ideas, policies and programs.[6]

Whilst women have a long history of participation in such organizations, their involvement has increased greatly over the past two decades and they have achieved notable successes in influencing the political agenda through such organizations and through movements for social change. Women's participation in development agencies, projects and programmes has had an impact on development policies.

HOW FAR HAVE WOMEN COME? □

Contrasting views exist on the progress women have made in terms of their political participation. On the one hand, a study on women's political participation by the United Nations Economic Commission for Latin America and the Caribbean (ECLAC) presents an optimistic view:

Since the turn of the century, women have come a long way as regards political participation ... their increased visibility, acquisition of full citizenship and greater education make it impossible to conceive of building a long-term future without their participation.[7]

It is also true, however, that far fewer women than men participate politically, economically and socially, and women have far less decision-making power. As the *Human Development Report 1993* states:

Women are the world's largest excluded group. Even though they make up half the adult population, and often contribute more than their share to society, inside and outside the home, they are frequently excluded from positions of power.[8]

An examination of gender discrimination, that is, discrimination against women, reveals enormous gaps between men and women in all societies, and many of the obstacles that prevent women's equal social participation. Without statistics, however, it is difficult to obtain systematic information on the extent of gender discrimination, or for governments, intergovernmental agencies and other planning and policy-making bodies to assess the situation and respond to the needs of women and their families in ways which improve gender equality. For instance, lack of accurate information on women's role in agricultural production has resulted in the failure of development programmes and projects because they did not address the needs of women farmers. On the other hand:

At the village or community level, an accurate reflection of the contribution of women farmers in statistics will further provide the justification for fundamental changes in policy, plans and the allocation of agricultural resources so that all farmers, both female and male, benefit. This would effectively remove many of the constraints women farmers face in increasing their productivity.[9]

Statistics also provide women's organizations with an important instrument with which to pressure and lobby national and international bodies, to influence policies and programmes, and to make the case for the need for further gathering of statistics.

Over the past few decades, women researchers, activists and organizations have called attention to the fact that economic and social advances and development do not necessarily benefit all people equally, and to the need to disaggregate statistics by sex. When statistics distinguish between men and women, they reveal that the position of women lags far behind that of men, and that in some countries gender disparity is even growing. As the former Secretary-General of the United Nations, Javier Pérez de Cuéllar, says in introducing the book *The World's Women 1970–1990*:

It is clear from these data and indicators that, although there have been some improvements for women over the past 20 years, the majority still lag far behind men in power, wealth and opportunity. Data are needed to generate awareness of the present situation, to guide policy, to mobilize action and to monitor progress towards improvements.[10]

The World's Women 1970–1990 is a collaborative effort by many United Nations bodies to present as clear and comprehensive a picture as possible of women's condition and how it has or has not changed over the two decades in the areas of: family and households; public life and leadership; education and training; health and child-bearing; housing, human settlements and the environment; women's work and the economy. On women's participation in public life and leadership, the report reaches the following conclusion:

Women are poorly represented in the ranks of power, policy and decision-making. Women make up less than 5 per cent of the world's heads of State, heads of major corporations and top positions in international organizations. Women are not just behind in political and managerial equity, they are a long way behind. This is in spite of the fact that women are found in large numbers in low-level positions of public administrations, political parties, trade unions and businesses.[11]

Growing awareness of gender disparities has led to increased efforts by United Nations bodies, governments and non-governmental organizations to gather statistics on women and to pinpoint the male-female discrepancies. For instance, the United Nations Children's Fund (UNICEF) produces an annual report, *The Progress of Nations*, which ranks the nations of the world according to their achievements in health, nutrition, education, family planning and the progress of women in terms of literacy, maternal mortality and participation in politics. UNICEF is also collecting age and sex-disaggregated data, and some countries

TABLE 1.1
DIFFERENCE BETWEEN HDI AND GENDER-DISPARITY-ADJUSTED HDI

COUNTRY	HDI VALUE	GENDER-DISPARITY-ADJUSTED HDI	DIFFERENCE BETWEEN HDI AND GENDER-DISPARITY-ADJUSTED RANKS
SWEDEN	0.977	0.921	4
NORWAY	0.978	0.881	1
FRANCE	0.971	0.864	5
DENMARK	0.955	0.860	8
FINLAND	0.954	0.859	8
AUSTRALIA	0.972	0.852	1
NEW ZEALAND	0.947	0.844	9
NETHERLANDS	0.970	0.826	1
USA	0.976	0.824	–3
UNITED KINGDOM	0.964	0.818	0
CANADA	0.982	0.816	–9
BELGIUM	0.952	0.808	3
AUSTRIA	0.952	0.782	1
SWITZERLAND	0.978	0.768	–10
GERMANY	0.957	0.768	–4
ITALY	0.924	0.764	3
JAPAN	0.983	0.763	–16
CZECHOSLOVAKIA	0.892	0.754	4
IRELAND	0.925	0.720	–1
LUXEMBOURG	0.943	0.713	–3
GREECE	0.902	0.691	0
PORTUGAL	0.853	0.672	3
CYPRUS	0.890	0.656	0
COSTA RICA	0.852	0.632	2
HONG KONG	0.913	0.618	–5
SINGAPORE	0.849	0.585	1
KOREA, REP. OF	0.872	0.555	–3
PARAGUAY	0.641	0.546	1
SRI LANKA	0.663	0.499	–1
PHILIPPINES	0.603	0.451	0
SWAZILAND	0.458	0.344	0
MYANMAR	0.390	0.297	0
KENYA	0.369	0.241	0

A positive difference shows that the gender-disparity-adjusted HDI rank is higher than the unadjusted HDI rank, a negative the opposite.

Source: UNDP, **Human Development Report 1993.**

and organizations are disaggregating data by race and ethnic origin as well. The Inter-Parliamentary Union (IPU) has been compiling statistics on the representation of women in parliaments and other political bodies (see Chapter 4).

Since 1990, the UNDP has been issuing an annual *Human Development Report* with extensive statistics, disaggregated by sex, in a number of areas: percentage of the population; life expectancy; literacy; mean years of schooling; enrolment at the primary, secondary and tertiary levels; and labour force participation. Statistics on maternal mortality, fertility rates and contraceptive use are also presented. The reports are designed to give a comparative rating of the world's countries on the basis of a human development index (HDI). This measure is obtained by combining indicators such as real purchasing power, education and health, and is thus able to present a more comprehensive picture of a country's development than ratings based only on the gross national product (GNP). Each country is assigned an HDI value and the countries are ranked from highest to lowest. According to the *Human Development Report 1993*, Japan ranked first with a HDI value of 0.983, while Guinea was in

GENDER DISPARITY IN JAPAN

Japan, despite some of the world's highest levels of human development, still has marked inequalities in achievement between men and women. The *Human Development Report 1993* human development index puts Japan first in the world. But when the HDI is adjusted for gender disparity, Japan slips to number 17. Here's why.

In tertiary education, the enrolment for females is only two-thirds that of males. Similarly in employment, women are considerably worse off. Women's average earnings are only 51 per cent of those of men, and women are largely excluded from decision-making positions: they hold only 7 per cent of administrative and managerial jobs. Their representation is even lower in the political sphere. Women obtained the right to vote, and to be elected to parliament, only after the Second World War. Yet today, only 2 per cent of parliamentary seats are held by women, and at the ministerial level there are no women at all (compared with 9 per cent for industrialized countries as a whole and 13 per cent for the other countries of Asia). Nevertheless, one or two women have achieved important political positions, and a number of women were among the founders of the Social Democratic Party.

In terms of legal rights in general, Japan's patrilineal society is only gradually changing to offer women greater recognition and independence. Only in 1980 was the inheritance right of a Japanese woman raised from one-third to one-half of her late husband's property (the rest goes to the children). In other aspects the law is still not gender-neutral. Thus, the legal minimum age of marriage is eighteen for men, but sixteen for women. And after divorce, a man can remarry immediately, but a woman has to wait six months.

Japan now has political and non-governmental organizations pressing for change. The League of Women Voters, for instance, is lobbying for a correction in the disparity of seat distribution in parliament, and for greater participation of women in policy making.

UNDP, *Human Development Report 1993*, New York, 1993, p. 26

last place with a HDI rank of 173 and an HDI value of 0.045.

For a number of countries the *Human Development Report 1993* presents a gender-sensitive HDI, measured on the basis of indicators for women (see Table 1.1). The changes in the countries' HDI value and rank are very revealing:

When the HDI is adjusted for gender disparity, no country improves its HDI value – The meaning: no country treats its women as well as it treats its men, a disappointing result after so many years of debate on gender equality, so many struggles by women and so many changes in national laws ... But some countries do better than others, so adjusting for gender disparity makes a big difference to the rankings: Japan falls from number 1 to 17, Canada from number 2 to 11 and Switzerland from number 4 to 14. By contrast, Sweden improves its rank from number 5 to 1, Denmark from number 16 to 7.[12]

The *Human Development Report 1993* indicates the gaps between men and women in life expectancy, population, literacy, mean years of schooling, primary, secondary and tertiary education enrolment, and labour force participation (see Table 1.2 at the end of this chapter). According to the report:

In industrial countries, gender discrimination (measured by the HDI) is mainly in employment and wages, with women often getting less than two-thirds of the employment opportunities and about half the earnings of men. In developing countries, the great disparities, besides those in the job market, are in health care, nutritional support and education. For instance, women make up two-thirds of the illiterate population. And South and East Asia, defying the normal biological result that women live longer than men, have more men than women. The reasons: high maternal mortality and infanticide and nutritional neglect of the girl-child. According to one estimate, some 100 million women are 'missing'.[13]

Attempts to relate statistics and indicators of women's status to development goals show that the status of women rises hand in hand with economic and social development. For instance, as UNICEF reports:

Girls' education correlates positively with several important national and international goals, including universal primary education, economic productivity, social development, inter-generational education, social equity and sustainability of development efforts.[14]

*GIRLS' EDUCATION AND DEVELOPMENT GOALS**

There is a positive correlation between primary education enrolment rates of girls and GNP per capita. In addition, there is definitely an overall impact of education on the economic well-being of women, their families and society, although the relationship is both multidimensional and complex ... Girls who complete primary school education participate more in the labour force and are employed in different types of occupations in that labour force. This leads to greater wage employment opportunities and more participation in self-employment and in the informal sector, which in turn leads to higher productivity, higher wage earnings, more access to credit and higher entrepreneurial earnings. For those women who do not join the formal or informal sector but

* UNICEF, **Strategies to Promote Girls' Education**, New York, 1992, pp. 12–19

remain in non-market and home production, primary education still leads to more efficient performance of domestic work, child care and production of goods for home consumption. On the other hand, larger gender disparities in education appear to reduce GNP, and the widest education gender gap exists in the lowest-income countries, where girls' enrolment in school lags behind boys' by an average of 20 per cent ... Educated mothers have healthier families. First, an inverse relationship exists between girls' education and infant mortality, and this relationship is particularly strong in low-income countries. Each added year of maternal education tends to translate into a reduction in child mortality rates. (The mortality-reducing effect of a father's education is smaller, especially in rural populations.) Further, a mother's education explains more of the variation in child mortality than many other variables, including family income, access to health care, cost of health care or total family income that can be allocated to health care. Since the mother carries the main burden of looking after the health of her children, how well she performs this task depends on the knowledge and confidence that she gains from getting an education ....

There is also a correlation between mean years of female schooling and family health. Higher levels of schooling for girls increase children's chances of getting immunized and therefore increase their chances of survival. The mothers' education appears to reduce the negative effects of poor community sanitation and water supply .... High female literacy rates correlate with lower fertility rates .... Educated women generally marry later, are more likely to practice family planning and have smaller families than their uneducated counterparts ....

Education empowers women. By increasing women's ability to earn an independent income, education increases women's status in the community and leads to greater input into family and community decision-making. Perhaps more importantly, education provides girls with a basic knowledge of their rights as individuals and as citizens of their nation and the world. Having knowledge, income and decision-making power can place women on a more equal footing with their male counterparts .... Education also provides people with the knowledge and skills to contribute to and benefit from development efforts, especially in areas of health, nutrition, water and sanitation, and the environment. Efforts in these areas are more likely to be successful if women understand the new concepts and their potential benefits, possess the skills needed to implement new ideas, and are willing to test these concepts with their families and communities .... Girls' education is a necessary condition to ensure that development efforts will be sustained. ●

FACTORS AFFECTING WOMEN'S POLITICAL PARTICIPATION ☐ Many interrelated factors affect women's ability to participate in politics and the life of society. A number of major factors have already been mentioned:

- household status
- employment and remuneration
- work-related rights (maternity leave, job security, provision of child care)
- double burden of work
- education and literacy
- health
- ability to control fertility.

In addition, there are a number of other significant factors:

PHOTO: LAUREN GOLDSMITH/UNICEF

Girls' education is essential for sustainable development

- access to financial resources
- legal rights
- tradition, cultural attitudes and religion
- socialization and self-confidence
- violence against women
- the mass media.

ACCESS TO FINANCIAL RESOURCES

Women face obstacles in accessing financial resources, such as credit and funding, to carry out political activities, whether in the field of electoral politics or in organizations.

LEGAL RIGHTS Women often face legal discrimination and restrictions that inhibit their participation in many spheres of life. Constitutional and legislative guarantees of women's rights are not always implemented, and religious laws, customary laws or personal status laws that discriminate against women may be allowed to override such constitutional declarations and legislation. Moreover, women are not always aware of their rights under the law. As an expert meeting on legal literacy pointed out:

In situations where there is de jure recognition of women's rights, the need may arise to increase awareness of such rights. Where there is no such recognition, the need to raise awareness for the purpose of agitating for such rights becomes necessary.[15]

Legal guarantees and knowledge of one's rights are not sufficient, however, unless these rights are enforced. People also need the means to be able to claim their rights, and women are the least likely to have access to the justice system.

TRADITION, CULTURAL ATTITUDES AND RELIGION Gender discrimination often stems from tradition, conservative cultural attitudes and religion or religious interpretations. In many places women are still perceived as subordinate to men. Appeal is sometimes made to tradition to justify discriminatory practices. Yet, it is invariably in relation to women that tradition is invoked, while traditional practices that interfere with men's modernization or advancement are easily done away with. Religion plays a major role in determining cultural attitudes towards women and religious interpretations can be used to inhibit women's participation.

SOCIALIZATION AND SELF-CONFIDENCE In nearly all societies, girls are socialized to identify with the family and the private sphere, while boys are brought up to act in the public sphere. Both at school and at home, girls are conditioned for roles as wives and mothers, while boys are trained in skills and encouraged to develop the self-confidence needed for public life. Gender stereotyping in educational materials, the bias against women in history books, and the lack of women leaders as role models all reinforce this. Thus, women often lack the self-confidence and skills to function in the public forum – such as the ability to speak up and voice their opinions, that men have been given the chance to develop.

VIOLENCE AGAINST WOMEN In recent years violence against women, in its many forms, has come to be recognized as a major obstacle to women's participation. Occurring in all regions of the world, violence prevents women from becoming active and causes them to pull back from participation. According to a report from the United Nations Development Fund for Women (UNIFEM):

Violence against women is often a direct obstacle to women's participation in development projects. For example, a revolving fund project of the Working Women's Forum in Madras almost collapsed when the most articulate and energetic participants started to drop out because of increased incidents of domestic violence against them after they had joined. Faced with the same problems, the Association for the Development and Integration of Women (ADIM) in Lima succeeded in its work by initiating programmes that combined income generating schemes with legal aid to battered wives and women abandoned by their partners.[16]

Similarly violence or the threat of it, in both its blatant and more subtle forms, can severely curtail women's participation in political life.

THE MASS MEDIA The mass media both reflect and perpetuate discriminatory stereotypes and negative images of women and reinforce cultural attitudes that inhibit women's participation. Moreover, the male-dominated media often fail to give attention to women's needs, concerns and achievements.

WOMEN'S DIVERSITY

☐ It is not surprising that women through their political participation have put all these factors on the agenda, whether in electoral politics or through their collective action in women's organizations and other types of organizations and movements. The following chapters will examine the ways in which this is being done.

Although all women are affected by these factors, women are not a homogeneous mass and the way they are affected varies greatly depending on their diverse situations, including their age, nationality, ethnic identity, class and income level, and

PHOTO: OLGA YOLANDA LOPEZ/ISIS INTERNATIONAL

Collective awareness building leads to action and empowerment

many other particularities. For example, a study carried out by the United Nations Economic Commission for Latin America and the Caribbean found that class significantly affects both opportunities and forms of participation. According to the study, upper-class women tend to participate in politics through the vote and often defend their privileges. Middle-income urban women are more heterogeneous and their participation takes a greater variety of forms, depending on their access to material goods, their education and their participation in the labour force. Whether they are housewives or employed, middle-income women tend to accept the status quo. Their political options are limited and their vote is easily and often manipulated.[17]

There are notable variations to this pattern. Middle-income urban women in Latin America and the Caribbean, as in other regions of the world, are often in the forefront of and/or deeply involved in social movements and campaigns such as the human rights movement, the environmental and peace movements, and women's movements. Women from low-income groups often mobilize in response to specific situations, in spontaneous movements that are sparked by repression or an immediate concern in the workplace, in the neighbourhood or community. Low-income women may also organize as the result of external encouragement by such mobilizing forces as a political party or a trade union. Once the immediate cause for mobilization is over, women's participation often decreases. The participation of lower-income women, whether urban or rural, is most often collective, as part of wider organizations, and is frequently linked to survival or the obtaining of basic needs.[18]

POLITICAL PARTICIPATION AND THE EMPOWERMENT PROCESS

□ In participating in politics, whether through electoral politics, public life, or non-governmental organizations and movements, women are empowering themselves. 'Empowerment' is a word widely used, but seldom defined. Long before the word became popular, women were speaking about gaining control over their lives, and participating in the decisions that affect them in the home and community, in government and international development policies. The word 'empowerment' captures this sense of gaining control, of participating, of decision making. More recently, the word has entered the vocabulary of development agencies, including international organizations and the United Nations.

Empowerment is a process and is not, therefore, something that can be given to people. The process of empowerment is both individual and collective, since it is through involvement in groups that people most often begin to develop their awareness and the ability to organize to take action and bring about change. Women's empowerment can be viewed as a continuum of several interrelated and mutually reinforcing components:

- Awareness building about women's situation, discrimination, and rights and opportunities as a step towards gender equality. Collective awareness building provides a sense of group identity and the power of working as a group.
- Capacity building and skills development, especially the ability to plan, make decisions, organize, manage and carry out activities, to deal with people and institutions in the world around them.
- Participation and greater control and decision-making power in the home, community and society.
- Action to bring about greater equality between men and women.

In short, empowerment is a process of awareness and capacity building leading to greater participation, to greater decision-making power and control, and to transformative action.

EMPOWERMENT

At a workshop of Pacific women entitled 'Women, Development and Empowerment', Vanessa Griffen spoke about what empowerment means to her:

'To me, the word simply means: adding to women's power .... To me, power means:

- having control, or gaining further control;
- having a say and being listened to;
- being able to define and create from a women's perspective;
- being able to influence social choices and decisions affecting the whole society (not just areas of society accepted as women's place);
- being recognised and respected as equal citizens and human beings with a contribution to make.

Power means being able to make a contribution at all levels of society and not just in the home. Power also means having women's contribution recognised and valued.'

Vanessa Griffen (ed.), *Women, Development and Empowerment: A Pacific Feminist Perspective,* Asian and Pacific Development Centre, Kuala Lumpur, 1987, pp. 117–18

TABLE 1.2
FEMALE – MALE GAPS

DEVELOPING COUNTRIES

	FEMALES AS A PERCENTAGE OF MALES (SEE NOTE)									
HDI RANK	LIFE EXPECTANCY 1990	POPULATION 1990	LITERACY 1970	LITERACY 1990	MEAN YEARS OF SCHOOLING 1990	PRIMARY ENROLMENT 1960	PRIMARY ENROLMENT 1988–90	SECONDARY ENROLMENT 1988–90	TERTIARY ENROLMENT 1988–90	LABOUR FORCE 1990
High human development	110	100	90	98	86	95	100	99	80	42
20 Barbados	107	109	–	–	93	–	98	92	–	92
24 Hong Kong	107	94	71	–	63	85	99	106	56	57
27 Cyprus	107	101	–	–	86	–	100	102	114	60
30 Uruguay	109	103	100	99	110	100	98	–	114	45
31 Trinidad and Tobago	107	101	94	–	101	98	100	104	68	38
32 Bahamas	–	106	–	–	94	–	–	–	–	90
33 Korea, Rep. of	109	100	86	94	61	90	100	97	53	51
36 Chile	110	102	98	100	92	96	92	108	82	45
42 Costa Rica	106	98	99	101	97	98	100	105	68	40
43 Singapore	108	97	60	–	66	93	100	104	–	64
44 Brunei Darussalam	–	94	–	–	83	–	–	–	–	–
46 Argentina	110	102	98	100	105	101	107	113	117	27
50 Venezuela	109	98	90	103	97	100	103	–	91	27
51 Dominica	–	–	–	–	91	–	–	–	–	72
52 Kuwait	106	76	65	87	79	78	98	94	129	16
53 Mexico	110	100	88	94	96	94	97	102	76	46
55 Qatar	107	60	–	–	93	–	98	112	–	8
Medium human development	105	96	59	80	65	83	99	82	57	66
Excluding China	105	99	–	87	75	–	95	88	75	54
56 Mauritius	108	102	77	–	68	90	102	100	52	54
57 Malaysia	106	98	66	81	91	77	100	105	95	45
58 Bahrain	106	73	–	84	67	–	98	101	–	11
59 Grenada	–	–	–	–	93	–	–	–	–	94
60 Antigua and Barbuda	–	–	–	–	80	–	–	–	–	–
61 Colombia	109	99	96	98	106	100	103	119	108	69
63 Seychelles	–	101	–	–	92	–	99	100	–	74
65 Suriname	107	102	–	100	92	–	100	119	113	41
67 United Arab Emirates	106	48	29	–	101	–	100	114	–	7
68 Panama	106	97	100	100	106	96	106	109	–	37
69 Jamaica	106	101	101	100	97	101	98	111	75	45
70 Brazil	109	101	91	97	94	96	–	90	100	54
71 Fiji	107	99	–	–	83	–	101	104	57	23
72 Saint Lucia	–	106	–	–	96	–	–	–	–	–
73 Turkey	105	95	49	79	50	64	93	64	55	49
74 Thailand	106	99	84	96	76	90	–	97	–	88
75 Cuba	105	97	101	98	103	100	99	112	–	46
76 Saint Vincent	–	–	–	–	95	–	–	–	–	–
79 Saint Kitts and Nevis	–	–	–	–	97	–	–	–	–	–
81 Syrian Arab Rep.	106	98	33	–	60	44	93	72	72	18
82 Belize	–	–	–	–	93	–	98	–	–	49
84 Saudi Arabia	106	84	13	66	26	–	81	75	73	8
85 South Africa	110	101	–	–	90	90	–	–	–	50
86 Sri Lanka	106	99	81	89	80	90	100	107	71	59
87 Libyan Arab Jamahiriya	106	91	22	67	23	26	90	–	–	10

89	Ecuador	107	99	91	95	92	91	98	104	68	43
90	Paraguay	107	97	88	96	88	86	99	107	88	70
91	Korea, Dem. Rep. of	110	101	–	–	63	–	–	100	–	85
92	Philippines	106	99	96	99	89	95	98	104	–	59
93	Tunisia	103	98	39	76	41	49	91	80	67	15
94	Oman	106	91	–	–	22	–	94	81	80	9
95	Peru	106	99	74	86	80	75	96	–	24	49
96	Iraq	103	96	36	71	69	38	87	64	64	6
97	Dominican Rep.	107	97	94	96	87	99	100	–	–	17
98	Samoa	–	–	–	–	78	–	–	–	–	–
99	Jordan	106	95	45	79	66	63	–	–	–	11
100	Mongolia	104	99	85	–	95	99	103	110	–	83
101	China	105	94	–	73	60	–	100	77	50	76
102	Lebanon	106	106	73	83	66	94	92	71	44	37
103	Iran, Islamic Rep. of	101	97	43	67	68	48	91	73	45	21
104	Botswana	111	109	–	78	97	–	106	–	76	55
105	Guyana	109	99	–	98	91	–	100	105	76	27
106	Vanuatu	–	92	–	–	71	–	–	–	–	86
107	Algeria	103	100	28	65	18	67	88	80	44	5
108	Indonesia	106	101	64	85	58	67	96	84	–	66
109	Gabon	107	103	51	66	33	–	–	–	41	61
110	El Salvador	111	104	87	92	98	–	103	100	73	81
111	Nicaragua	104	100	98	–	110	102	104	–	121	51
Low human development		103	97	44	59	39	50	99	62	41	39
Excluding India		105	100	45	65	43	50	81	63	35	42
112	Maldives	–	–	–	–	77	–	–	–	–	25
113	Guatemala	108	98	73	75	86	78	85	68	–	34
114	Cape Verde	103	112	–	–	39	–	95	100	–	41
115	Viet Nam	107	104	–	91	59	–	94	93	28	88
116	Honduras	107	98	91	94	93	99	106	–	65	22
117	Swaziland	107	103	–	–	82	–	105	96	68	67
118	Solomon Islands	–	–	–	–	70	–	–	–	–	–
119	Morocco	106	100	29	62	36	40	68	70	59	26
120	Lesotho	117	108	–	–	–	–	119	–	–	78
121	Zimbabwe	106	102	75	82	40	–	100	85	36	54
122	Bolivia	109	103	68	83	60	64	90	84	–	31
123	Myanmar	106	101	67	81	72	85	98	92	–	60
124	Egypt	104	97	40	54	42	65	79	75	53	12
125	Sao Tome and Principe	–	–	–	–	39	–	–	–	–	–
126	Congo	110	103	38	63	35	51	–	–	20	64
127	Kenya	107	100	43	–	42	47	96	70	45	67
128	Madagascar	106	102	77	83	65	78	98	90	82	66
129	Papua New Guinea	103	93	62	58	50	12	85	63	38	64
130	Zambia	104	103	56	81	45	67	98	56	37	40
131	Ghana	107	101	42	73	46	48	81	65	26	67
132	Pakistan	100	92	37	45	25	28	55	45	41	13
133	Cameroon	106	103	40	64	33	49	86	68	–	42
134	India	101	93	43	55	34	50	97	61	47	34
135	Namibia	104	101	–	–	–	–	–	–	–	31
136	Côte d'Ivoire	107	97	38	60	31	35	–	44	27	52
137	Haiti	106	104	65	80	63	84	100	95	35	67
138	Tanzania, U. Rep. of	107	102	38	–	45	55	104	80	33	93
139	Comoros	102	102	–	–	65	–	83	75	–	69
140	Zaire	107	102	36	73	36	79	50	56	–	56
141	Lao People's Dem. Rep.	106	99	76	–	59	47	80	68	50	81

142	Nigeria	107	102	40	63	26	59	93	77	38	25
143	Yemen	101	108	15	50	18	–	–	20	–	15
144	Liberia	105	98	30	58	26	40	–	55	31	44
145	Togo	107	102	26	54	31	38	68	30	15	58
146	Uganda	107	102	58	56	41	–	88	44	36	71
147	Bangladesh	99	94	33	47	30	39	88	50	22	7
148	Cambodia	106	101	–	46	71	–	–	–	–	64
149	Rwanda	107	102	49	58	31	–	100	67	20	92
150	Senegal	104	102	28	48	29	–	75	52	26	35
151	Ethiopia	107	102	–	–	43	27	75	71	23	71
152	Nepal	98	95	13	35	32	5	51	40	–	51
153	Malawi	103	103	43	–	46	–	95	50	27	72
154	Burundi	107	104	34	65	33	33	84	67	33	–
155	Equatorial Guinea	107	103	–	–	20	–	–	–	–	56
156	Central African Rep.	111	106	23	48	32	23	65	35	20	86
157	Mozambique	107	103	48	47	54	60	82	44	33	92
158	Sudan	105	99	21	27	45	40	71	74	68	41
159	Bhutan	97	93	–	–	32	–	65	29	–	48
160	Angola	107	103	44	51	52	–	82	–	15	64
161	Mauritania	107	102	–	45	29	23	70	45	14	28
162	Benin	107	103	35	49	29	39	52	38	15	31
163	Djibouti	107	98	–	–	33	–	73	67	–	–
164	Guniea-Bissau	108	105	–	48	27	–	55	44	–	72
165	Chad	107	103	10	42	31	14	44	25	11	21
166	Somalia	107	110	20	39	31	–	57	58	22	64
167	Gambia	108	103	–	41	23	–	73	45	–	69
168	Mali	107	106	36	59	27	43	58	44	14	20
169	Niger	107	102	33	82	40	43	61	44	17	89
170	Burkina Faso	107	102	23	32	54	42	64	56	27	96
171	Afghanistan	102	94	15	32	12	13	52	45	18	9
172	Sierra Leone	108	104	44	37	26	–	75	57	20	49
173	Guinea	102	102	33	38	20	36	50	36	12	43
All developing countries		104	96	54	72	58	61	94	74	51	52
Least developed countries		104	100	38	58	43	44	81	58	28	48
Sub-Saharan Africa		107	102	42	64	46	52	85	64	32	55
Industrial countries		110	106	–	–	99	–	–	–	–	77
World		106	99	–	–	72	–	–	–	–	56

INDUSTRIAL COUNTRIES

FEMALES AS A PERCENTAGE OF MALES (SEE NOTE)

HDI RANK		LIFE EXPECTANCY 1990	POPULATION 1990	MEAN YEARS OF SCHOOLING 1990	UPPER SECONDARY EDUCATION ENROLMENT 1988	UPPER SECONDARY EDUCATION GRADUATES 1988	TERTIARY EDUCATION FULL-TIME EQUIVALENT ENROLMENT RATIO 1988	TERTIARY EDUCATION ENGINEERING AND RELATED SCIENCE ENROLMENT 1988	LABOUR FORCE 1970	LABOUR FORCE 1985–91	UNEMPLOYMENT 1990–91	WAGES 1990–91
1	Japan	108	103	98	104	108	–	16	64	68	110	51
2	Canada	109	102	97	102	105	114	29	–	–	90	63
3	Norway	109	102	98	112	113	118	27	38	81	85	85
4	Switzerland	109	105	93	85	90	48	42	52	60	125	68
5	Sweden	108	103	100	109	102	130	25	61	92	77	89
6	USA	110	105	102	105	113	116	29	59	83	91	59
7	Australia	109	100	99	71	–	115	40	42	71	93	–
8	France	111	105	102	105	109	119	–	54	75	168	88
9	Netherlands	109	102	104	84	106	81	25	–	–	179	78
10	United Kingdom	108	105	102	106	105	93	–	55	74	–	67

11	Iceland	108	99	103	–	–	–	–	–	–	131	80
12	Germany	109	108	90	91	96	86	24	–	–	120	74
13	Denmark	108	103	98	100	115	120	24	58	85	130	82
14	Finland	111	106	98	130	139	119	35	73	89	62	77
15	Austria	110	109	90	85	110	89	25	–	–	112	78
16	Belgium	109	105	100	–	–	120	34	42	70	201	64
17	New Zealand	108	102	104	106	–	103	48	38	77	87	81
18	Luxembourg	109	105	95	96	117	–	–	35	53	236	65
19	Israel	105	100	82	–	–	–	–	–	–	156	–
21	Ireland	108	99	102	125	112	84	48	36	44	64	62
22	Italy	109	106	99	104	113	95	53	–	–	234	80
23	Spain	108	103	92	115	113	105	28	24	54	194	–
25	Greece	106	103	89	–	–	–	–	–	–	255	68
26	Czechoslovakia	111	105	88	–	–	–	–	80	87	124	71
28	Hungary	111	107	102	–	–	–	–	70	85	83	–
39	Malta	105	103	92	–	–	–	–	27	34	56	–
40	Bulgaria	108	102	84	–	–	–	–	79	86	–	–
41	Portugal	110	107	76	129	–	–	37	34	76	206	76
48	Poland	112	105	92	–	–	–	–	85	83	–	–
77	Romania	108	103	89	–	–	–	–	83	86	–	–
78	Albania	107	94	93	–	–	–	–	–	–	–	–
	Aggregates											
	Industrial	110	106	99	–	–	–	–	59	77	–	–
	Developing	104	96	58	–	–	–	–	–	52	–	–
	World	106	99	72	–	–	–	–	–	56	–	–
	OECD	109	105	99	103	109	106	29	55	75	128	66
	Eastern Europe incl. former USSR	112	109	–	–	–	–	–	–	–	–	–
	European Community	109	105	96	103	106	98	34	46	70	168	75
	Nordic	109	103	99	112	115	123	27	59	88	89	84
	Southern Europe	108	104	90	110	113	99	43	26	58	220	80
	Non-Europe	109	104	101	103	110	115	26	60	76	98	59
	North America	110	105	101	105	112	116	29	59	83	91	59

Note: All figures are expressed in relation to the male average, whch is indexed to equal 100. The smaller the figure the bigger the gap, the closer the figure to 100 the smaller the gap, and a figure above 100 indicates that the female average is higher than the male.

1. United Nations Development Programme (UNDP), *Human Development Report 1993*, UNDP, New York, 1993, p. 1.
2. Ibid., p. 21.
3. Ibid., p. 22.
4. Ibid.
5. Ibid.
6. Arvonne Fraser, *Women and Public Life*, IWRAW, Minneapolis, 1993, p. 11.
7. United Nations Economic Commission for Latin America and the Caribbean (ECLAC), *Women and Politics in Latin America and the Caribbean*, ECLAC, Santiago, 1989, p. 6.
8. UNDP, p. 25.
9. Alexandra Stephens, 'Decolonising agricultural information', FAO Regional Office for Asia and the Pacific, Bangkok, 1992, p. 2.
10. United Nations, *The World's Women 1970–1990: Trends and Statistics*, UN, New York, 1991, p. v.
11. United Nations, p. 6.
12. UNDP, p. 16.
13. Ibid. pp. 16–17.
14. UNICEF, *Strategies to Promote Girls' Education*, UNICEF, New York, 1992, p. 11.
15. Brigette Mabandla, 'Increased awareness by women of their rights', paper for the Expert Group Meeting on Increased Awareness by Women of their Rights, including Legal Literacy (UN Division for the Advancement of Women – DAW, Vienna, 1992), p. 1.
16. Roxanna Carrillo, *Battered Dreams*, UNIFEM, New York, 1992, p. 12.
17. ECLAC, pp. 13–15.
18. Ibid.

2 WOMEN'S PARTICIPATION IS NOT NEW

Increasing numbers [of women] are entering political life through non-governmental organizations, women's movements and associations of professional women. And women are increasingly active in the politics of their communities and locales. Community and grassroots participation have long been an extension of women's traditional place in the community and responsibility for the health and well-being of their families. The past 20 years have seen a burgeoning of groups headed by or heavily made up of women .... Women in both the developed and the developing regions have discovered that they can translate their efforts to protect themselves into effective political action.[1]

GROUPS AND ORGANIZATIONS are one of the principal means through which women participate in the life of society. While women are poorly represented in political bodies and power structures, they have learned to use other avenues to turn their aspirations into political action. Thus, they frequently form the majority of community and grassroots organizations and play leading roles in movements for social change. And they have increasingly formed women's groups, organizations and networks to empower themselves and participate in the economic, political and social spheres.

Whilst the past two decades have witnessed the flourishing of women's groups and organizations and an upsurge of women's participation in other non–governmental organizations, women's participation is not new. Throughout history, women have been both leaders and unsung participants in their communities and in social movements.

Much of women's participation is hidden from history, however: unrecorded, barely mentioned, or forgotten. Today, women researchers and writers are recovering this history to create awareness of women's contributions to society and to social change around the world. Women's studies courses and departments at universities and other educational institutions have helped to give women a sense of their history and to show the historical roots of women's contemporary participation. As the feminist scholar and historian, Mary R. Beard, has written:

... the personalities, interests, ideas, and activities of women must receive an attention commensurate with their energy in history. Women have done far more than exist and bear and rear children. They have played a great role in directing human events as thought and action. Women have been a force in making all the history that has been made.[2]

Whilst a great deal of historical study to date has focused on women in ancient civilizations and in the Western world, there is a growing body of research on the historical roles of women in the religious, political, economic and social life of many other societies as well.[3] Studies of African societies, for instance, show that women often wielded considerable political and economic influence. One example:

Among the Yoruba, a major trading people of southwestern Nigeria, women as a group had official public representation through a variety of institutions including the office of the Iyalode, an influential woman appointed to the ruler's council of chiefs, who functioned as the leader and

spokesperson for the women of the city. The Iyalode had her own court and council of subordinate female chiefs to make decisions and adjudicate disputes connected with women's dominant role in trade and markets as well as domestic concerns. These roles were complementary to those of the male chiefs; the Iyalode participated in all the judicial and political affairs of the royal council, and some Iyalode were major political powers in their states.[4]

There are also many instances of women activists who fought for the emancipation of women and asserted themselves in spite of legal and cultural restrictions. Nineteenth-century Asia is a case in point:

Some of the lesser-known early agitators on women's rights were Pandita Ramabai (1858–1922) of India, who attacked Hindu religious orthodoxy and spoke up for women's freedom as early as the 1880s and who herself led an independent life; Kartini (1879–1904), a pioneer of women's education and emancipation in Indonesia, who defied tradition to start a girls' school... Jiu Jin of China (1875–1907) who left home to study in Tokyo and to involve herself in revolutionary politics and women's issues.[5]

Women's participation in political and social movements is also rooted in the past. Women have played significant roles in revolutionary movements, from the march of over 5,000 women to Versailles in 1789, one of the major events of the French Revolution, to the twentieth-century liberation movements. The militancy of women workers during the Industrial Revolution in Europe and North America is well-documented: as early as the 1830s women textile workers in the factories of Lowell, Massachusetts, went on strike and marched through the streets to protest against working conditions, and in 1844 they formed the Lowell Female Labor Reform Association.[6] The nineteenth-century demonstrations of women workers helped inspire and give rise to the annual celebration of International Women's Day on 8 March. Women workers in many regions have a long tradition of activism: women in China, Sri Lanka and India, for instance, were active in the labour movements of the 1920s and were in the forefront of strikes and other agitation.[7]

Women's pre-eminent role in today's environmental movements also has antecedents in earlier times. For instance:

As long ago as the seventeenth century in India, women were at the forefront of the fight against forest destruction. Led by a woman, Amrita Devi, 300 people of the Bishnoi Community in Rajasthan gave their lives to save the sacred Kherji trees by clinging to them, an act which inspired the modern Chipko Movement throughout the Himalayas.[8]

Various types of women's organizations have existed in the past. Women of the nobility and intellectual women have organized circles for literary, artistic and other intellectual and educational pursuits. And religious sisterhoods and associations have provided women with opportunities for education and careers, particularly in times when women had few alternatives to marriage or other possibilities to develop their intellectual abilities.

NEW WOMEN'S ORGANIZATIONS EMERGE ☐ The late nineteenth and early twentieth centuries saw the emergence of many new kinds of women's organizations, and a look at this period reveals the rich and diverse heritage of many contemporary groups. It was a time of social ferment leading to the establishment of many organizations: the revolutionary, socialist and radical social

PHOTO: M. EUGENIA JELINCIC/ISIS INTERNATIONAL

Women today get inspiration from women activists in the past

reform movements gave rise to revolutionary women's clubs and political associations, while the militant workers' movement spun off women workers' associations. A time of new educational and professional opportunities for women, especially women of the upper and middle classes, the period also gave rise to professional and educational associations of women, to women's rights and suffrage movements, and to women's welfare, service and social reform organizations.

Many debates of the age were similar to ongoing ones today: whether to demand equality with men within the existing system or to restructure society; whether to work for slow reform or for radical change in the political and social system; whether to form alliances with male-dominated organizations or to build strong and separate women's organizations to fight for women's rights.

For example, in their 'Message to Future Generations' two leading activists of the women's suffrage movement in the United States, Elizabeth Cady Stanton and Susan B. Anthony, articulated their frustrations in trying to work for women's rights within the male-dominated abolitionist or anti-slavery movement:

Our liberal men counselled us to silence during the war, and we were silent on our own wrongs; they counselled us again to silence in Kansas and New York, lest we should defeat 'Negroe Suffrage', and threatened if we were not, we might fight the battle alone. We chose the latter and were defeated. But standing alone we learned our power; we repudiated men's counsels forevermore; and solemnly vowed that there should never be another season of silence until woman had the same rights everywhere on this green earth as man.'[9]

Although the women's suffrage movement

went its own way, it nevertheless took several decades before women obtained the right to vote. In the meantime, different tendencies developed within it: a more radical stream took up questions of women's social status, particularly marriage laws and customs, and supported the workers' movement. But the suffrage movement as a whole gradually became more conservative, middle-class oriented and focused on the single issue of the vote. One of the reasons for this was, ironically, the attempt to enlist the support of the dominant middle-class men to the cause of women's right to vote.[10]

This was not the first or the last time women have faced the dilemma of whether or not to work within a political or social movement that considers women's demands to be secondary or to be put in abeyance until other goals have been achieved. On the one hand, when women have chosen to form separate women's organizations to struggle for their rights, they have run the risk of isolating themselves from other issues and movements. On the other hand, remaining within other movements has often meant compromising on their own demands for women's rights. To work on several fronts at once may appear to be the common-sense solution, but it has not proved to be easy in practice. For one thing, such a struggle can be exhausting and, for another, the interlinkages between different types of oppression, such as those of gender, race and class, are not always clear or well understood.

The nineteenth and early twentieth centuries saw the growth of welfare-oriented organizations in both the South and the North, which offered urban upper- and middle-class women a way of organizing and becoming involved in the life of the community and society. Advocating education and social reform to improve the status of women, these organizations provided assistance in the fields of health, education and other community services. As middle- and upper-class organizations, they were sometimes elitist and patronizing, and promoted conservative middle-class values including the traditional image of women as the homemaker and helper. However, as these forerunners of contemporary service-oriented women's organizations evolved, so did their views on women's identity, relationships and solidarity between women of different classes. A study on the role of women in public life in Asia reports thus:

In many countries in Asia, women's early attempts at influencing policies that affected them concerned the issue of female education as a tool of modernisation and development. There was also a realisation of the need for social reform to rid the society of the evil practices which undermined the status of women. Traditionally, the early women's organizations devoted specifically to 'social work' aimed at ameliorating the distress of the disadvantaged womenfolk in the society. The task was undertaken by elite women and the approach was one of social welfare. Women's organizations also raised the issues of women's backward status in society and focused the communities' attention to the social evils which afflict women. These organisations were articulate in voicing women's identity when later the country passed through national liberation movements. These were, in many cases, the precursors of the latterday women's movements. In many Asian countries, e.g. India, the Philippines, Malaysia, Sri Lanka, Pakistan and Bangladesh, this was the broad pattern of the growth of women's organizations.[11]

In Europe and North America, where nineteenth-century industrialization brought social tensions and made urban poverty highly visible, many middle-class women took part in social reform movements and organized clubs, associations and services for working women. These included such initiatives as the settlement houses which brought social work centres to cities in the United States, and accommodation for working girls that later grew into the World Young Women's Christian Association (YWCA). The clubs and associations of professional and university women that arose in this period concerned themselves not only with the advancement of women in the professions and educational spheres but also with service work for more disadvantaged women, a tradition they carried on into the twentieth century.[12]

INTERNATIONAL WOMEN'S ORGANIZATIONS □ International associations of women also arose in this period. Among the oldest of these is the International Council of Women, founded in 1888 for the purpose of uniting women's organizations in different countries in promoting equal rights for women as well as women's participation in politics and public life. Dozens of other international non-governmental women's organizations came into existence in the first decades of the twentieth century, uniting women in a variety of professional, academic, religious, civic, service and peace organizations. In their early years these international organizations were made up mainly of women from North America and Europe, but as the twentieth century progressed, affiliates were established in other regions of the world. By the end of the First World War, millions of women belonged to international women's organizations, with their headquarters mainly in Europe and North America. One study reports: 'Although forty-five million women were represented by the women's international organizations a leadership cohort of middle and upper-class British, Scandinavian and American women who met on a regular basis in London or Geneva coordinated women's international work.[13]

These organizations mobilized their memberships to press for women's participation in international politics in an attempt to exert women's influence in questions of peace, war and international political bodies, organizing conferences and meetings at the site of world politics and conferences. Today most of these international women's organizations have members in all regions. Although their international headquarters are still found mainly in Europe and North America, and especially near United Nations bodies, many of the national and local affiliates operate autonomously.

Throughout this century the promotion of women's political participation and social reform have remained major issues. While many of the early women's rights organizations favoured a gradualist approach to reforms, other more confrontational equal rights organizations emerged in the 1920s. The question of whether to work within or outside the political structures has been a topic of ongoing debate. Many international women's organizations are convinced of the need to work within the structures and have mobilized their energies to influence international political bodies in two ways: first, to increase the number and participation of women within inter-governmental organizations; and, second, to pressure these organizations to give attention to women in their work. The efforts of the women's international non-governmental organizations to influence first the League of Nations and then the United Nations, as well as their initiatives in organizing non-governmental meetings to coincide with United Nations conferences, are recounted in Chapter 6.

PHOTO: ANNE WALKER/IWTC

Training courses for women emphasize empowerment

The question of women's difference, still a matter of intense discussion today, was much debated among the early women's organizations: some emphasized that women were different from men in being more concerned with humanitarian, service and welfare issues, while the opposite extreme rejected such notions as detrimental to the equality of women with men. Other views recognized that women had different needs and perspectives that should be incorporated into political and public life.

Throughout the twentieth century, times of more militant women's rights advocacy have alternated with periods when these issues have faded into the background. In industrialized countries following the Second World War, when most women had obtained the right to vote and when basic social, welfare and labour reforms had been instituted, women's activism ebbed. In the same period, the energies of women in colonized countries were directed to the struggle for independence. The 1970s saw a renewal of activism among women, workers and other oppressed groups in countries around the world. Many burning issues of earlier decades forcefully re-emerged, including those of women's participation in political and workers' movements and issues of legislation, women's status in the household, marriage, traditions and attitudes, economic participation, education, health and women's rights.

Other continuing concerns of international women's organizations have been social reform, and service and welfare-oriented activities. Over the past two decades, an evolution can be seen, with a shift from activities designed to bring welfare programmes to passive recipients, to strategies of promoting self-reliance, leadership, awareness and capacity building, sustainable development and empowerment. Education and training programmes have also shifted from top-down to participatory ones. This can be seen in activities such as the workshop organized by the International Federation of University Women (IFUW) for women in Africa in 1993. Entitled 'Leadership, Organizational Development, Management and Programme Development for Women as Decision Makers and Agents of Change', it was designed to give 'training that would enable [women] to strengthen and manage effective organizations and develop viable, sustainable projects and programmes at local, regional and national levels'.[14]

Women's international NGOs are also framing their economic projects in terms of empowerment. For example, Zonta International sees its work as that of 'women empowering women' through projects that aim 'to improve women's productivity and their access to resources, thus enabling them to participate actively in national development, and to enable low-income and disadvantaged women to gain access to training and technical support for their productive and reproductive activities'.[15] Local programmes of other service organizatons are oriented to putting their resources into helping to meet needs identified by the recipients. An example is the work of Soroptimist International, which includes literacy programmes, positive support systems for carers (who are mostly women), support for the victims of violence against women, parenting skills, and aid and rehabilitation for refugees.[16] Leadership training for girls and young women, aimed at preparing them for participation in the political and public life of their countries, is a major concern of organizations such as the World YWCA, the World Association of Girl Guides and Girl Scouts (WAGGS) and Associated Country Women of the World (ACWW).

THE WOMEN'S PEACE MOVEMENT

This movement illustrates many of the strategies used by women's organizations throughout the years. Women have been peace activists in societies all over the world for many centuries. The history of the contemporary organized women's peace movement can be traced back to the 1820s and 1830s, when women in the United States and Europe formed women's peace societies. Women actively participated in various international peace organizations and meetings in the mid-nineteenth century, and in 1852 the first international women's magazine, *Sisterly Voices*, was published by women's peace groups, the Olive Leaf Circles, in the United States and England.

In the late nineteenth and early twentieth centuries, many women prominent in other social reform and women's rights movements were active participants in the peace movement. Best known as the author of the American Civil War song 'The Battle Hymn of the Republic', Julia Ward Howe was among the first women's rights activists to promote a separate women's peace movement. When her attempt to organize an international women's peace congress failed, she helped organize local women's peace festivals in cities throughout the United States and Europe, and Istanbul.

Another prominent woman was Bertha von Suttner of Austria, an anti-war activist and writer whose novel *Lay Down Your Arms!* was written to promote the international anti-war movement. A close friend of the wealthy Swedish dynamite manufacturer Alfred Nobel, she inspired him to establish the Nobel Peace Prize, and in 1905 became the first woman to receive the award. Many leading social reformers and more radical social activists took an anti-war stance and promoted non-violence and international sisterhood, including Jane Addams, Clara Zetkin and Rosa Luxemburg. As a member of the Anti-

Imperialist League, Jane Addams joined with women in their own organizations who launched an anti-war protest against the Spanish-American War in 1898, including a protest against the annexation of the Philippines and the continuing war against Filipino guerrillas.[17]

Recognizing that getting the vote would not be sufficient for women to influence world politics, many women activists in the movement for women's suffrage simultaneously worked to promote peace. On the eve of the First World War, a number of these women in Europe and the United States stepped up their activities for peace. With the outbreak of the war in 1914, they protested against the killing and destruction and pressed for the neutral countries to bring the belligerents to the negotiating table. An International Congress of Women held in The Hague in 1915 gave birth to the Women's International League for Peace and Freedom (WILPF), an international women's NGO which has continued to play a significant role in women's peace activities to this day. In spite of the restrictions and difficulties of travelling during wartime, nearly 1,200 women met in The Hague and thousands more supported the congress. A book on the history of WILPF recounts:

These intelligent and sensitive women first came together in World War I from neutral countries and from countries whose men were slaughtering each other on the battlefield, yet the women warmly embraced as sisters. The symbolism of the moment must never be lost, for the surmounting of artificial barriers in the spirit of reconciliation is the most essential message and the most needed attribute for our time.[18]

It is significant that these women also linked their work for peace with work for women's rights and international justice and independence:

Those who met at that first International Congress of Women saw that a permanent peace could be built only on the basis of equal rights, including equal rights between women and men, of justice within and between nations, of national independence and of freedom.[19]

At the close of the war, another International Congress of Women was convened in Zurich in May 1919. Although it was not possible to hold it at the same place as the official peace conference, as originally hoped, the congress was able to telegraph to the heads of state meeting at Versailles its resolution protesting that: the proposed terms of peace violated 'the principles upon which alone a just and lasting peace can be secured ... deny the principles of self-determination, recognise the right of the victors to the spoils of war, and create all over Europe discords and animosities, which can only lead to future wars.'[20]

While recognizing differences of race, nationality and social–political points of view, the congress none the less achieved remarkable unity on issues including disarmament, international politics, and economics. At the same time, the women called for the inclusion of a women's charter, which would guarantee equal rights for women, in the peace agreement. In addition to equality in political participation, the congress discussed such issues as violence against women, birth control, trafficking in women, the elimination of double moral standards between men and women and remunerative recognition of women's activities in both production and reproduction.

For women, peace has always meant more than the absence of war and violence. Although opposition to war and campaigns for disarmament were and are major activities, throughout the years women

PHOTO: ANNE WALKER/IWTC

Women in the USA protest against nuclear weapons

continued their efforts to get their male partners in the peace movement to recognize the struggle for women's rights as part of the struggle for peace and to create the conditions for women to participate in society on an equal footing with men.

In the years following the First World War, the predictions of the International Congress of Women that an unjust peace would lead to future war soon appeared to be coming true. However, women continued their efforts for peace in many organizations (one of these was the War Resisters League which, although not a women-only organization, was founded by three women in 1923), and between the two world wars women actively campaigned for peace and disarmament. In 1932, women gathered 9 million signatures on a petition urging steps towards total and universal disarmament, for presentation at the World Disarmament Conference held that year. A driving force of the women's peace movement has always been fierce opposition to militarism and war because of the negation of life and nature and because of the high level of destruction that war and militarism bring. The struggle for disarmament, therefore, has always been an essential part of the ongoing peace work by women.

Since the Second World War, a major focus of the peace movement has been nuclear disarmament. The book, *Women and War,* by Jeanne Vickers, traces women's participation in this:

Women have been in the forefront of the anti-nuclear movement since the dropping of bombs on Hiroshima and Nagasaki. In 1959 a conference on the responsibility of women in the atomic age was held in Brunate, Italy, by the newly formed European Movement of Women against Nuclear Armament, which grouped women of all political persuasions from both east and west. Women played a significant role in arousing and organizing the public in massive educational and petition campaigns in support of a treaty to ban nuclear testing, which resulted in the Partial Test Ban Treaty of 1963. In 1964 a new peace movement was started in the United States, calling itself Women Strike for Peace, and in the same year women from many countries demonstrated at a NATO conference in Scheveningen, in the Netherlands, against plans to set up a multilateral nuclear force. In April 1978, in preparation for the First Special Session of the UN General Assembly Devoted to Disarmament, some 80 women from different countries met in Vienna to discuss action and to formulate a message to the United Nations.[21]

Throughout the 1970s and 1980s women took part in countless signature campaigns, marches, demonstrations, conferences and meetings. Peace camps sprang up in different parts of the world: a huge demonstration of women and an International Women's Peace Camp was organized at the time of the Second Special Session of the United Nations devoted to Disarmament in 1982 and was reactivated in 1985. In 1981, Welsh women marched from Cardiff to the US Air Force base at Greenham Common, England, to protest against the proposed installation of cruise missiles. The women's peace camp at Greenham Common continued for several years. In 1983, Australian Women for Survival organized a peace camp outside a US satellite communications base at Pine Gap. Elderly Japanese women set up a peace camp at the foot of Mount Fuji to protest against the military takeover of their land. All across the Pacific, women have protested against nuclear testing in the region.[22]

While much of the early international peace movement was concentrated, or at least most fully documented, in Europe and other industrialized countries, women

PHOTO: GABRIELA

A demonstration of women in the Philippines links military spending to lack of social services

in other regions of the world were also engaged in peace activities. As these women became more active internationally, they brought new issues to the movement, including development, the environment, the global economy and the debt crisis. They thus helped to place the issue of peace back into an enlarged context of international justice. Women in Latin America and Asia are leading protest movements against the arms trade, against the large percentage of national budgets directed to the military, against militarism and military violence against women, against the presence of foreign military bases. They are also organizing around issues of prostitution, drugs and AIDS, which all flourish around such bases.

As old conflicts continue and new ones develop, women continue to alert public attention, organize help for the victims of war and war crimes, and put issues onto the international peace agenda, often joining hands with women on the other side of the conflict. For instance, numbers of Palestinian and Israeli women met together peacefully for years to build bridges between them. An Israeli peace organization, Women in Black, demonstrated for peace together with Palestinian women, in silent vigils of women dressed in black in public places. This symbolism has been taken up by women in other countries and conflicts. While organizing assistance to women and children victims of the conflict in former Yugoslavia, women have also drawn public attention to the human rights abuses of women in conflict situations and in 1993 brought the issue of systematic rape and forced prostitution as war crimes to the international agenda of the World Conference on Human Rights.

Women are also active in peace education and research: the International

Peace Research Association (IPRA) was headed for many years by a leading women's rights advocate, Elise Boulding, and Ruth Leger Sivard produces World Military and Social Expenditures, a series of reports that give statistics on military and arms spending and show how this spending lessens the possibilities of meeting human needs.[23] Women are also tracing the common thread that links violence against women in the family to the violence of military force; they are analysing the effects of militarism on the lives of women around the world and the links between militarism and the global economy.

Women's peace organizations have always made the links with issues of justice in a broad sense and they see peace as a comprehensive whole and as a global security issue. The Women's International League for Peace and Freedom, for instance, campaigned to bring the issue of military activities, in peace and wartime, and their effects on the global environment and development to the agenda of the 1992 United Nations Conference on Environment and Development. Although this struggle did not succeed, it nevertheless helped raised global awareness of this vast problem. Women's groups continue to lobby the United Nations Disarmament Commission in Geneva on an ongoing basis and have called on the Commission to expand its relations with NGOs to allow them to have much more input into the Commission's work. While it is difficult to measure the achievements of the women's peace movement in terms of direct results, it has had a major impact in sensitizing public opinion and pressuring governments and international bodies. Still more needs to be done, however, particularly to place more women in the seats of power where decisions are made on war and peace, military spending and policy.

WOMEN NOBEL PEACE PRIZE LAUREATES

- 1905 *Bertha von Suttner (1843–1914)* international peace activist
- 1931 *Jane Addams (1860–1935)* social worker and international women's peace activist
- 1946 *Emily Greene Balch (1867–1961)* international women's peace activist
- 1977 *Mairead Corrigan and Betty Williams* co-founders of the Community of Peace People in Northern Ireland
- 1979 *Mother Theresa* founder of a women's religious order devoted to relief work
- 1982 *Alva Myrdal* researcher and activist on disarmament
- 1991 *Aung San Suu Kyi* political leader of the non-violent struggle for democracy in Burma
- 1992 *Rigoberta Menchu Tum* indigenous peoples' leader and social justice worker in Guatemala

1. United Nations (UN), *The Women's World 1970–1990: Trends and Statistics*, UN, New York, 1991, p. 6.
2. Mary R. Beard, *Women as a Force in History*, Collier Books, New York, 1973, p. 10.
3. See, for example, Elise Boulding, *The Underside of History*, Westview Press, Colorado, 1976; and Margot I. Duley and Mary I. Edwards (eds.), *The Cross-Cultural Study of Women*, Feminist Press, New York, 1976.
4. Duley and Edwards, p. 324.
5. Kamla Bhasin and Nighat Said Khan, *Some Questions on Feminism and its Relevance in South Asia*, Kali for Women, New Delhi, 1993, pp. 5–6.
6. Eleanor Flexner, *Century of Struggle*, Atheneum, New York, 1972, pp. 55–7.
7. See Kumari Jayawardena, *Feminism and Nationalism in the Third World*, Zed Books, London, 1986.
8. Alexandra Stephens, 'Women's participation in environmental management', paper for the Food and Agriculture Organization Regional Office for Asia and the Pacific (FAO/RAPA), September 1992, p. 2.
9. Quoted in Sheila Rowbotham, *Women, Resistance and Revolution*, Vintage Books, New York, 1974, p. 108.
10. See, for example, Eleanor Flexner; Rowbotham.
11. Najma Chowdhury, 'Role of women in public life in developing countries', paper for Expert Group Meeting on the Role of Women in Public Life (UN Division for the Advancement of Women, Vienna, 1991), pp. 16–17. See also Jayawardena.
12. See Boulding; Flexner.

13. Carol Miller, 'Lobbying the League: women's organizations and the League of Nations', unpublished thesis, Oxford University, 1992, p. iii.
14. International Federation of University Women (IFUW), 'IFUW programme focus', 1993.
15. Miriam Vieyra, 'Empowering women', *Zontian*, December/January/February 1992–93, p. 10.
16. Soroptimist International, 'Programme focus', 1991–95.
17. See Gertrude Bussey and Margaret Tims, *Pioneers for Peace: Women's International League for Peace and Freedom 1915–1965,* Alden Press, Oxford, 1980; Jeanne Vickers, *Women and War*, Zed Books, London, 1993, pp. 121–2; and United Nations Library of Geneva, *1843–1993 Bertha von Suttner and Other Women in Pursuit of Peace,* UN, Geneva, 1993. Information for this section was also supplied by Edith Ballantyne of the Women's International League for Peace and Freedom.
18. Kay Camp, 'Foreword to the 1980 edition', in Bussey and Tims, p. 3.
19. Ibid.
20. Women's International League for Peace and Freedom, *Report of the International Congress of Women,* Zurich, May 12 to 17, 1919, WILPF, Geneva, 1919, p. 242.
21. Vickers, pp.121–2.
22. Ibid., pp. 122–4.
23. Ruth Leger Sivard, *World Military Expenditures*, World Priorities, Washington, D.C.

3 WOMEN MOBILIZING AND ORGANIZING

Women
We have a purpose in our lives
to be part of history, of a new dawn
to be an overflowing river
that waters the world
which belongs to all, equally.[1]

It is this experience of continuously being marginalized in mainstream politics that leads us to believe that there is a continuous need for participating in feminist activity and politics.[2]

SPEAKER AT AN AWARENESS BUILDING WORKSHOP, SOUTH ASIA

IN THE LATE 1960s, a new militant feminist consciousness and movement emerged on a global scale and gave rise to thousands of new women's groups, organizations and networks in both the North and the South. The movement is fuelled by the realization that, in spite of gains in the social, economic and political spheres, women are still far from participating equally in society.

The present-day feminist movement did not spring up in a vacuum: the seeds were planted by our mothers, grandmothers and great-grandmothers who fought for women's rights as strong individual women, as part of movements for the right to vote or for education of women, as part of social reform movements, workers' movements, independence and national liberation and other struggles. For instance, a Latin American feminist writes:

Feminism is not a recent phenomenon in Latin America, but formal history has always chosen to obscure the presence and achievements of women, both in terms of their specific demands and their participation in the overall political struggles. Early this century, women's right to vote, access to education and paid work, together with calls in favor of changing laws that discriminated against married women, were just some of the issues of concern to the first wave of feminists in Argentina, Chile, Venezuela, Colombia, Mexico, Peru and Puerto Rico. In 1910 the First International Feminist Congress was held in Buenos Aires, Argentina, to be followed nine years later by the formation of a National Feminist Party. Chile in 1910 saw the birth of the Pan-American Feminist Federation ...[3]

In Latin America, the feminist movement was strongly influenced by the influx of women militants from political or social movements who were no longer prepared to occupy traditional servicing roles in these movements or to accept the marginalization of women's issues. Another font of feminism in the region is the movement of grassroots women's organizations formed for survival needs, such as the people's kitchens and other community and neighbourhood groups that began to flourish in the 1970s and 1980s. While women's roles in these organizations are frequently extensions of their traditional household ones, the activities have raised women's awareness of their oppression and built their organizational skills.

A pattern of the growth of feminism that contains both similar and different elements is illustrated by the re-emergence of feminism in Sri Lanka:

In Sri Lanka, the women's movement was not imposed on women by the United Nations or by Western feminists, but has had an independent history. Women participated in the cultural

revival of the late 1880–1910 period, educated themselves and began to enter the professions (the first woman doctor qualifying in 1899), and in the 1920s the Women's Franchise Union led the demand for the female vote, which was obtained in 1931. In subsequent years, many organizations, including the Women's Political Union, and the All-Ceylon Women's Conference, agitated for equal rights. Women were also active in trade unions in the 1920s and in the first Leftist party of the 1930s where they participated in the anti–imperialist struggle and the battle for basic economic and social changes. The first autonomous women's feminist socialist group was the Eksath Kantha Peramuna, formed in 1948, led by women of the Left parties... The 'Year of the Woman' proclaimed in 1975 by the UN served to bring the issue to the forefront again. Almost all political parties, trade unions and non–governmental organizations celebrated the event. Feminists travelled around Sri Lanka speaking on the women's issue and meeting with a good response from all classes of women. Feminist literature from abroad also influenced many local women who began to write on the issue and to translate feminist writings. New organizations arose ranging from liberal to Marxist, which represented various shades of feminism. Foreign funders, pressured by their own feminist movement, began to support local women's movements and projects both at governmental and non-governmental level. The result of the activity was a forging of links internationally between women's movements.[4]

Similar patterns can be found in other countries and regions. In Africa, strong women's organizations emerged in many countries as part of independence movements, liberation struggles and movements for democracy. Increasingly, these women's groups fought for women's rights within other political struggles. The United Nations World Conference on Women and Non-Governmental Forum, held in Nairobi, Kenya in 1985, gave impetus to a women's movement with a feminist perspective. Women also created new associations for development and survival in the face of economic crises.

Modernization and social reforms paved the way for the emergence of a new feminist movement in Islamic countries of North Africa, the Middle East and Turkey in the 1980s. This happened, for example, in Algeria, Egypt, Tunisia and Turkey, where reform or revolutionary movements had given women a number of legal rights, particularly in the realm of marriage and the family, and opened opportunities for them in education and work. When these rights were threatened by the rise of Islamic fundamentalism, feminist groups emerged in protest.

In some countries, such as Algeria, feminist groups formed as a response to Islamist movements or state attempts to change family law. At two crucial points – in the early 1980s when the Algerian family code was being formulated, and in 1990 when the FIS (Islamic Salvation Front) was making political inroads – Algerian feminists were organized, militant and audacious.[5]

Across North Africa and in Turkey, the feminist movement has pointed out the gap between legal reforms and the implementation of the law and has given rise to research, writing and activism on the issue. And, whilst women are a mainstay of Islamist movements, stirrings have been reported among Islamist women:

PHOTO: M. EUGENIA JELINCIC/ISIS INTERNATIONAL

Women from Islamic countries exchange views at an international women's meeting

... some Islamist women question and criticize the secondary status of women in Muslim communities, and they blame men for oppressing women and limiting their activities. An unintended outcome of their participation in Islamist movements is that Islamist women become more participatory, more political, and more demanding of the men within their own movements. We have seen that in Iran, Islamist women are asserting their right to criticize gender discrimination and are using language similar to that used by women's rights activists in other countries. Such women are not only more open to change but more willing to engage in dialogue with persons outside their movements.[6]

WHAT IS FEMINISM? □ The diversity and richness of the new wave of feminism make it difficult to define. Most simply and basically, the following can be said:

Present-day feminism is a struggle for the achievement of women's equality, dignity and freedom of choice to control our lives and bodies within and outside the home.[7]

It differs from earlier feminist or women's rights movements in that it seeks more than equality or equal rights with men. According to Kamla Bhasin and Nighat Said Khan, the main difference is this:

... earlier, the struggle was for the democratic rights of women. It included the right to education and employment; the right to own property; the right to vote; the right to enter parliament. In other words, earlier feminists fought for legal reform, for a legally equal position in society. Today, feminists have gone beyond mere legal reforms to end discrimination.[8]

Feminism today seeks to root out the causes of women's oppression, to empower women to participate in decision making at all levels of society, and to transform society through the inclusion of women's participation and perspectives. While in practice there are many different kinds of feminism, attempts to classify it according to ideological streams, such as liberal, radical, socialist, Marxist and postmodern, run into difficulties because feminism is characterized by the rejection of rigid ideological categories and by an ongoing exchange and development of ideas on the causes of women's oppression, the nature of women's difference, gender roles, the relation of women's oppression to other oppressions, and strategies for the empowerment of women. Nevertheless, some significant elements and sources of feminist ideas and strategies can be distinguished. From liberal thinking come ideas of equality and equal rights and strategies of reform within existing structures. Radical streams of thought contribute a celebration of feminine values and traits, such as nurturing and closeness to nature, and a stress on respecting, valuing and incorporating these everywhere in society, as well as the identification of patriarchy, or pervasive male domination of society, as a root cause of women's oppression. Streams of thought often identified as socialist feminism emphasize the interconnectedness of the oppression of women with oppression based on class, race and other social, cultural, economic and political factors, and the need to work on different levels and with different means to attain the goal of women's empowerment. As articulated by Rhoda Reddock of the Caribbean Association for Feminist Research and Action (CAFRA):

Feminists are those who recognize the exploitation of women and its relationship to other forms of oppression and who work actively to change it.[9]

An international workshop entitled 'Feminist Ideology and Structures in the First Half of the Decade for Women', which brought together women from both the South and the North in 1979, expressed this intertwining of oppressions and identified two long-term feminist goals:

The oppression of women is rooted in both inequities and discrimination based on sex and in poverty and the injustices of the political and economic systems based on race and class. First the freedom from oppression for women involves not only equity, but also the right of women to freedom of choice, and the power to control their own lives within and outside of the home. Having control over our lives and bodies is essential to ensure a sense of dignity and autonomy for every woman. The second goal of feminism is ... the removal of all forms of inequity and oppression through the creation of a more just social and economic order, nationally and internationally. This means the involvement of women in national liberation struggles, in plans for national development, in local and global strategies for change.[10]

In this widely held view, feminism aims not simply for equal rights but for a transformation of all oppressive relationships in society. While certain commonalities of women's oppression have been identified, there is also a recognition and appreciation of the diversity of women and of their oppression. An emphasis on the complexity of and changing nature of gender roles (that is, the socially defined roles of men and women) and oppression is characteristic of postmodern feminist thinking. Feminism, then, is not simply one big global sisterhood, uniting women in their oppression as women across barriers of class, colour, race, religion or nationality. Nevertheless, feminists are attempting to find common ground to work on specific issues and the overall goal of women's

PHOTO: CENTER FOR WOMEN'S GLOBAL LEADERSHIP/DOUGLASS COLLEGE, RUTGERS UNIVERSITY

Women from many countries come together to network and strategize

empowerment as part of a global women's movement.

FEMINISM IN PRACTICE ☐ Whilst feminist visions of a fairer, more just and humane world may at times be utopian, these are balanced by very concrete goals and practical strategies to empower women, particularly in specific situations. Rejecting a top–down approach, the new wave of feminism has been especially strong in starting at the grassroots and working on very particular problems on the local level. The organization and mobilization of women are thus central to feminist strategy. However, there is a recognition of the need to work at the policy-making level and to develop macro strategies as well. While greater emphasis is now placed on bringing women and women's issues and perspectives into the mainstream, maintaining strong women's groups and networks is still considered a crucial strategy in the effort to change policy and to transform society.

Awareness building, which is a basic component of the process of empowerment, has been an important part of feminist strategies and practice nearly everywhere: for instance, in the middle-class feminist consciousness-raising groups that were widespread in Europe and North America in the early 1970s, in village women's groups and, in the form of gender sensitivity training, in mainstream development institutions.

Unlike the earlier phase of the women's movement, with its international organizations, headquarters and memberships, the new wave of the women's movement comprises thousands of diverse groups and organizations without organic linkages. Networking has thus emerged as a strategy to link these many diverse efforts around the globe, breaking their isolation, promoting the exchange of ideas and

LEGACY OF ACTIVISM BRINGS HEALTH SERVICES TO URUGUAYAN PROVINCE

One of the poorest departments in Uruguay, Cerro Largo is located 400 kilometres north of the capital city of Montevideo. Through meetings, presentations, and group reflection, we gradually discovered the 'knots' in ourselves that held us back and began to untie them and stir ourselves into action. In July 1987, the process led to the foundation of the Casa de la Mujer (Women's Center), conceived as a system of integrated services for women in Melo, the main city of Cerro Largo. In April 1990, we founded the Las Flores Community Center in a working-class suburb of Melo. Both the Women's Center and the Community Center offer the following services:

- Child care services that enable mothers to leave their children and work outside the home or take care of other business. The objective is to provide a climate of affection with non-sexist educational and developmental content that stimulates integral growth, independence among children of both sexes, and new forms of human relations. We attempt to provide an important service to women while at the same time promoting feminist perspectives in the children's formal education.
- Small business promotion to generate income for women. The Women's Center, for example, has a design and layout workshop and a photocopier. In the Las Flores Community Center, a group of women are working to recover traditional textile handicrafts.
- Legal aid and counselling in cases of domestic violence, divorce, etc.
- The alternative Clinic for Mental, Sexual, and Reproductive Health at the Women's Center. In March 1990, the Women's Center opened this clinic, where women's health problems are handled from a gender perspective with the aid of a multidisciplinary team consisting of a sex educator, a psychologist, a bacteriologist and a gynecologist.

The Casa de la Mujer (Women's Center) is a project both of and for the women of Cerro Largo. It is a space where we can grow together, where we can learn of our femininity from the inside and turn it outward, crossing barriers of color, income, and class, and identifying with each other as women.

It is a space for expressing our feelings and thoughts without fear, for learning to work together collectively, creatively and critically, through horizontal relationships that encourage reflection on our roles within the family and society ... a space for discovering our potential to change and to emerge as new women, capable of participating and acting decisively ... a space in which solidarity among women allows us to broaden our knowledge and strengthen permanent values such as love, liberty, peace, tolerance and happiness.

We believe, as Paulina Luisi did, that the feminist program 'seeks to make things more just and natural, conceives of women as something more than child-bearing machines and house-keepers ... and believes that the real mission of preserving the species must be a task not only for her body but also for her mind and heart.'

Maria Cristina Sosa and Leda Pesce, *Women's Health Journal*, No. 1, 1992, Isis International, Santiago, Chile experiences, and strengthening and supporting their work. A more informal way of linking than through membership, networking is facilitated today by global communications and transportation technologies, which enable women to meet and communicate with relative ease. Whilst global communications facilitate networking, the globalization of industry, tourism and mass media and the international linkages in political and economic decision making make it imperative for women to link together globally on a regular basis. Women cannot challenge these structures on the local level alone, but need to undertake collaborative efforts and campaigns to lobby, pressure and influence structures and policy making at the national, regional and international levels.

Many of the issues that feminist groups and organizations have put on the agenda recently, such as violence against women, reproductive rights, sexuality, child care, recognition of the value of household work, discrimination in educational and job opportunities, customary attitudes and traditions, are not new, but had been taken up by women's organizations in the first half of the twentieth century. However, many had faded from the limelight in the years following the Second World War when women had made many advances in the political, social and economic spheres. When it became apparent that despite gains in the field of women's rights in politics and public life, deep-seated discrimination against women remained, groups and organizations took up what they perceived to be burning but neglected issues with renewed militancy. In the evolution of contemporary feminism, the focus has widened to include global concerns such as the economy, environment and sustainable development.

The feminist approach to birth control and family planning, places it in the framework of reproductive rights, women's right to control their own bodies and women's overall health needs. At the grassroots, the feminist health movement has sparked off thousands of women's health centres in villages and urban communities which work from the feminist perspective. One such group, the Women's Centre in Cerro Largo, Uruguay, illustrates several of the concerns and strategies of the women's health movement at the grassroots. Inspired by Paulina Luisi, in 1908 the first woman to receive a medical degree in Uruguay and a women's suffrage activist, and by feminists in other Latin American countries, a group of women decided to open a women's centre and health clinic (see box). Combining health care and other services, the centre was designed as a place for women to meet with each other and develop their awareness and capabilities in a supportive atmosphere.

Hundreds of similar initiatives can be found in countries of both the North and the South. Networking enables such groups to link up with each other, share their experiences and information and carry out health campaigns. Several women's health and reproductive rights networks have been created in the past two decades, some international, such as the Women's Global Network for Reproductive Rights, some regional, such as the Latin American and Caribbean Women's Health Network. Others are focused on specific issues, such as the Feminist International Network of Resistance to Reproductive and Genetic Engineering (FINRRAGE). Through these networks feminist health groups and organizations not only debate issues among themselves but also lobby health and population bodies at the national and international levels, and promote dialogue between health researchers, policy makers, and grassroots activists. Since the late 1970s an International Women's Health

PHOTO: M. EUGENIA JELINCIC/ISIS INTERNATIONAL

International Women and Health Meetings are a forum for women to discuss reproductive rights

Meeting has been held every four years, organized in turn by women's health groups and networks in Europe, Latin America, Asia and Africa. The strategy of rotating the responsibility for organization of international meetings among women's groups in different regions is part of the effort of the international feminist movement to broaden the participation of women. Regional and international women's health networks also collaborate on an annual women's health campaign focusing on issues such as maternal mortality and abortion. These campaigns provide the opportunity for awareness building and lobbying at both the grassroots and the policy-making level.

While working extensively in the area of health and reproductive rights at the grassroots, the feminist movement has, at the same time, been very active in its attempts to influence health and family planning policies at governmental and inter-governmental levels. Although a wide range of views are represented in the feminist health movement, on the whole, it has been very vocal in expressing criticism of the policies of population programmes. As explained by Naila Kabeer in a presentation at a 'day of dialogue', organized by the Population Council, the controversy is centred not so much on the provision of reproductive technology as on the motives of population organizations and the ways in which their programmes are carried out: 'In the Third World context, opposition has often taken a radical anti-imperialist stance. Some critics have seen population programmes as the product of fears among Northern countries of the politically destabilizing effects of unchecked population growth; others as an attempt by the North to deflect attention from the fact that if underdevelopment resulted from an imbalance between consumption and resources, overconsumption was a characteristic of the wealthy elites and nations rather than of the world's poor. While the population establishment is not monolithic, there does appear to be a shared emphasis on the urgency of fertility reduction as a route to poverty alleviation and environmental sustainability.'[11]

In contrast, feminists view reproductive technology in a broader perspective of the right of women to control their bodies and their lives and in the context of their overall health needs. According to Kabeer:

If feminist interpretations of women's reproductive needs were adopted, the provision of reproductive technology would be geared to enhancing women's choices and health and supporting their reproductive rights. This would entail a significant recognition that as bearers and carers of children, women have a particular stake in the conceptualization, formulation and implementation of family planning programmes. The idea of the user's perspective in the planning of contraceptive provision would help to highlight that different groups of women have different needs at different stages of their lives so that reproductive choice requires a range of family planning methods. Critical to effective choice is information: about what is available, the risks in terms of women's health and of probabilities of contraceptive failure, the screening check-up and follow-up practices which should accompany each form of contraception. Evaluation methods which encourage sensitivity to women's needs would need to replace those which are merely acceptance-related. Finally, it would be important to broaden the focus of family planning programmes to encompass men. Women's reproductive rights should not be premised on the denial or neglect of men's reproductive responsibilities.[12]

As with the issue of health and reproductive rights, the feminist approach to violence against women places it in the global context of women's lives. Multiple strategies are used: at the grassroots, groups are organizing refuges for women victims of violence, counselling and legal advice and aid centres, media campaigns to sensitize public opinion, and legal actions. They have also led concerted campaigns on the national and international levels to have violence against women recognized as a violation of women's rights and to develop legal and policy instruments to prevent this violence. The story of how the Women's Crisis Centre in Magomeni Mapipa, Tanzania, is working together with the Media Watch of the Tanzanian Media Women's Association (TAMWA) (see box) illustrates some of the strategies women are using to combat violence against women at the grassroots and national levels.

Likewise with other issues: the increasing international dimensions of trafficking in women, for instance, demand new approaches to forced prostitution, on which women's organizations have been focusing attention since the early days of the equal rights and peace movements. With the growth of international sex tourism, the mail-order bride business and the recruitment of women migrants into prostitution, women's organizations today are dealing with trafficking in women on a global level. Moreover, critical of an approach that reduces prostitution to a matter of violence against women, feminists are making efforts to develop an integrated framework for the issue 'which takes into consideration the global, social and economic realities and in particular the unequal North–South relations.'[13] Strategies for dealing with trafficking in women and sex tourism encompass education and awareness raising, economic development, legal actions, creation of infrastructure, networking, lobbying and political action at grassroots, national and international levels, and international solidarity campaigns and actions.

Action for women's legal rights has also taken on new dimensions, and new

WOMEN'S CRISIS CENTRE, MAGOMENI MAPIPA, TANZANIA

The focus which the centre has adopted has been counselling and legal aid, which serves as a broad outline of the clinic's work. On the whole, help is made available to women and children in need of advice and counselling at the clinic. The centre offers medical, legal and social services to women and children. It offers a wide range of expert advice on all matters including employment rights, property rights, child maintenance, as well as the main issue it has specifically vowed to address, that of sexual and domestic violence. There are lawyers, social workers, journalists, academicians, and trade unionists available for consultation during the clinics who offer advice to clients on specific problems. The questions we discuss among ourselves are:

- Can changes in laws relating to sexual offences and battery reduce the incidence of violence against women?
- Would separate courts like the proposed tribunal we are lobbying for help victims?

We intend to discuss these questions publicly over the radio and in the print media in order to ascertain public opinion. We hope that soon we should come up with a more concrete plan for the campaign for legal reforms in the country.

We feel it necessary to challenge NGOs, especially those which specifically address issues pertaining to women and children, to help find ways of sensitizing police, policy makers and legal personnel on gender biases.

One of the major recommendations ... is that education at all levels ought to be geared to sensitize people, especially youth, the adults of tomorrow, on the gender-related causes of violence. Popular education programmes ought to go hand in hand with legal reform. This should be implemented in the community, in schools, among religious organizations and with police departments. We feel it is important for our centre to co-ordinate with the police, NGOs and National Commissions to address the issue of women's rights charters to which Tanzania is a signatory and which it has ratified. So far, splinter groups have been working in isolation. We feel it is imperative that these groups form a cohesive movement so that human rights charters are implemented to the letter.

We have mounted a massive campaign in conjunction with TAMWA's Publicity Unit to protest against the negative portrayal of women in the media which encourages men to view women as inferior and as sexual objects.

Tanzanian Media Women's Association (TAMWA), *Sauti ya Siti,* November 1992, pp. 30–31

women's rights organizations and networks have emerged to respond to changing needs. Out of the realization that the gains made in obtaining constitutional and legislative guarantees of women's rights are not in themselves sufficient, women's groups and organizations are taking up with renewed attention strategies to ensure the implementation of these guarantees, including legal literacy, legal action and counselling. To strengthen this work on the regional and international levels, networks such as the Asia Pacific Forum on Women Law and Development (APWLD) and

PHOTO: SARVESH/WOMEN'S FEATURE SERVICE

Marching for women's rights, India

Women in Law and Development Africa (WiLDAF) link women's groups and organizations working at both local and policy-making levels. International solidarity campaigns and actions are important components in the strategy of networks such as the Women Living Under Muslim Laws Network which links women in countries across Africa, Asia, the Middle East and Europe. Increasingly, women's organizations are using existing international mechanisms that guarantee women's rights. These instruments and some of women's actions to strengthen them are described in Chapter 6.

'All issues are women's issues', a feminist slogan, means that women's groups and organizations organize around an extensive range of questions, including traditional practices and female genital mutilation, the environment, development, structural adjustment and the debt crisis. Many urban women's centres and grassroots women's groups, often concerned with day-to-day survival, are involved simultaneously with a whole range of problems women face.

THE POWER OF INFORMATION □ One effect of the burgeoning of women's groups and organizations is an enormous amount of new information, publications and other media generated by it. In a world where 'information is power', access to, control over and sharing of information and knowledge are crucial elements in women's participation and empowerment. Out of this understanding have sprung a number of the developments and strategies of the past decades: alternative women's media, the use of grassroots media for awareness building and action, women's resource centres and information networking, women's studies, and action to influence mainstream media.

Although we live in an age of information overload and mass communication, women's groups and organizations nevertheless lack relevant information and communication channels. Consequently they have created their own communication channels and are producing thousands of alternative women's publications.[14] To meet the needs and demands of getting women's voices and research into print, women's publishing houses have been established in different parts of the world. Many publishing houses have series devoted to women's studies. One result of this growth of women's publishing has been the international feminist book fairs held every two years since the mid-1980s.

Other forms of media, such as radio, video, theatre, dance, songs and arts and crafts are widely used by grassroots groups and organizations, especially as tools for awareness building, education, expression and action. Street theatre is popular among many groups in India who use it to raise public awareness and start discussions on the problems facing women. In both Asia and Africa women are using traditional drama, song and dance to illustrate and help find solutions to community problems. One of the best-known initiatives by women to use drama for awareness and organization building is Sistren, a Caribbean women's theatre group that has won worldwide acclaim. Formed in 1977 by working-class women, Sistren develops its plays from the concrete problems that women encounter daily. In addition to full-

THE GLEN NORAH WOMEN'S THEATRE GROUP

A member of the Zimbabwe Association of Community Theatre (ZACT), the group is a result of the Women in Theatre Conference which was held in 1990 at the University of Zimbabwe and attended by women theatre artists from Jamaica, Zambia, Botswana, Tanzania, South Africa and Zimbabwe. Created mainly as a full-time women's group, the Glen Norah Women's Theatre Group tries to use theatre to articulate women's issues, especially those which touch on the role of women in the country's socio-economic development. The formation of the group was an important event in the history of theatre in Zimbabwe. Up until then most theatre groups were headed by men and their attempts to include women's issues in their plays were always from a man's point of view. The Glen Norah Women's Theatre Group intends to try to show women's problems and issues from a women's point of view.

Who Is To Blame? is a play about unemployed women school leavers in Zimbabwe. It traces the life of a rural girl from her studies to employment. Her friend's brother tries to rape her as payment for assisting her to find a job. She becomes up a prostitute, but in the end, she leads the women out of prostitution to form a co-operative in which they are able to use their performing-arts talent to earn a decent living. *Who Is To Blame* uses traditional music and dance in an approach that succeeds in involving the audience. Glen Norah Women's Theatre Group has scheduled performance tours in Zimbabwe and Botswana. The group plans to hold theatre workshops for women, especially in teacher training colleges. It is working on a play on AIDS dealt with from a woman's perspective. Another theme the group plans to explore is that of co-operatives and some of the reasons they fail.

Adapted from
'Women's achievements', *Speak Out*,
No. 19 (1992), pp. 18–19.

PHOTO: SISTER NAMIBIA

Storyteller at a Women's Cultural Festival, Namibia

scale theatre performances, Sistren conducts workshops in both urban and rural communities, involving the participants in dramatizing their problems and organizing to take action to solve them. Similar techniques are used by other groups, such as the more recently established Glen Norah Women's Theatre Group in Zimbabwe.

Women's documentation and information centres have been established to meet both the need for information in the women's movement and to collect and preserve the wealth of women's alternative media productions and resource materials. Some centres serve only the work of their own organization or network while others are regional or international; some specialize in a particular area, such as health, while others cover a wide range. Most, however, share a number of common objectives:

- to recover, preserve and give value to women's knowledge and history;
- to gather women's alternative resource materials – books, magazines, bulletins, pamphlets, packets and non-print media – that are not generally found in libraries;
- to make these materials accessible to action-oriented groups and organizations and to women at the grassroots, who may not have access to or experience in using more formal academic and institutional libraries.

Many women's resource centres service the information needs of other women's groups and organizations not only through their collections, but through repackaging information, producing new resource materials, promoting research on concerns not generally found in academic research and information centres, and providing a space for women to meet, plan and develop strategies. Some are themselves engaged in action. International information exchange and networking is a primary objective of a number of organizations such the International Women's Tribune Centre (IWTC) and ISIS, which, originally based in Rome and Geneva, has evolved into two organizations: Isis International, in Santiago and Manila, and Isis–WICCE (Women's International Cross Cultural Exchange), in Kampala, Uganda.

Another strategy for increasing women's access to relevant information is to increase women's presence and perspectives as well as the coverage of women in the mass media. Efforts in this direction include women's news and feature services directed to the mass media, education and training of women in media, and action to increase women's employment in the media.

WOMEN EMPOWERING COMMUNICATION An assessment of women's media-related activities and the development of future strategies was undertaken at an international conference, 'Women Empowering Communication', held in Bangkok in February 1994. Organized by the World Association for Christian Communication (WACC), Isis International, Manila, and the IWTC, it brought together over four hundred women communicators from media organizations and networks working in both alternative and mass media in eighty countries in all continents of the world. Although women's media organizations and networks have grown tremendously over the past two decades and have taken action at all levels, much more remains to be done to counter the negative effects of the mass media on women. The conference identified the negative aspects of the mass media and counterposed its own vision of communication that would empower women:

The so-called 'mainstream' media are a male-dominated tool used by those in power. At the global level they are controlled by the North; nationally they are in the hands of the local elite. As they are now structured, the media propagate unsustainable lifestyles ... and consumption patterns which turn people into consumers not only of goods but of ideas and ideologies: women, children and the majority of men are invisible and their voices are unheard. There is particular lack of respect for the integrity and dignity of women: stereotyped and dehumanized, we have been turned into commodities. The excessive use of violence in these media is destroying the sensibilities of all humanity. For all these reasons it is essential to promote forms of communication that not only challenge the patriarchal nature of media but strive to decentralize and democratize them: to create media that encourage dialogue and debate; media that advance women and peoples' creativity; media that reaffirm women's wisdom and knowledge, and that make people into subjects rather than objects or targets of communication; media which are responsive to people's needs.[15]

The conference identified the following strategies aimed at strengthening and empowering women's communications:

- strengthening of peoples', and more specifically women's media, including storytelling, visual and performance arts, which build on their knowledge, wisdom and creativity;
- integration of humane values into women's media creations, such as harmony with nature, co-operation, nurturing, caring, love and compassion, and women's struggles for freedom, to ensure that women's alternatives do not become hierarchical, undemocratic and elitist;
- development of education and training to enable women's organizations and community groups to access existing media in order to communicate effectively their own messages and concerns;
- increased opportunities for technical training for women in the area of communications;
- incorporation of gender sensitivity, local history and cultural diversity in the education and training of communications professionals;
- expansion of gender-specific media research and documentation at the local level;
- promotion of lobbies and campaigns directed at opinion makers and media consumers to raise public awareness on how issues of development affect women;
- strengthening of monitoring networks with legal backing to guarantee the democratic functioning of media;
- strengthening of women's links with potential allies throughout hierarchies (government, politicians, corporations, donors, media managers) to turn strategies into concrete actions;
- building of links and solidarity between women and gender-sensitive men working in media at all levels;
- continuation of efforts to build links among women's networks and forge broader links with other people-oriented networks;
- pinpointing of special networking considerations and the strengthening of information exchanges: between urban and rural groups and organizations, across language barriers, at varied levels of consciousness and access to technology, in oppressive conditions;
- efforts to ensure the widest and most appropriate dissemination of information related to United Nations meetings

that concern people's lives and futures, including training in methods of using this information;

- efforts to assure women's participation and the inclusion of women's perspectives in all stages of preparations for these meetings.

Participants also called on the conference organizers to spearhead the following activities:

- a worldwide effort to document all forms of women's communication practices, and the organization of workshops on how they can be used effectively;
- exploration of possibilities for establishing a women's satellite network;
- swift global dissemination of women's views at the 1995 World Conference on Women and NGO Forum in Beijing via satellite communications;
- the building of support for one day during the Beijing conference of worldwide media programming by and about women;
- the monitoring of all worldwide media during one day at the start of 1995, the data to be used as the basis of an analysis of women's position;
- efforts to have 1996 declared International Year of Women Communicating.

The conference further recognized that to achieve the goal of social justice and participatory democracy, it is necessary to bring pressure to bear on those who now hold power. In this respect, the conference identified the need to pressurize governments and policy makers to implement the numerous international conventions and agreements relating to women including the Nairobi Forward-looking Strategies, the Convention on the Elimination of All Forms of Discrimination Against Women, the Vienna Declaration on Human Rights, and Agenda 21. The conference likewise identified the need to press donors to re–examine their funding policies and give priority to strengthening women's media and communications networks through support that is relevant, practical and substantial.[16]

WOMEN'S STUDIES Women's empowerment requires not only information, but also the development of critical theory. Women's studies in universities, institutes and research associations have developed in response to the challenge of finding new theoretical frameworks and methodologies for data collection and analysis as a part of critical social theory. Multidisciplinary in nature, women's studies have sought to bring an analysis of women's situations and a new analytical framework to the social sciences. A distinguishing characteristic of women's studies and other critical social theories is their normative approach and combination of research, study and activism. Women academics and researchers have joined together in action-oriented organizations and networks to carry out participatory research, develop theory and build links with the global women's movement.

WOMEN IN TRADE UNIONS AND WORKERS' MOVEMENTS □

Women have a long history of militancy in workers' movements, dating from the nineteenth century. Today, women comprise nearly one-third of union members worldwide, but hold few leadership positions in trade unions. Even where women are found in relatively large numbers in parliaments, they lag behind in the decision-making bodies of unions. In Denmark, for instance, where women hold about 30 per cent of the parliamentary seats, in 1990 they held only 17 per cent of the leadership positions in trade unions affiliated to the International Confederation of Free Trade Unions (ICFTU). In Sweden, where women hold about 30 per cent of elected positions in national political bodies, they comprise only 20 per cent of the trade union leadership.[17]

Among the obstacles to women's participation in trade unions are the male-dominated unions themselves, which often prevent women from reaching leadership positions and which fail to take up women's issues. The trade union agenda is generally constructed from a male perspective and women's concerns, such as child care and equal opportunities for promotion, are not given priority. Women, moreover, often are not able to find the time, because of their double burden of work outside and inside the home, to participate in union activities. When they do, they frequently face difficulties because of lack of training and practice in leadership. And both men and women lack awareness of the needs and rights of women workers. The situation stems in part from the history of the trade unions, which emerged first in heavy industrial sectors which employed men almost exclusively. Today, large numbers of women workers, particularly in the export processing zones (EPZs) of the newly industrialized countries (NICs), remain unorganized: sometimes legislation or government regulations prevent unions from organizing in particular areas; in other cases, traditional unions have shown little interest in organizing women.

Strategies to increase women's participation in the trade unions and workers' organizations include awareness building, leadership training, networking among women workers and international solidarity. Where there are no unions or where they are failing to represent women workers, women have often formed strong women's sections or branches, or independent associations, or even their own unions.

The Self-Employed Women's Association (SEWA) of India is an outstanding example of how a women workers' association can give unorganized women the opportunity to participate actively and to develop leadership and decision-making skills. Since its founding in 1973, tens of thousands of Indian women, urban and rural, have been active members of SEWA, demonstrating that when a labour organization takes into consideration women's issues and responds to women's needs, women will participate.

The experience of SEWA demonstrates the opposition that women workers often receive from male union leaders. Growing out of an initiative of Ela Bhatt of the Textile Labour Association (TLA) and self-employed women labourers in the informal sector in Ahmedabad, India, SEWA tackled the urgent problems confronting the women: exploitation by moneylenders, police harassment, and bureaucratic regulations. Early initiatives included the establishment of a co-operative bank managed and run by the women themselves; the organization of pressure groups to take direct action for the protection of the workers; and the setting up of child-care centres, a maternity and health insurance scheme and a housing scheme. These efforts were run by the women themselves, enabling them to learn decision-making and management skills, how to deal with banks, insurance companies, the police and the municipal authorities, and the power of collective strength.

As SEWA women became stronger and their success began to attract attention nationally and internationally, a rift began to grow between SEWA and the TLA, which culminated in 1981 when the TLA expelled SEWA and Ela Bhatt from its organization and premises and asked its unions to withdraw their money from the SEWA bank. An account of the break in

PHOTO: INTERNATIONAL LABOUR OFFICE

During a workers' demonstration, UK

Setting up of a Women Section in the Trade Union

CAW AND KWWA, *WHEN THE HEN CROWS ... KOREAN WOMEN WORKERS EDUCATIONAL PROGRAMS* (CAW, HONG KONG, 1991)

the Indian women's journal, *Manushi*, identified the underlying causes as the male-dominated leadership of the TLA, the distance of its leaders from the workers, and its policies of collaboration and compromise.[18]

Ela Bhatt, the founder of SEWA, wrote at the time: 'SEWA owes its existence to TLA, but when SEWA women slightly show their little bit of independence and self-dignity, it is being destroyed.'[19]

SEWA overcame the crisis and continues today as a registered federation of trade unions with a membership of 40,000, fighting for their rights through direct action and in the courts. While continuing to provide a co-operative bank and services for women labourers, SEWA has also taken up lobbying to change policy at the state and national level. Its example has become an inspiration for women in the informal sector worldwide.[20]

Another strategy is illustrated by the efforts of women in South Korea who are attempting to build an independent women workers' organization strong enough to make the trade unions accept women's issues as the issues of all workers. In response not only to the sharp decline in women's participation in trade union leadership in the 1980s, but also to the failure of the unions to recognize women's specific problems or to take action on them, and to attitudes typified by comments such as: 'If workers are liberated, women would automatically be liberated' or 'To talk about women's issues in the labour movement is to cause confusion and division in the movement', the Korean Women Workers Association (KWWA) was founded in 1987. In its inaugural statement, the KWWA said:

Women workers must join together and struggle in order that the special problems women suffer become the problems of all workers and so that all workers will join together to destroy the discrimination and the oppression of women. We have come to the stage where independent activities for women workers should be realised... Women workers, as women and as workers, must be aware of the reality we are facing ... to bring more awareness to the masses and to build a broader basis for the labour movement. In addition, women workers have to achieve our own progress through our own free and independent efforts.[21]

Women's forums and gender awareness training have been initiated within unions to support women and increase the sensitivity of male workers to women's needs and concerns. Dorothy Mokgalo, who was hired by the Congress of South Africa Trade Unions (COSATU) to build women's leadership in the union federation and to educate men on women's issues, recounts the efforts to create the position:

Women's forums were set up in the unions in 1989. Then in 1990 it was agreed that COSATU would employ a full-time women's coordinator to help organize women. It seemed a victory, but two months later the decision was

changed because two unions were against it. We were shocked and upset by this. We all asked what sort of democracy this was. But we took it up again with the same spirit and we succeeded! ... It was agreed men had to be educated on women's issues. The attitudes of men needed to be challenged at the same time as we build women in COSATU so men must be part of this process.[22]

Thus it was decided to call the new officer 'gender coordinator', a title which includes both men and women, rather than 'women's coordinator'. Gender subcommittees were formed to take up issues and the first problems to be identified as obstacles to women's participation in union meetings were lack of childcare facilities and men's lack of co-operation in housework.[23]

In some unions, progress has been made in putting the issue of women's double burden on the union agenda. Measures to alleviate this usually consist of provision of childcare and other social services. Some unions have taken up the relatively new concept of shared parental responsibility and shared housework between men and women.

SHARING THE LOAD

The idea of 'sharing the load' is gaining acceptance in the South African Commercial, Catering and Allied Workers' Union (SACCAWU) which went beyond its demand for maternity leave and obtained a parental rights agreement with a company. This provided paid leave to both men and women to care for their children.

As recounted in *Sharing the Load*, a book published by the union: 'With the agreement, the union hoped to change the way in which men and women see their roles in society. The union believes that without the re-organisation of family life in such a way that it is shared between both parents, we cannot talk about freedom for both men and women. For as long as women are seen only as mothers, cooks and cleaners, there can be no equality between men and women in society.'

The union publication recognizes the difficulties in changing age-old attitudes and practices: 'The challenge that faces the union now is to ensure that the fight for women's equality does not remain at the level of confronting management. We have to ensure that each and every comrade in the union begins to examine his/her own practice.' Union members recognize that such basic changes in attitude and practice take time: 'It is still a new idea, but people will get used to the idea and accept it. Today there are a few men who share, but in ten years' time there will be many more!'

Speak Magazine, No. 34, 1991

The efforts of women within unions and worker's organizations on the local and national levels have given rise to and are strengthened by regional and international networking. As a result of the growing consciousness and activism of women workers and the greater awareness generally of women's issues, the International Confederation of Free Trade Unions (ICFTU) has encouraged its affiliates to recruit women to union leadership and to take up women's issues. At its Fifth World Women's Conference in Canada in April 1991, the ICFTU called for women's and equality issues to be made part of the mainstream trade union agenda and for unions to bring women's demands to the negotiating table and train women workers for leadership positions.[24]

Grassroots networking is another significant strategy. One organization that uses it is the Committee for Asian Workers (CAW), which links women workers, women labour organizers and women workers' organizations in Asia, especially in the newly industrialized zones. CAW publishes research and manuals, and organizes workshops to enable women workers to come together to discuss their problems, educational and organizing methodologies, and strategies for dealing with management. In addition to building links and strengthening local actions through the solidarity and support of women in other factories, industries and export processing zones, international networking enables women workers to bring their concerns to international attention and gives them forums to discuss global problems.

Further discussion of women workers and their activities in trade unions is found in the book *Women and Work*, prepared by Susan Bullock, in the Women and World Development series.

RELIGIOUS GROUPS ☐ Throughout history, religion has been one of the main vehicles for women's participation in community life and in society.

Women in the English-speaking Caribbean have been members of women's organizations since the 19th century. In the main, these have been religious-based organizations, especially of the various denominations of the Christian Church. The large-scale organization of women continues to take place within religious bodies. On the one hand religion represents a legitimate space within which women can freely participate outside the home, without question or need for justification. On the other it provides that spiritual solace and community in a world in which hard work, social and economic and physical or emotional violence are the order of the day.[25]

Women's role in the world's major religions today varies tremendously between and within religions. Some religious organizations are founded on funda-mentalist principles which promote a traditional or even regressive social position for women, while others are welfare-oriented and charitable organizations, and still others are progressive and in the forefront of promoting women's rights. Despite this diversity, women are focusing their attention on a number of common trends: the spread of fundamentalism, new interpretations of sacred writings, and greater access to leadership roles.

The rise of religious fundamentalism has been identified as a trend that may limit women's participation in religious organizations and in society. This concern was raised by women from different countries and religions who participated in the Women's Global Leadership Institute on Women, Violence and Human Rights held at the Center for Women's Global Leadership, New Brunswick, USA, in June 1992. The participants appealed to the international human rights community to launch a worldwide investigation into the violations of women's human rights through fundamentalism.

A common trend in the combatting of religious discrimination against women in the major religions is the study and reinterpretation of sacred scriptures and writings from a feminist or women's perspective. Women theologians and women's theological groups are examining texts in order to counteract interpretations of religious writings and traditions that repress women and their rights. According to Sisters in Islam, a group of professional women in Malaysia who study the Koran and its relation to the status of women in Islam:

It is not Islam that oppresses women, but people who have failed to understand the true intentions of Islam and who have misinterpreted its texts.[26]

Sisters in Islam has published booklets, based on the study of Koranic verses, explaining to women their rights. The organization also gives assistance to Muslim women on issues related to marriage, divorce, polygamy and domestic violence.

Groups of Jewish women are advocating an interpretation of the Halachah or traditional law that permits women equal decision-making power with men in marriage and divorce and greater participation in religious rites. Orthodox Jewish women are trying to break down the strict segregation in religious practice that prevents them from becoming part of the quorum of ten men (the *minyan*) in the synagogue to recite the Kaddish (mourner's prayer). In asserting themselves, these women are not rejecting the Halachah, according to a report by Leila Seigel, former president of the International Council of

STATEMENT ON RELIGIOUS FUNDAMENTALISM

We, the participants of the Women's Global Leadership Institute on Women, Violence and Human Rights, including women from six continents of Hindu, Buddhist, Muslim, Jewish, Christian and secular backgrounds, compared the experiences of women in our respective countries, and shared our concerns about the increasing phenomenon of fundamentalism and its impact on women's human rights.

Whereas we come from countries or communities in which the relationship of religion and the state takes various forms ranging from state religion or minority religious laws within secular or non-secular states in which one or several of the above mentioned religions is rapidly expanding in a way that shapes the national political agenda or affects some minority/migrant communities' identities within the country; and whereas the religious as well as ethnic, cultural, class, personal and political differences among us do not prevent us from identifying common issues of concern, namely:

– the use of religion as an effective means to control people and particularly women in our various national contexts which prevents us from reaching our full potential as human beings and constitutes a violation of our human rights;

– our local governments and/or political leaders merging state function with religion and manipulating religion in order to oppress minority groups, worsen inter-minority conflicts and/or strengthen their undemocratic power;

– the way in which fundamentalist groups are increasingly using economic resources to achieve popular support and increase their influence in national politics;

– the use of foreign aid, overseas charity work, development funds to foment and import fundamentalism to other countries; and whereas we respect religion as a matter of personal belief and practice:

we are opposed to any forms of legislation and policy formulation in the name of religion; and we strongly feel that a secular environment is the only means that can provide a comparatively safe space for women's human rights since the use of religion by existing power structures leads and has led to obvious human rights violations in many countries.

Therefore, be it resolved that we request that the human rights community immediately launch an investigation into the violation of women's human rights through fundamentalism worldwide, by means of case studies of each major religion as well as comparative surveys.

Adopted June 24, 1992 by women from the following countries: Algeria • Argentina • Bangladesh • Chile • China • Colombia •Dominican Republic • Ecuador • France • The Gambia • Germany • India • Ireland • Kenya • Mexico • Netherlands • New Zealand/Aotearoa • Nigeria • Peru • Philippines • Puerto Rico • South Africa • Sri Lanka • Turkey • Uganda • United States • Zimbabwe

Center for Women's Global Leadership,
Douglass College,
New Brunswick, New Jersey

Jewish Women: 'On the contrary, through knowledge, they are showing the way to a more just interpretation that is not based on male superiority.'[27]

Women's access to leadership positions varies greatly, even within a religion. In Judaism, for instance, the Reform and the Reconstructionist streams recognize women as equal partners and women have the right to become rabbis, whilst the Conservative stream is divided on these questions and the Orthodox stream strictly disapproves of equality. In various Christian denominations, women have been striving for many years to open the church hierarchies to the participation of women and to increase women's representation in church decision-making bodies. Whilst the Roman Catholic and Orthodox churches have all-male hierarchies, most Protestant denominations admit women to the clergy and to decision-making positions. In the Church of England, women have been ordained as deacons since the 1980s. In November 1992 the General Synod, the governing body of the church, passed a vote to admit women to the priesthood, based on a two-thirds majority. This has, nevertheless, provoked much discord among the church hierarchy and membership. In general, women are found mostly in the lowest levels of religious hierarchies and in serving roles.

As in other spheres, the strategy of strong women's organizations and international solidarity is sometimes used to promote more equality between men and women in religious organizations. An example comes from the Lutheran World Federation (LWF) which in 1952 called for full partnership of men and women. It was not until twenty years later, however, when women personally took the lead, that significant progress was made in reaching equal representation between men and women in decision-making bodies. By 1984 the LWF Assembly recommended that all decision-making bodies and meetings sponsored by the LWF should include a minimum of 40 per cent women and, following the next Assembly, 50 per cent. In addition, 40 per cent of training resource funds were to be allocated to women. These targets were achieved by 1989 and a monitoring system has been implemented.

With a critical mass of women in decision-making bodies and meetings, the LWF Office of Women in Church and Society was able to draw up a Plan of Action for the 1990s that shifts the focus from percentages of women in leadership positions 'to an examination of the long-term commitment of the churches in addressing the actual issues affecting women in the life of church and society.' Strategies for implementing the plan include building alliances and working together with men as well as 'international networks of women who can analyse problems and build coalitions in church and society.'[28]

WORKING WITH MEN IN INTERNATIONAL NGOS ☐ Women of course participate in many international non-governmental organizations comprising both men and women. Such organizations frequently reflect the unequal relationships between men and women in the larger society: women generally fill the service roles while more men than women are found in the leaderships. Growing gender awareness and the influence of the women's movement, however, are making themselves felt in the composition of leaderships, in the goals of the organizations and in their ways of working. Women have also succeeded in working through such NGOs to promote women and to respond to women's needs.

Many international NGOs and donor agencies have appointed gender officers, established women's focal points and instituted gender awareness training programmes. Others have given greater attention to women in their work. For instance Amnesty International, which

IBFAN, *FIGHTING FOR INFANT SURVIVAL*

reports on human rights abuses around the world and supports the rights of prisoners of conscience, is giving greater priority to the violation of women's human rights now that the international women's movement has succeeded in putting this on the international agenda.

The International Baby Food Action Network (IBFAN) is an example of how women have successfully worked with men in international NGOs to promote the rights of women. IBFAN was created in 1979 by six non-governmental organizations: Berne Third World Working Group (Switzerland), Interfaith Centre on Corporate Responsibility (USA), Infact Formula Action Coalition (INFACT, USA), International Organization of Consumers Unions (IOCU), Oxfam (UK) and War on Want (UK). With a large number of women in its membership, IBFAN has carried out a complex and multilayered international campaign, including a successful international boycott of multinational corporations, while simultaneously lobbying the World Health Organization (WHO) and UNICEF to adopt the International Code of Marketing of Breast-milk Substitutes. To accomplish this, IBFAN used its grassroots network around the world to gather evidence both about the advertising and promotional techniques used by the corporations to persuade women to use breastmilk substitutes, and about the negative, often fatal effects of this on the health of babies; it then used the grassroots network to monitor the implementation of the code. In its focus on the practices of multinational corporations and on babies, the campaign in its early stages sometimes lost sight of the mothers. But women in IBFAN brought a third focus to the activities of the network: that of promoting, protecting and supporting breastfeeding and working to create conditions to make it possible for women, with their multiple responsibilities inside and outside the home, to breastfeed their infants. IBFAN is also significant in the way it has been able to mobilize women and men at the grassroots to have a direct effect on giant multinational corporations:

IBFAN and the Code set an important precedent for several international campaigns by involving grassroots groups, giving them the opportunity to participate in debates on the international scene when matters affecting their people were being decided, and bringing the recommendations back to local communities.[29]

IBFAN is also an encouraging example of how international NGOs can incorporate women's perspectives, prioritize their needs, and effectively mobilize international action to campaign for them.

1. From the song 'Women', by the Shakti Group, quoted in Isis International, *Women Envision*, No. 5, 1993, p.2.
2. Nandita Gandhi and Vasantha Kannabiran, 'Current developments in feminism', in *Pressing Against the Boundaries*, Report of an FAO-FFHC/AD South Asia Workshop on Women and Development, FAO, New Delhi, 1989, p. 12.
3. Ana Maria Portugal, 'Introduction: On being a feminist in Latin America' in 'The Latin American Women's Movement', *Isis International Women's Journal*, No. 5, p. 5.
4. Kumari Jayawardena, 'Feminism in Sri Lanka in the decade 1975-1985', *Voice of Women*, Vol. 11, No. 4, 1986.
5. Valentine M. Moghadam, *Modernizing Women: Gender and Social Change in the Middle East*, Lynne Reiner Publishers, Boulder, 1993, p. 251.
6. Ibid., p. 255.
7. Kamla Bhasin and Nighat Said Khan, *Some Questions on Feminism and its Relevance in South Asia*, Kali for Women, New Delhi, 1993, p. 3.
8. Ibid., pp. 2-3.
9. Quoted in Ayesha Imam, 'Women's liberation: myth or reality?', in *Women, Struggles and Strategies*, Isis International, Rome, 1986, p. 69.
10. Report of the International Workshop on Feminist Ideology and Structures in the First Half of the Decade for Women (1979), Asia and Pacific Centre for Development Women's Programme, p. 1.
11. Naila Kabeer, 'Bridging the divide', *People and the Planet*, Vol. 2, No. 1, 1993, p. 27.
12. Ibid., p. 28.
13. Statement by participants in the IsisWicce 1991

Exchange Programme on Poverty and Prostitution.
14. See *Directory of Third World Women's Organizations, Isis International, Manila and Santiago*, 1991.
15. 'Bangkok Declaration', Women Empowering Communication Conference, Bangkok, Thailand, February 1994.
16. Ibid.
17. Virgina Willis, 'Public life: women make a difference', paper for the Expert Group Meeting on the Role of Women in Public Life organized by the UN Division for the Advancement of Women, Vienna, 1991, p. 4.
18. *Manushi*, No. 8, 1981, p. 8.
19. Ibid., p. 15.
20. See Kalima Rose, *Where Women Are Leaders: The SEWA Movement in India*, Zed Books, London, 1992.
21. Committee for Asian Women and Korean Women Workers Association, *When the Hen Crows: Korean Women Workers' Educational Programs*, CAW, Hong Kong, 1992, pp. 12–13.
22. *Speak, No.* 40, 1992.
23. Ibid.
24. International Confederation of Trade Unions (ICFTU), *Equality: The Continuing Challenge – Strategies for Success*, ICFTU, Belgium, 1992.
25. Rhoda Reddock, 'Women's organizations in the Caribbean community from the nineteenth century to today', *Womenspeak!*, Nos. 26 and 27, 1990.
26. S. Masturah Alatas, *True Picture on Rights of Muslim Women*, Sisters in Islam, Bangear Park, Malaysia.
27. Leila Seigel, 'Jewish women in Judaism', unpublished article, 1993.
28. Lutheran World Federation, *A Clear Plan of Action*, LWF, Geneva, 1992.
29. IBFAN, *Fighting for Infant Survival: An Information Kit on the Promotion, Protection and Support of Breastfeeding*, Penang.

4 PARTICIPATION IN POLITICS AND PUBLIC LIFE

The political space belongs to all citizens; politics is everyone's business and affects the lives of each of us ... the more women are associated, in numbers corresponding to their percentage of the population, in the political decision-making process, in parties, in elected bodies in governments and in international bodies, the more they can be associated with this process as protagonists and the more they can change the modalities and outcomes of politics. Only then will the concept of democracy find concrete and tangible expression ... democracy and the participation of women go hand in hand and promote each other mutually.[1]

If women's participation in the politics and decision making of their countries is a measure of democracy, then all countries still have a long way to go to achieve true democracy. Although women are participating in ever greater numbers in politics and public life all over the world, they still remain largely outside the realms of power and decision making in governments. The gaps between men and women's participation in political life have narrowed somewhat but remain huge, as figures on women as heads of governments, holders of ministerial positions and members of parliaments show.

One hundred years of struggle for the vote ☐ Beginning with New Zealand in 1893, women have gained the right to vote almost everywhere, although often only after long and difficult struggles. The long fight for women's suffrage in the United Kingdom and the USA, for example, began in the mid-nineteenth century and lasted well into the first quarter of the twentieth century. In the Philippines, women began organizing to get the vote in the early years of the twentieth century and obtained it only in 1937. The Indian women's movement demanded the vote from the British colonial authorities in the 1920s and lobbied their political parties for support, but it was not until 1950 that women in India finally gained the right to vote.

The Inter-Parliamentary Union (IPU) has gathered data on 150 countries with parliaments (see Table 4.4). In some countries the right to vote was granted in stages or with restrictions: first on the local level, then on the national level; or only to certain categories of women to begin with, such as literate or property-holding women. In some countries, the right to vote was given to women of European descent but not to indigenous women, as in Australia, Kenya, South Africa and Southern Rhodesia (Zimbabwe). Today such restrictions no longer exist in these countries and, of the countries in the world with parliaments and elections, only Kuwait still denies the right to vote to women.

While women in twenty-one countries of Europe and North America were enfranchised before the Second World War, fourteen countries of Europe did not give the vote to women until after the war. Women in Switzerland had to wait until 1971 to vote on federal issues. In other regions of the world, only eleven countries had extended the vote to women before the Second World War: Bolivia, Brazil, Cuba, Maldives, Mongolia, Philippines, Sri Lanka, Thailand and Uruguay. In a number of countries that had been colonized, women received the right to vote at the time of independence. See Table 4.4

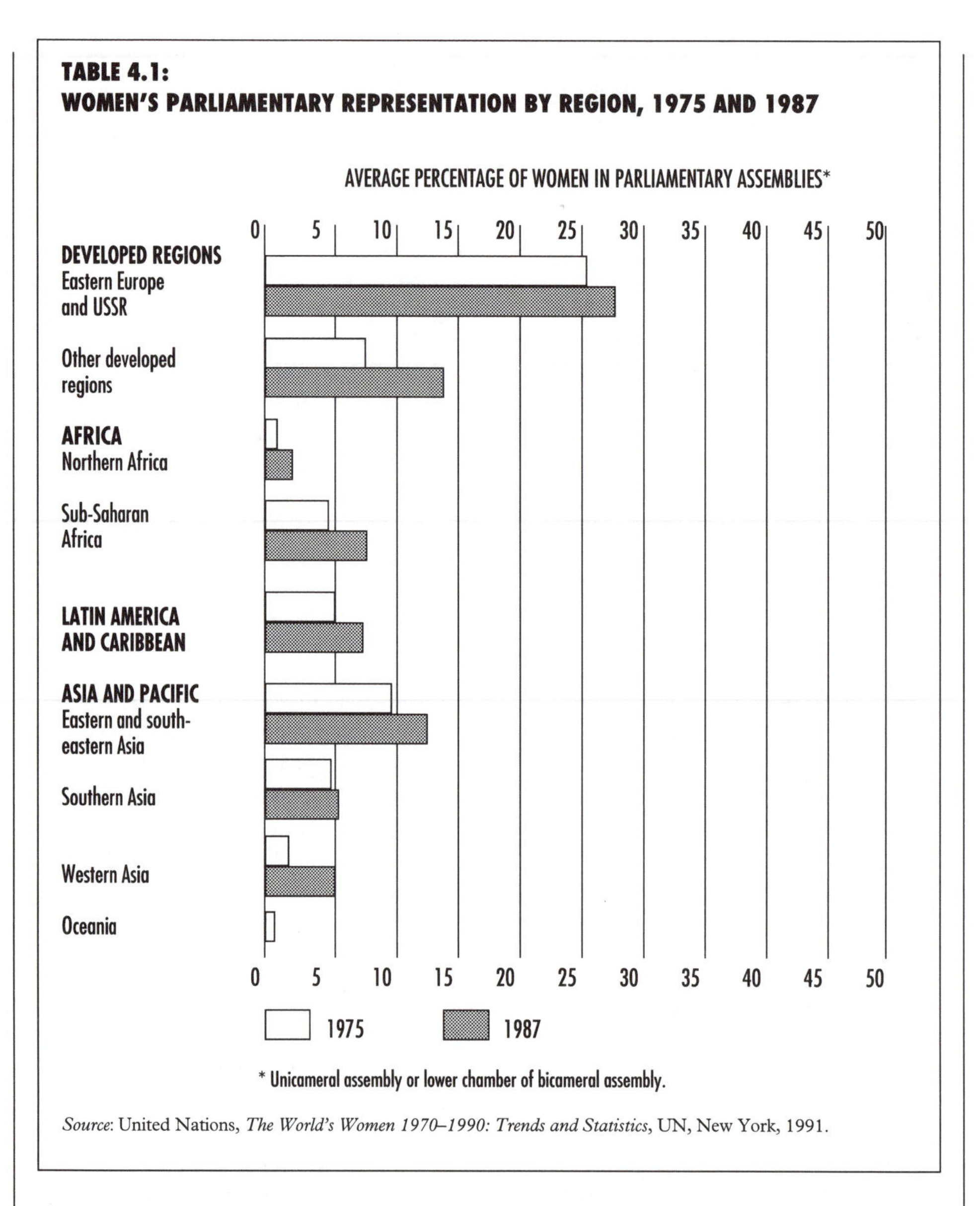

Source: United Nations, *The World's Women 1970–1990: Trends and Statistics*, UN, New York, 1991.

at end of this Chapter.[2]

WOMEN IN PARLIAMENTS □ The right to vote was a necessary step but, despite expectations, it was no guarantee that women would be able to participate in politics on an equal basis with men. In most countries, the right of women to be elected to parliament was granted at the same time as the right to vote, and in many places they were elected to parliament in the first general elections following the granting of the right to be elected (see Table 4.4). But in some countries there were gaps – ranging from three years (Denmark) to forty-two years (Australia). By 1993, women had been elected to the parliaments of most countries of the world.

TABLE 4.2:
WOMEN'S PARLIAMENTARY REPRESENTATION IN EASTERN EUROPE AND THE FORMER USSR, 1987 AND 1990

	WOMEN IN PARLIAMENT(%)	
	1987	1990
BULGARIA	21	9
CZECHOSLOVAKIA	30	6
GERMANY		
former German Dem. Rep.	32	21
HUNGARY	21	7
POLAND		
Senate	..	6
Lower House	20	4
ROMANIA	34	4
USSR		
Congress of People's Deputies	..	16
Soviet of Nationalities	31	14
Supreme Soviet	35	14

Source: *The World's Women 1970–1990.*

Only the parliaments of Comoros, Djibouti, Kiribati, Kuwait, the Solomon Islands, and the United Arab Emirates had never had women members.[3]

Women's participation in parliaments grew in every region between 1975 and 1987, as shown by Table 4.1. The greatest increases were in sub-Saharan Africa and in developed regions. However, the pace of the increase has been uneven, and overall women hold an average of only 10 per cent of parliamentary seats.

This trend has continued in the 1990s with the notable exceptions of the former socialist countries of eastern and central Europe where the number of female members has dropped dramatically following the political change from one-party to multi-party systems (see Table 4.2). Under one-party socialist governments, women held a relatively high percentage of parliamentary seats (over 30 per cent) in many countries, but a low percentage of positions in the decision-making bodies at government level (below 5 per cent). One explanation given is that the parliaments in these political systems were weak in comparison to the governments, where the real decisions were made.[4]

As can be seen from Table 4.5 at the end of this chapter, in 1993 women held more than 20 per cent of parliamentary seats in only 11 out of 170 countries: Seychelles (45.8%), Finland (39%), Norway (35.8%), Sweden (33.5%), Denmark (33%), the Netherlands (29.3%), Iceland (23.8%), Cuba (22.8%), Austria (21.3%), China (21%) and Germany (20.5%). In Sweden, the percentage of women in parliament rose to 41 per cent as a result of the September 1994 elections. In 36 countries, women held less than four per cent of the seats in parliament in 1993.

WOMEN AT MINISTERIAL LEVEL □

Worldwide women held only 4 per cent of ministerial-level positions in 1990. Women held more than 20 per cent of the positions only in Bhutan, Colombia, Norway and Sweden. Women filled 10 per cent or more of ministerial posts in seventeen countries, and in over eighty

PHOTO: LEHTIKUVA OY

Finnish Government Ministers of Housing, Environment, Social Issues and Health, Defence, Justice, Cultural Affairs, and Education, 1991

countries, women held no positions at ministerial level at all.

Most women in ministerial positions were responsible for health, welfare, education, culture or women's affairs – areas that are traditionally considered to be women's concerns. These ministries are marginalized in many countries and have limited power and resources. Economic, political and legal areas remain almost exclusively a male preserve, with a few exceptions: women have been ministers of foreign affairs in Botswana, Canada and Colombia, of political affairs in the Republic of Korea, of defence in Finland, and of finance in New Zealand.

WOMEN HEADS OF STATE OR GOVERNMENT □ The twentieth century has seen few women heads of state or government, either elected or appointed.

Many women who have reached the top came from families which are deeply involved in politics, including Corazon Aquino, Siramavo Bandaranaike, Benazir Bhutto, Indira Gandhi, Isabelita Peron and Khaleda Zia. Some of them gained power following the death of a political parent or spouse. For instance, Benazir Bhutto is the daughter of a former prime minister of Pakistan; Corazon Aquino was the wife of an opposition leader assassinated in the Philippines; and Khaleda Zia is the widow of a former president of Bangladesh. Nevertheless, women heads of state and government have distinguished themselves in their own right, and several have been considered strong leaders. Most of them have been 'lone women at the top': they have not, on the whole, been connected to women's movements or made special efforts to promote women's issues or open the way to other women to participate in politics. Notable exceptions to this are Gro Harlem Brundtland of Norway, whose cabinet of

WOMEN HEADS OF GOVERNMENT OR STATE IN THE TWENTIETH CENTURY

Presidents

- Corazon Aquino — Philippines
- Violeta Chamorro — Nicaragua
- Vigdis Finnbogadottir — Iceland
- Lidia Geiler — Bolivia
- Ertha Pascal-Trouillot — Haiti
- Isabela Peron — Argentina
- Mary Robinson — Ireland

Prime Ministers

- Siramavo Bandaranaike — Sri Lanka
- Benazir Bhutto — Pakistan
- Gro Harlem Brundtland — Norway
- Kim Campbell — Canada
- Eugenia Charles — Dominica
- Tansu Ciller — Turkey
- Edith Cresson — France
- Indira Gandhi — India
- Chandrika Kumaratunga — Sri Lanka
- Maria Liberia-Peters — Netherlands Antilles
- Golda Meir — Israel
- Maria de Lourdes Pintasilgo — Portugal
- Hanna Suchocka — Poland
- Margaret Thatcher — United Kingdom
- Khaleda Zia — Bangladesh

ministers was composed equally of men and of women, and the Irish head of state, President Mary Robinson, who acknowledged the importance of the women's movement in Ireland.

MAKING A DIFFERENCE □ Do women politicians have different concerns or behave differently from men in politics and does women's participation make a difference to political issues and the way politics are carried out? Drude Dahlerup, lecturer at the Institute of Political Science, University of Aarhus, Denmark, who has carried out extensive research on women in politics, says:

Don't expect us to make much difference as long as we are only a few women in politics. It takes a critical mass of women to make a fundamental change in politics.[5]

When significant numbers of women are present in politics, as in the Nordic countries where women hold a relatively high percentage of elective positions in government, studies show that they do make a difference. However, women are subject, just as men are, to prevailing political practices and to global economic and political forces that affect their possibilities for action. As Dahlerup says:

... women politicians are just as powerless when it comes to the global economic changes as are the male politicians. But the many women in politics in the Scandinavian countries have to some extent changed people's attitudes towards women as leaders, have changed the political discourse somewhat, have placed women's issues on the agenda, and have to some extent changed the political culture. As an expression of this cultural change, let me tell you a story of a little boy three years of age, living in Norway where the prime minister and many party leaders are women. The boy asks his mother: 'Mamma, can a man become prime minister?'[6]

A study on women in public life, carried out by the United Nations Division for the Advancement of Women (DAW), also argues that only a critical mass of women allows female politicians to bring different values to public life: 'The fewer the number of women in public life ... the less they are likely to be able to confidently assert distinctively female values, priorities and characteristics. As a minority operating in a male domain, most women public figures, to be accepted and to function on a basis of equality with men, have had to adapt to and adopt the male priorities predominating in public life. Minorities, such as women who are successful in a male world, according to a classic theory of minority behaviour, absorb the dominant culture to such an extent that they tend to dissociate themselves from other women, to underrate their own success and to perceive any discrimination they meet as a result of their own shortcomings. It takes a minority of a certain minimum size, 30–35 percent, to be able to influence the culture of groups and to facilitate alliances between group members. That theory may explain why lone women who reach high office have often appeared not to bring distinctively female values to their office.'[7]

What are these 'distinctively female values'? While bearing in mind that the question of whether or not women have distinct biologically or socially determined values is a controversial one, as well as the dangers of gender stereotyping, several studies of women in politics show that women's experiences, particularly as mothers and in their traditional roles in the home and the family, make them more acutely aware than men of the needs of other people and thus more able and likely to take into account in their work the needs and rights of women, children, the elderly, the disabled, minorities and the disadvantaged. Women are also more likely to advocate measures in the areas of health and reproduction, child care, education, welfare and the environment, and are generally less militaristic and more supportive of nonviolence and peace. Women tend to be more realistic and practical in their work, more able to initiate and accept changes in methods and targets, and more willing to work collectively. Women generally also consider the impact of their decisions on others more carefully. All of these factors constitute a different attitude to political culture.[8] According to DAW:

Where women are in power in sufficient numbers there is evidence that they do indeed behave differently from their male colleagues. On a broad canvas, the new political movement, the Greens, in which from the beginning women have played a leading role, has tried new forms of politics and collaborative, non-hierarchical systems that better reflect women's ways of working. A report of the working of the local council of a suburb in Sweden showed how an increase in women's representation to 40–48 percent led to changes in the political climate, with debates reported to be more to the point, language more concrete and accessible, male officials daring to acknowledge family obligations and give them priority over political obligations, as the basis of decision-making broadened to include women's perspectives.[9]

OBSTACLES □ The United Nations Division for the Advancement of Women (DAW) has identified a number of obstacles to women's participation in politics which prevent them from reaching parliamentary and ministerial positions:

- the relatively short historical tradition of women's political participation and lack of experience in campaigning, public debate, exposure to media;
- prevailing negative attitudes towards women's participation in public life, lack of confidence and support for female candidates and politicians on the part of the electorate, including women;
- the difficulty women experience in com-

PHOTO: OLGA YOLANDA LOPEZ/ISIS INTERNATIONAL

When women participate in sufficient numbers, they can make a difference

bining a political career with the traditional woman's role in the family and often in society;

- economic dependency or lack of financial means;
- insufficient education in general and political education in particular;
- women's reluctance or diffidence to participate in politics, particularly at a high level.[10]

Political parties, parliaments and trade unions are major vehicles for political careers and the low participation of women in these organizations, especially at the leadership level, closes important paths for advancing to decision-making positions in government.[11]

WOMEN IN POLITICAL PARTIES □

Political parties are a major path to participation in elected and appointed political bodies. Whilst women comprise a substantial part of the membership of political parties in many countries, they are regularly excluded from leadership. Although only a limited number of countries, especially in Africa, Asia or Latin America, were able to give statistics on party membership in response to a 1991 questionnaire of the Inter-Parliamentary Union, many of those that did respond reported female membership of between 30 and 50 per cent in political parties: Austria, Belgium, Canada, Dominica, Finland, Gabon, Greece, Iceland, Ireland, Italy, Japan, Kenya, Luxembourg, Malta, New Zealand, Panama, Republic of Korea, Sweden, and the United Kingdom.[12]

The percentage declines considerably in leadership positions. There are a few exceptions: in Sweden, almost all parties have at least 40 per cent women in their governing bodies, and in Australia, Iceland,

and New Zealand some parties reported a significant percentage of women in leadership. In Norway, three major parties were headed by women and women figured among the top leadership of several other parties. The Green parties of Germany, New Zealand, Sweden and Switzerland have an equal balance of men and women in leadership, due in part to quota systems. Zimbabwe reports that 30 per cent of the central committee of ZANU (PF) are women and Nicaragua estimates that 20 to 30 per cent of party leaders are women. For the rest, few countries report more than 20 per cent of women in party leadership and many report considerably less.[13]

Major obstacles to women's participation were identified by the Inter-Parliamentary Union as lack of child care and time conflicts between political party meetings and family responsibilities:

The structuring of political working time, conceived by men for men, creates a time conflict between certain political activities and the time which women wish to or must devote to family activities, and sometimes to professional activities as well. This is true for women in all countries, and more particularly for women in Third World countries where the traditional division of tasks between men and women remains strict.[14]

A study of measures taken by parties to counter these difficulties revealed that political parties in only a few countries occasionally provide childcare facilities and/or rearrange meetings to schedule them at times convenient for women: for example, in Australia, Belgium, Egypt, Italy, Japan, Morocco, New Zealand, Sweden, the United Kingdom, the United States of America and Vietnam.[15]

NATIONAL AND INTERNATIONAL CIVIL SERVICE □ Statistics that exist on female employment rates in the public sector show that women make up at least 50 per cent of public sector employees in Denmark, Finland, Sweden and the Philippines. In Argentina, Mexico, Indonesia, Iraq and Thailand women also comprise a sizeable proportion of the public administration.[16] One reason for female prevalence in the public sector is that salaries in the civil service are generally lower than those in the private sector, making the civil service less attractive to men. Moreover, according to *The World's Women: 1970–1990*, 'Educated women work in the public sector because it offers them white collar conditions, employment security, benefits, and possibly some opportunity to advance.'[17]

However, women tend to be concentrated at the lowest hierarchical levels and in the lowest-paid jobs of the civil service. This is a cause for concern not only because it demonstrates inequality of opportunity, but because political power is increasingly exercised by technocrats in the upper ranks of the civil service. A study of women in European politics states:

In the Western political scene as a whole, the very small number of women civil servants at the highest levels of the state is perhaps the most worrying aspect of their marginalisation. When we know that parliamentary power is declining and is being replaced by the power of technocrats, it is worrying to see women making progress in the former and not among the latter.[18]

Where women have succeeded in reaching high levels in the state civil service, doors have opened to greater political power through appointment to government positions. For instance, in France, most of the women who comprise one fourth of the positions in ministerial cabinets entered through the path of the civil service.[19]

DAW has found that the usual obstacles that women face in any job – discriminatory attitudes and customs, less access to education, the difficulties of combining paid employment with household and childcare responsibilities – restrict women's career path in the civil service. In addition, recruitment, promotion and appeals mechanisms, training and career development opportunities and job classifications all tend to channel women to 'female' job categories with few prospects for advancement. Women confront appointment systems that may be based on patronage, and are not transparent, and recruitment panels and entrance requirements and exams that are directly or indirectly biased. Frequently women with the same or higher qualifications than men are placed on lower levels and salary scales. It is ironic that one area in the civil service where women are often marginalized without opportunities for advancement is in jobs related to the implementation of affirmative action, that is, measures to increase opportunities for those who have faced discrimination in the past.[20]

As in national civil services, women in the international civil service are concentrated in secretarial and administrative jobs or in low-level professional occupations such as editorial, library and language positions with little room for advancement. A pertinent question raised by the Australian Permanent Representative to the United Nations at the UN General Assembly on November 1991 is:

Why is it that a standard-setting organization like the United Nations is following rather than leading the world on an important issue of equality?[21]

TABLE 4.3
WOMEN PROFESSIONAL STAFF IN THE UNITED NATIONS SYSTEM

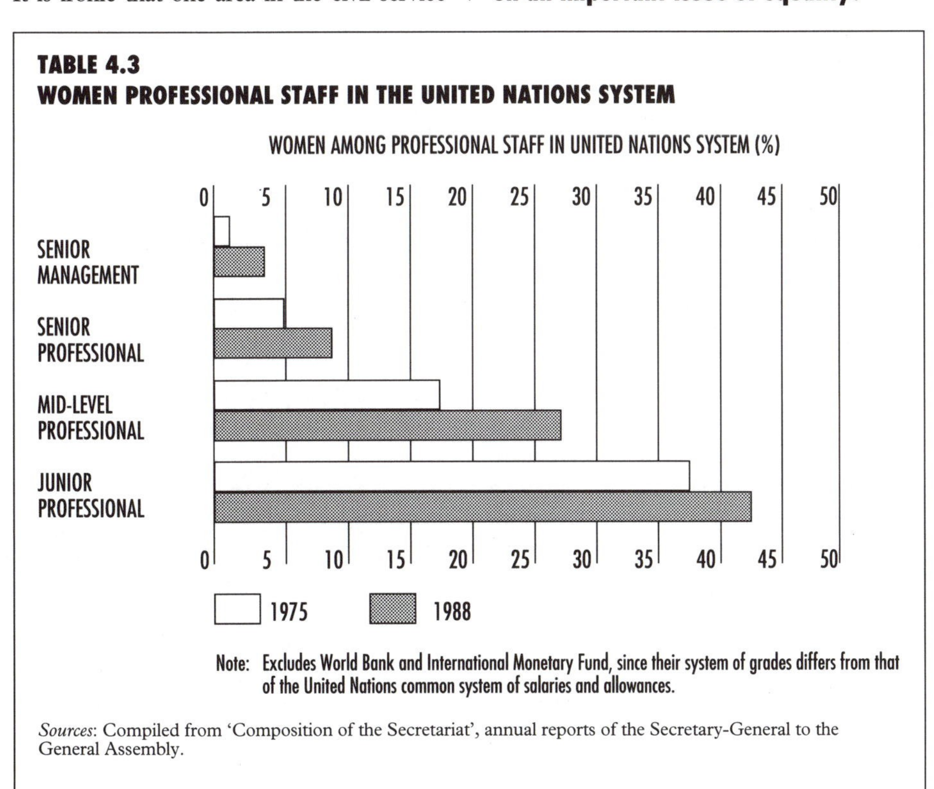

Note: Excludes World Bank and International Monetary Fund, since their system of grades differs from that of the United Nations common system of salaries and allowances.

Sources: Compiled from 'Composition of the Secretariat', annual reports of the Secretary-General to the General Assembly.

While the United Nations has undertaken many initiatives and come out with numerous documents and recommendations to promote equality and the advancement of women around the world, it has neglected to put its own house in order. Women are very poorly represented in the upper echelons of the organization's management and barely present in the higher professional positions.

A look at the statistics on the professional staff in the United Nations system shows that while the number of women increased at all levels between 1975 and 1988, women still made up less than 5 per cent of the senior management and less than 10 per cent of the senior professional staff in 1988. Women were better represented among mid-level professionals (25–30 per cent). Only at the entry level did women comprise a substantial percentage of the staff: more than 40 per cent of the junior professionals (see Table 4.3).

Recruitment methods affect the percentage of women at the various levels. At the entry level, where staff are recruited on the basis of competitive examinations, more than 40 per cent of staff are women. At the senior levels where staff are recruited from among the mid-level professionals or from outside, women are decidedly at a disadvantage. Few governments put forward women as candidates for higher-level jobs and women within the United Nations face the same obstacles to advancement as women in national civil services and other occupations. With the same qualifications as men, women are often appointed to lower job and salary levels; they wait longer than men for promotion; they are not given the same opportunities to gain the experience necessary for promotion to management positions; they face negative attitudes from supervisors and department heads; and they have insufficient access to training programmes, participation in substantive meetings and travel. This situation is, of course, compounded by women's household and family responsibilities. To remedy this situation, the United Nations General Assembly set targets to be achieved: women should hold 30 per cent of all posts subject to geographical distribution by 1990 and 35 per cent by 1995, including 25 per cent at the top levels.

On International Women's Day, 8 March 1993, Mr Boutros Boutros-Ghali, Secretary-General of the United Nations said:

By the time of the fiftieth anniversary of the United Nations, in 1995, I expect to see the numbers of women working in professional posts at the UN to be reflective of the world population as a whole.[22]

To back up this statement, special measures were taken to quicken the pace of achieving gender balance in policy-level positions in the United Nations Secretariat.[23]

MECHANISMS FOR INCREASING WOMEN'S PARTICIPATION ☐ An expert group meeting on Equality in Political Participation and Decision-Making organized by DAW made the following recommendations to improve women's status in political parties:

- as an interim measure, substantial targets, such as quotas or similar forms of positive action to ensure women's candidacy for office and participation in political posts should be applied;
- training programmes should be developed to increase the political and management skills of women in politics, both as candidates and as elected or appointed officials, especially making use of the experience of other women

who have achieved public office;

- women's sections of parties should be evaluated and strengthened to enable them to influence party policy and promote female candidacy;
- information on potential women candidates should be compiled, maintained on a systematic basis and made available when candidacy or appointments are considered;
- parties should be encouraged to examine the criteria used to select persons for political functions to ensure that the varieties of experience possessed by women are taken into account in selection;
- training activities should be developed to sensitize party members to the needs and potentials of female members;
- as an interim measure where the electoral system might make it useful, parties should undertake special measures to provide funding for women candidates for office.[24]

Other important mechanisms include networking, participation in the campaigns of other politicians, lobbying, membership in the same clubs, professional and academic associations. Women's participation in politics and decision-making positions in government is highest in countries where women have developed strong networks, have access to higher education and training in political science, law and management, and to developed social support services.[25]

Similarly, the following strategies to improve the participation of women in national and international civil services have been identified by DAW:

- all civil services should have clear statements on all personnel practices (recruitment/appointment, promotion, training and development, leave entitlements and other conditions of service, including appeals mechanisms);
- where possible, women should serve on all committees (especially appointment and promotion committees);
- civil services should accept that equal employment opportunity and affirmative action strategies are a necessary part of human resource management;
- the disadvantages that women experience in their pursuit of career development vis-à-vis men should be mitigated;
- equitable distribution of women throughout all levels in the administrative hierarchy should be promoted (to avoid concentrations at the lowest levels) and in all function areas (especially in areas regarded as non-traditional for women);
- the number of women in decision-making positions in all civil and foreign services (including international and intergovernmental organizations) should be improved.[26]

QUOTAS In some countries, quotas have been successfully used to increase women's participation in the leadership of political parties and in party lists for public elections. For instance, the Norwegian Labour Party stipulates that at least 40 per cent of all candidates for election must be women; the Danish Social Democratic party has a similar provision for municipal and county elections.[27] According to the Norwegian Labour Party's Secretariat:

Quotas for women is the most efficient strategy we ever used to increase women's political representation.[28]

A study on the effectiveness of the quota system in the Nordic countries produced the following findings:

It takes about three elections to implement a new quota system fully... First and foremost because it is a problem to throw a man out in order to get a woman in. It is much easier to wait for vacant seats. Today the parliamentary fraction of the Norwegian Labour Party consists of about fifty-fifty men and women. In the Danish Social Democratic Party women's share of the candidates for the local elections increased from 28% in 1985 to 33% in 1989 after the introduction of quotas. The percentage of women elected increased from 25% to 29%. This example shows that a rule of 40% women on the list does not secure women 40% of those elected, even if implemented. Depending on the electoral system and whether preferential votes are allowed for, you can have 40% women on the list – and no women elected! That will happen, e.g. if all the 40% are placed on the bottom of the list and men are given priority on the top of the list. Quotas for women in elections is a very controversial measure. There will always be great resistance. It takes power in advance as well as good alliances with men in order to introduce this rather efficient measure for empowerment of women.[29]

Quotas are more frequently established by political parties than by governments. A survey by the Inter-Parliamentary Union showed that, in 1991, 56 political parties in thirty-four countries had some kind of a quota system either for legislative elections (22 parties) or executive posts of the party (51 parties). On the other hand, the constitutions or legislation of only a few countries provide for quotas for women in parliament, including those of Angola, the former Union of Soviet Socialist Republics (USSR) and Nepal. In addition, the 1991 electoral law of Argentina establishes a compulsory 30 per cent quota for women candidates for all elective posts. Establishment of quotas for women in parliament has also been debated in Belgium, France, Germany, Peru and Switzerland. Related to the quota system is the mechanism of reserved seats: Bangladesh, Egypt, Nepal, Pakistan and the United Republic of Tanzania are among the countries that have or have had in the past a certain number of seats in their national parliaments reserved for women.[30]

Possible drawbacks of the quota system are: quotas may be interpreted as a ceiling or limitation to the number of women or may be used to appoint token women with little or no power, especially in bodies that do not have real decision-making power. However, quotas or reserved seats can be one of the few ways to ensure some representation for women where this is nonexistent or very low; they can also be used effectively where women have already achieved a measure of political power, as in the Nordic countries, to push for even greater representation of women.

Quotas are sometimes established for appointments to government bodies: in the Netherlands, for example, Cabinet Office guidelines aim for an equal balance of men and women in advisory bodies; in Norway the law specifies that 40 per cent of public appointees to government commissions must be women. In Australia the National Agenda for Women has targeted the year 2000 to achieve equal representation of men and women on government-appointed boards and bodies.

AFFIRMATIVE ACTION A mechanism closely related to quotas is affirmative action, which is used to redress past discrimination against women and give them equal opportunities with men in access to jobs and promotions. In India, affirmative action measures taken to increase the numbers of women in the civil service include: media campaigns and training incentives to recruit women; inclusion of at least one woman on every government recruitment board; a separate register for women at all employment exchanges; the inclusion of at least 30 per

QUOTAS: PROS AND CONS

In response to a survey carried out by the Inter-Parliamentary Union in 1991, a number of parliaments reported on the debate on quotas going on in their countries. Here are excerpts from some of the replies.

Belgium: The possibility of introducing quotas for women on voting lists does not meet with unanimity, even among women. However, it is noted that the party which first had a well-structured and powerful women's organization, having fixed quotas for women in its structure and on voting lists since 1973, is the party with the most women parliamentarians. This encouraging achievement is the result both of fixing quotas and of the presence of a strong group of women politicians who are well integrated in the party at all levels.

Egypt: There are many opinions regarding the effects of implementing a quota system on women's participation in political life. Some people think that such a system would be prejudicial to equality between men and women as far as rights and responsibilities are concerned, because it demonstrates a lack of understanding of the capacity of women to occupy key posts on the basis of their own efforts and popularity. The other view is that the system is capable of ensuring greater participation by women in political life, particularly where women's social situation and the prevalence of certain traditions and customs hamper their participation, especially in rural areas. It should be emphasized that practice has shown that the abolition of the quota system in Egypt led to a reduction in the number of women candidates at elections.

Inter-Parliamentary Union,
Women and Political Power
(1992) pp. 100-101.

cent women on recruitment lists, if they are available. In spite of these efforts, the percentage of women in the public sector is still small in India, and women comprise less than 10 per cent of the Indian administrative and foreign services.[31]

In some countries governments are carrying out systematic affirmative action programmes. The International Labour Organization (ILO) has given the following report on Zimbabwe:

In all the ministries and other public services of Zimbabwe, the objective is to guarantee that 30 per cent of middle and senior management positions be occupied by women, as they constitute 30 per cent of staff at entry level in the public sector. After a period of research and planning, the programme in the public services began in 1991: identification of women who could be promoted or promoted after exposure to management training, more women students in educational institutions, and similar measures. It would appear that the impact of these measures is slow in making itself felt. In the second year of implementation, the programme still falls short of achievement of its goals. Still, gains have been made. In the space of some 18 months, the number of women in the highest positions went up from 19 to 32, although in percentage terms this means from a little more than 10 per cent to somewhat less than 15 per cent. In middle-management positions, there is as yet very little change.[32]

Factors hindering the success of the affirmative action programme in Zimbabwe included 'lack of clear and adequate information about the policy;

consequent resistance and resentment by some men; fear and lack of confidence by the women themselves; and family attitudes, expectations and responsibilities'.[33] In Australia an evaluation of the application of the Australian Affirmative Action Act carried out in 1991/92 concluded: 'The quality of affirmative action programmes will have to be improved if women are to achieve true equality with men on the job.'[34]

Affirmative action is also being used to remedy the lack of women in the United Nations. Measures specify that where the 1995 targets of 35 per cent women overall in posts and 25 per cent in senior management have not yet been reached, vacancies shall be filled by women, provided there are one or more fully qualified female candidates.[35] The question remains as to who decides whether or not they are fully qualified. It is essential that women be prominent in recruitment procedures if old prejudices and discriminatory attitudes are to fall away from the recruitment process.

Affirmative action programmes, like legislation on the equality of men and women, are not effective unless women know about them and unless there is strong pressure and organization to see that they are applied and enforced. Although affirmative action is a useful tool for increasing women's participation, it is only a part of a larger strategy necessary to break down barriers.

TRAINING Another mechanism for improving women's participation in the public sector and particularly for increasing women's access to the higher levels of the national and international civil services is training. Whilst training can be directed to improving women's skills in specific areas, particularly in management, in addition gender sensitivity training can be directed to both men and women to build awareness of the concrete and attitudinal barriers to women's participation and advancement. A United Nations survey and workshop on 'Men and Women in Management' led to the following conclusions:

- The key factors to the improvement of the status of women in an organization are top-level commitment, clear policies and a well-defined system of accountability. Training cannot substitute for these factors.
- Training can help to improve the working environment for women by promoting awareness of inappropriate behaviours and developing the supervisory and managerial skills needed to ensure that staff are perceived correctly and treated equitably.
- Awareness and skills training can either be done in independent workshops or incorporated into existing training activities such as supervisory and management training programmes.
- Independent training programmes need to be done on a fairly wide scale if they are to have a discernible impact, which could be costly. It is also difficult to make participation mandatory.
- Integrating a module on the status of women into supervisory and management training makes it necessary to treat the issue in a shorter period of time and focus on specific limited aspects, but it enables the issue to be dealt with in an overall organizational context.[36]

WOMEN'S SECTIONS OF PARTIES While many political parties around the world have women's sections, there is an ongoing debate about their usefulness. Parliamentarians in Gabon, for instance, say:

It has to be admitted that unanimity has not yet been achieved among the

PHOTO: ANNE WALKER/IWTC

With education and training, women can participate more effectively

female population in favour of establishing a women's branch in the political formation and parties. Some women think that such a structure is needed and must be maintained until the objective of equality has been achieved, which probably takes us to the year 2000. Others argue that, on the contrary, a women's branch enables women to be shut up in a ghetto.[37]

Unfortunately many women's sections are little more than the 'housekeeping' branch of the party or are too weak to make inroads into male political power. A survey of women's sections of parties in different regions found, for example, that although the women's wing of a Malaysian party had mobilized women voters and raised money for the party, it exerted virtually no power. In Latin America, women's sections in Mexico, Chile, and Peru were confined mainly to housekeeping tasks and had little clout in the party. In Colombia, women acknowledged that the women's branch was instrumental in giving them a start in politics, but few women gained more than token positions and their political careers in the party were short-lived: 'Women's numbers are simply too small for them to develop coalitions within for gender leverage.'[38]

The same survey paints an equally dismal picture of women's branches in Africa. In Zambia, women were limited to dealing with moral and ethical issues, while in Tanzania the women's section sponsored home economics, child-rearing and income-generating projects but rarely dealt with the issues of gender discrimination raised by its members. In Sierra Leone a women's branch mobilized women and raised funds for the party, but had little influence on party policy or candidates.[39] Another report found that the integration of Kenya's largest and oldest women's NGO, Maendeleo Ya Wanawake Organization (MYWO), into the ruling party in 1987, greatly decreased its power.[40]

However, women's sections can also provide a means to organize women and strengthen their ability to lobby for a different political agenda or greater involvement. Growing awareness of gender discrimination and imbalances has helped bring about change in some women's sections, as has happened in Canada:

The nature and organization of women's branches or women's committees within the national and provincial political parties in Canada have changed substantially over the years. In the early years, these organizations tended to be separate or auxiliary adjuncts to the main political parties. Often the tasks which women undertook within these organizations reflected the sexual division of labour in the larger society. Formerly, women's groups tended to be seen as sources of cheap labour. They were often relegated to activities such as addressing and stuffing envelopes, pouring tea at larger party meetings, organizing and facilitating party meetings, holding charity events for fund-raising, etc. However, in more recent years, there have been some dramatic changes. In the 1970s, women's groups tended to become more fully integrated into the larger federal party of which they were a part. During this period, the mandates, structures and roles of the organizations were altered. Many of the groups began to adopt affirmative action plans aimed at increasing the political participation of women in national party politics.[41]

WOMEN'S POLITICAL PARTIES The difficulties of working within political parties have led women in a number of countries to form women's parties to mobilize and involve women in politics. An account of the launching of the women's political party Kaiba (Women for the Motherland) in the Philippines in October 1986 reported:

Delegates stressed the importance of a venue for women to develop skills in political participation and felt that a women's political party would be a significant forum for women to organize and train themselves to be active in politics.[42]

Women's parties have also been formed in Canada, Germany, Spain, Nigeria and Iceland. While most of these have been short-lived and without much impact on electoral politics, their significance generally lies in giving women a space to discuss political issues. In Russia, the newly established Women of Russia party did remarkably well in the parliamentary elections of December 1993, gaining over 8 per cent of the vote. Only three other parties received a higher percentage.

WOMEN'S POLITICAL ORGANIZATIONS

Women have formed their own political organizations which aim to achieve greater representation of women in parliaments and political positions. Some organizations have several decades of experience, such as the League of Women Voters in the USA. More recently in the USA, feminist organizations such as the National Organization for Women and the National Women's Political Caucus have been working to build and to lobby for a women's agenda in politics, to mobilize women voters and to get more women elected at all levels. The Coalition for Women's Appointments, co-ordinated by the National Women's Caucus, has set up a databank of qualified women, and lobbies for high-level political positions for women.[43] Despite these efforts, the number of women in the US Congress remains low. In the elections of 1992, which women declared the 'year of the women' in politics, many more women ran and were elected to office, yet the number of women in the House of Representatives rose only from 28 to 47, just 10.8 per cent of the total of 435 representatives, while the number of women senators rose from 2 to 7 or just 7 per cent of the 100, and this more than seventy years after women got the vote.

Women's organizations in Europe have also been campaigning to increase the number of women in elected bodies. As early as 1965, the Centre Féminin d'Etudes et d'Information in France was demanding that women constitute one-third of the candidates for the European Parliament. In 1977 the National Council of Danish Women took up the call for an equal balance of men and women in this body. The National Council of Women in Belgium has campaigned for increased representation of women in local elections. In 1986 in France, DIALOGUE launched its campaign to increase the number of women candidates put forward by the conservative parties with the slogan 'Give a Seat to a Lady'. In the United Kingdom, the Three Hundred Group aims for an equal number of women and men among the 650 members of parliament.[44] In the Netherlands, the Association for Women's Interests, Women's Work and Equal Citizenship, which traces its history to the Association for Women's Suffrage, is campaigning for equal representation of men and women in political functions by the year 2000, with a goal of a 35 per cent share for women for 1994.

Political education and awareness building is intended to promote women's representation in the electoral process; to establish and lobby for a women's agenda; and to sensitize both women and men to women's issues and the role of women in

PHOTO: M. EUGENIA JELINCIC/ISIS INTERNATIONAL

Women's political education takes many forms: women in Chile sew political messages into *arpilleras* (wall hangings)

politics. Women's political organizations have carried this out in various ways. In Greece, for instance, the Women's Union organized regional seminars lasting several days to raise the political consciousness of women. Women in Nigeria (WIN) organized a series of seminars, workshops and conferences all across the country to involve women in political debate and present their views. These workshops reached a wide cross-section of women, including farmers, professionals and Muslim women. Women called for 50 per cent representation in legislative and executive posts, and recommended conditions they considered necessary for women's active participation in politics and decision making. WIN affirms the need for women to have political power in order to achieve democracy and development of the whole society, and quotes the saying that:

A society attempting to develop without the full participation of women is like a bird trying to fly with only one wing. It is bound to go off course.[45]

When the first elections for the Legislative Council of Hong Kong were held in 1991, women's organizations mobilized to educate women voters, encourage their participation in the elections, and to establish a women's agenda. For this purpose, five local women's groups united their forces: the Association for the Advancement of Feminism, the Hong Kong Association of Women Workers, the Hong Kong Women Christian Council, the Shaukeiwan Federation of Women and the Women's Centre. These groups launched the Women Voters Education Programme which included a 'conference on the women's platform' in which twenty-two of the total of fifty-four electoral candidates presented their positions on women's rights.[46]

Although the election of a woman, Corazon Aquino, to the presidency of the Philippines in 1986 did not open up politics to women as much as many had hoped, the return of democracy made it possible for women to organize politically. Within the government, the National Commission on Women led an energetic campaign and carried out extensive gender sensitivity training within government bodies on both the national and regional levels. Non-governmental women's organizations became very involved in lobbying the government on issues of concern to women.

There have also been attempts by autonomous women's movements to work within established political structures. One such effort took place in Peru, where feminist groups tried out a strategy of putting forward women candidates in the lists of the Izquierda Unida (United Left) in the elections of 1985, using the campaign slogan 'women vote for yourselves'. This attempt was the result of much debate in the autonomous feminist movement in Peru on whether or not to work within the established political structures and with political parties. According to Virginia Vargas, one of the candidates, the whole process was a learning experience which revealed both the limitations of working with the political parties and the formal political process and of the feminist movement to influence politics and gain wider support. On the one hand, the women found that they had too little strength to force the male-dominated political parties to make serious commitments to women's issues and needs. On the other, the women's platform, while giving much needed attention to women's specific issues, failed to focus sufficiently on wider economic and political issues. Moreover, the women found that the short time and great pressures of an electoral campaign made it difficult to convince the electorate of their cause. While some seeds were planted, much more groundwork and cultivation would be needed to make them grow.[47]

In Mexico, the women's movement is conducting a campaign Ganando Espacios (Gaining Spaces) to ensure that the constitutional right of equality is put into practice through legislation that guarantees women 50 per cent representation in all decision-making bodies in society. The campaign bases itself on the Convention on the Elimination of All Forms of Discrimination against Women, which has been ratified by Mexico. In Paraguay, the Coordinacion de Mujeres, an umbrella organization of women's groups, brings together women in an annual forum and tries to build gender awareness among women who already are politicians as well as to facilitate the entry of more women into electoral politics. In Argentina, women are monitoring the recent legislation requiring parties to include 30 per cent women in their electoral lists. The need to develop greater expertise in the political process has brought women from different countries in Latin America together in seminars to discuss issues such as 'Feminismo, poder y practicos politicos' (feminism, power and political practice) and 'Mujer y democratizacion del poder' (women and the democratization of power). As a result of one of these seminars, a Network of Women in Politics in the Southern Cone of Latin America was formed.[48]

Experiences with political education campaigns for women have shown that for lasting effects, the programmes must be ongoing and organizationally and financially sustained. Likewise, while one-off efforts to elect women candidates can focus attention on women in politics during an election campaign, long-term sustained

PHOTO: M. EUGENIA JELINCIC/ISIS INTERNATIONAL

Eritrean women in exile demonstrate in Rome on International Women's Day, 1983. The banner reads: 'Equality Through Participation'

efforts and financial resources are required to make a significant impact. Once women have reached high political positions, they are often able to open the way for other women, especially if they are connected to and supported by a critical mass of women in government and/or by strong connections with women's organizations and grassroots movements.

On the international level, women members of the Inter-Parliamentary Union (IPU) have instituted a twice-yearly Meeting of Women Parliamentarians which serves the purposes of increasing the number of women in delegations to IPU meetings and on its executive bodies and committees, influencing the agenda of IPU meetings, and providing women parliamentarians with the opportunity to share their experiences in strengthening the participation of women in politics in their countries. Among its achievements are the following:

- changes in the IPU statutes to the effect that delegations to IPU meetings from every parliament with women members should include at least one of them;
- election of women to the executive bodies and committees of the IPU, and changes in rules to the effect that the composition of any drafting committee should take into account gender balance;
- bringing to the IPU agenda issues of violence against children and women, health, and the well-being of the elderly;
- the development of a special IPU programme on the participation of women in political life which carries out regular surveys on the number of women in parliaments worldwide and on the factors that promote or hinder their participation in politics. This programme is also preparing a plan of action aimed at correcting the present imbalance between men and women in political life.

WOMEN IN MOVEMENTS FOR LIBERATION AND DEMOCRACY □

In times of political upheaval, in all regions of the world women have come forward to defend or struggle for national independence and liberation and for greater democracy. Resistance or liberation movements have given women the opportunity to leave their homes and participate alongside men for radical political changes. Women played significant roles in the revolutionary movements of the eighteenth, nineteenth and early twentieth centuries, and continued to do so in the resistance and partisan movements of the Second World War, in independence movements against colonialism, in national liberation struggles in countries such as Algeria, China, Eritrea, Namibia, Nicaragua, Mozambique, Palestine, Vietnam, and Zimbabwe, among others, and in movements of opposition to dictatorships and for greater democracy in the Philippines, South Africa and many countries of Latin America and other regions.

Recognizing the importance of mobilizing women, many liberation movements formed women's organizations to support and carry forward the revolutions. In these movements women, often portrayed with a baby in one arm and a gun in the other, have been sung as heroines who have taken up arms and proved their courage and daring. Indeed, many women have risked or given their lives, suffered detention and exile and participated in many ways in struggles for national liberation. Despite their significant contributions, however, women have mostly played supportive roles. Moreover, issues of particular concern to women, such as reproduction, child care, domestic work and discrimination against women, have usually been considered 'secondary' and women have been asked to subordinate them to the 'general good'. The assumption has been that the emancipation of women would automatically be achieved by the victory of the struggle.

At the end of the struggle, however, women were usually expected to assume their traditional roles or were largely limited to supportive positions in political and public life. Although most victorious movements proclaimed the equality of women and stamped out blatantly oppressive practices, women's issues continued to be considered peripheral. There were some exceptions: where women were essential to the building of the economy, newly liberated countries enacted legal measures to enable women to participate in the labour force. These measures generally included provisions for maternity leave, public childcare facilities, family planning and medical services. As economic and political changes have occurred over the years, however, these gains have been eroded.

Learning from these all too common experiences, as well as through interaction with the women's movement around the world, women in movements for liberation and democracy in the 1980s and 1990s began a parallel struggle for women's rights, and have been redefining the terms of their participation. The struggle for national liberation in Namibia illustrates the growing awareness of women and some of the strategies used to bring women's issues and perspectives to the agenda both during the struggle itself and in the new governments.

After years of struggle, spearheaded by the South West Africa Peoples' Organization (SWAPO), Namibia became independent on 21 March 1990 and SWAPO became a political party in the new government. Women's participation and the difficulties they faced are recounted by Nashilongo Elago, SWAPO member and former general secretary of the women's organization Women's Voice:

Women have been part of the struggle for liberation in Namibia as far back as can be remembered. Women fought alongside men during the time of the German occupation and women continue to fight today. In Namibia, December 10 is National Women's Day, a day on which women's role in the struggle is celebrated. Women fought for the liberation of Namibia because they felt it was their duty and they were committed. Within that struggle was the struggle for recognition of women as equal partners. Women were recognized and treated as equals in terms of the policy of SWAPO. But as individuals you have to deal with those male comrades in senior positions whose attitude may be something else. The person may not even be aware he is discriminating. Inside the country women in SWAPO never raised the question of sexism of men. In exile the Women's Council was more organized. And they had access to resources. The women could, for example, get scholarships. And these women could come and fill positions in the party. Our people in exile had a situation of exposure to the international community and they were very often confronted with questions relating to the participation of women. Not so at home. We were isolated. We did not have as much contact with the international community. In exile men and women shared the responsibility of child care, housework and such things.[49]

Now that the struggle is over, women in Namibia are facing the common situation in which there are few women in leadership positions, there is little opportunity for

NAMIBIA: THEORY INTO PRACTICE

The new Namibian Constitution contains some important statements about women's rights that can help women to have more equality in our society. As women of Namibia, we must speak out about our needs and our priorities. We must guide the government on women's issues so that women's rights will be applied in ways that are relevant to our lives.

The most important protection for women's rights is Article Ten. 'All persons shall be equal before the law. No person may be discriminated against on the grounds of sex, race'... This provision can be used to challenge any law, past or future, which discriminates against women. It can also be used to challenge government policies and practices which discriminate against women, and perhaps even to challenge sexual discrimination by individuals, employers or organisations.

Article 23, which is entitled 'Apartheid and Affirmative Action', authorizes Parliament to implement policies and programmes 'aimed at redressing social, economic or educational imbalances in the Namibian society arising out of past discriminatory laws or practices'. Women should take the initiative for suggesting affirmative action programmes which they believe will benefit them ...

There is also a section of the Constitution which contains principles of State policy: the state is to actively promote the welfare of the people by enacting laws 'to ensure equality and opportunity for women, to enable them to participate in all spheres of Namibian society' ...

The amount of attention given to women's rights in the Constitution is heartening, but it will be up to the women of Namibia to ensure that women's rights in the new Constitution are actually put into practice in meaningful ways.

Sister Namibia, Vol. 2, No. 1, 1990

PHOTO: JEAN SUTHERLAND/THE NAMIBIAN

Namibia: Nora Chase, now with Foreign Affairs, in the forefront of the women's march during the 1990 Independence celebrations

women to help determine the political agenda and, moreover, there is the usual tendency for men and women to revert to their old roles:

When the exiles returned they went to different villages all over Namibia. And we find that the pressure in society of traditional attitudes to women is being imposed. People are going back to the old ways of doing things. Women have not had a chance to set up their own agenda – the agenda of women has been dictated by men. Women must be part of making decisions in the new Namibia. Today in Namibia there are very few women at the top levels. They are very poorly represented in political parties, the church and in places where decisions affecting the lives of Namibians are made.[50]

Thus, when Namibia became independent in 1990, women faced the challenge of developing strategies to ensure their participation in the life of the country. Prime among these are the building of awareness about women's rights at the grassroots, leadership training and skills development, and mobilization of women into strong organizations that can monitor the implementation of women's rights and support women's efforts to participate in politics and public life. As articulated by Elago:

It is not enough having women's rights guaranteed in the constitution. Women's rights

which are a part of the constitution must filter down to the grassroots. We need a women's non-governmental organization as a powerhouse for women, and as a watch-dog for women's rights. We need some group where we can draw energy to put women in important positions.[51]

In addition to informing women about their rights under the new constitution, organizations are educating women about how the legal provisions can be applied to increase women's participation in the new society. For example, *Sister Namibia*, an activist women's publication, contributed to the information and educational campaign by publishing articles on the major constitutional provisions and their application.

MOVING TOWARDS DEMOCRACY □

As South Africa moved toward democracy in the early 1990s, women expressed very similar concerns about the lack of women in leadership positions, about the need to ensure that women's issues are not treated as secondary and about women participating in setting the agenda of the new government. For instance, Sizakele Nkosi, general secretary of the Alexandra Women's Congress, in Alexandra township, outside Johannesburg, said:

If you look at the participation of women in organizations it is very low. Women don't participate equally with men. They feel intimidated and inferior because of their background. There is a lot of sexism. We can't only blame apartheid. Men who think they are liberated will not allow their wives to get involved in organizations. These men are in meetings a lot, and are hardly at home. It is not right that only South African men decide on the future of South Africa. I don't want a parliament with men only. We want proper representation. We want women's issues discussed equally to other issues. For example, maternity rights should not be a secondary issue. Women must also decide for our country. We are the backbone of the nation.[52]

Part of the strategy for ensuring women's participation in politics and public life is the formation of strong women's organizations that can be both a school for leadership training and a means to bring women's voices and perspectives to the fore. As a result of two years of efforts by the African National Congress (ANC) Women's League, the ANC adopted a policy calling for one-third of the ANC candidates for the April 1994 elections to be women. Another initiative for making women's voices heard and for putting a women's agenda on the table at the national level was the establishment of a Women's National Coalition, bringing together both black and white women from sixty different organizations, including all the political parties. One of their primary goals was to ensure that women's rights were guaranteed in the constitution and laws of South Africa. Recognizing that equality of men and women will not come about automatically, the women who came together to form the Women's National Coalition declared:

The future depends on us whether there is to be a non-sexist South Africa. No one is going to give it to us.... Now we have to force open the doors through the voices of millions of South African women.[53]

Greater democracy does not automatically mean more opportunities for women, as is demonstrated in the transition of eastern European countries and the former Soviet Union to multi-party systems. Women's gains under the socialist systems are being cut back and their participation in politics and public life is declining to such an extent that it has raised the question: 'Does the beginning of democracy have to mean the end of women's rights?'[54]

Reports from Russia and Poland, for example, are not encouraging. According to information in a 1993 issue of *Women's Watch*, published by the International Women's Rights Action Watch (IWRAW), 70 per cent of the newly unemployed in Moscow were women aged forty-five to fifty-five, proposed legislation would restrict women's participation in the emerging market economy and childcare services are being severely reduced. The 20 per cent of women who are the sole wage earner in the household have been the hardest hit by this situation.[55] Citing setbacks in employment, labour laws and health care facilities in Poland, Helsinki Watch writes that:

... even the limited gains for women under communist rule are threatened. New political, economic and social pressures are emerging which, if allowed to develop unchecked, may mean that while democracy takes one step forward in Poland, women take two steps back.[56]

Moreover, as noted earlier, there has been a sharp drop in the number of women in legislative bodies in former communist countries. According to a study by Mira Janova and Mariette Sineau on women's political participation in eastern European countries: '... the significant drop in the number of women representatives in the different newly elected assemblies seems to be a direct consequence of the political changes and of the new importance of elections. For the first time in 45 years, elections are no longer a matter of masquerade and imitation, but represent a serious question of power; they consequently mean real competition between the candidates chosen by different parties. Artificially raised under Communist regimes, the percentage of women can seem, in fact, exceptionally low today.'[57]

The alarming lack of women's participation in determining the shape of the changing political system in Russia was expressed by a leader of a new alliance of women's organizations called the Women in Russia Movement: 'We are building a democratic society while women are excluded from the process of making decisions.'[58]

The establishment of the Women in Russia Movement is, however, one of the signs that women are mobilizing to counter the declining opportunities for and numbers of women in politics. While aiming broadly to increase women's participation in politics, Women in Russia is also advocating the restoration of social benefits such as free child care and medical care as well as measures to alleviate the painful effects of economic reform. As noted above, Women in Russia obtained the fourth largest percentage of votes in the December 1993 elections and obtained 24 seats in the Duma, or lower house, of the parliament.[59]

The study by Janova and Sineau on women in eastern European politics is optimistic:

There may be fewer women in politics – a consequence of the electoral 'market' – but women may have greater influence. Indeed, the intellectuals who fought hardest for political change are the very same ones who are most in favour of the rapid integration of women in politics. Furthermore, in creating opposition movements, intellectuals largely depended on the presence of well-known women as leaders and activists. In Bulgaria, women intellectuals, writers, painters, economists, lawyers, appeared at the head of all the opposition movements and formed the hard core of the opposition's electoral

campaign in 1990. The reaction of the former Communist Party (the Socialist Party) was almost instant: in order not to be left behind, the leaders forgot their macho attitude and placed competent women in prominent positions, to help boost party fortunes and give it a more positive image. The Bulgarian election campaign proved that, in certain conditions, women could provide one of the stakes of political combat.[60]

In Russia an Independent Women's Forum held in 1992 emphasized the need to empower women through compiling evidence on the reality of women's lives and the organization of awareness-building seminars.[61] Leadership training for women has also been identified as an urgent need to enable women to participate in the new political systems of the former Soviet Union and the countries of eastern Europe. One such initiative taken by the International Federation of University Women (IFUW) was a regional seminar for women from the Baltic countries entitled Leadership and Organizational Development which aimed to train women to identify the urgent problems facing them, develop strategies to address these problems and build networks to support each other in their efforts.[62] Reports from other countries, such as the Ukraine, whilst not minimizing the difficulties facing women also point to some initiatives that aim to promote women's participation in the new political structures.

In Latin America, women's participation in democratic movements during the 1980s differed in significant ways from their earlier participation, particularly in the greater awareness of gender issues and the need to make women's rights an integral part of the struggle for democracy. Women's experiences in grassroots movements and political parties in Uruguay, as the country moved toward civilian elections after twelve years of military rule, give insights into how this new awareness arose:

WOMEN'S POLITICAL PARTICIPATION IN THE UKRAINE

The overcoming of economic difficulties and further development of the Ukraine is impossible without the emancipation of women's political consciousness and possibilities for them to use their abilities. Among the positive results of the recent changes in the Ukraine are:

- the establishment of state structures and public organizations working with and for women;
- the desire of the government and the political parties for active collaboration with women's groups. For instance, the Green Party aims to promote the development of a women's movement, while the Christian Democratic Party is assisting the revival of women's organizations, and the Peasant Democratic Party programme calls for the improvement of working conditions both in the workplace and at home;
- the recognition of women's organizations as equal participants with other partners dealing with national revival.

However, women still remain removed from the mainstream of politics. Women are deprived of the opportunity to prepare themselves for leadership positions not only by political, socio-economic and cultural factors, but also by their own ideas about their place in society. This is shown by the decrease in the number of women in representative and executive bodies at all levels. For example, in the Supreme Soviet of the Ukraine, there are only 13 (or 3 per cent) women deputies. There is no woman in government and almost no women leaders of political parties. It is no accident, therefore, that there has been a very active process of the formation of women's organizations lately to defend women's interests, help them with their survival and develop their consciousness.

I.I. Shupick, 'Women in Ukraine: Participation and Decision Making: From Economy to Politics' (unpublished paper, Poltava, Ukraine, 1993.

Towards 1980 new forms of organization began to flourish, like the running of popular soup kitchens, cooperative movements and groups to help the mothers and families of political prisoners. At the same time,

PHOTO: M. EUGENIA LORENZINI

Chile 1983: the feminist movement demonstrates for 'Democracy Now'

neighbourhood women's groups began to appear, most of them initiated by housewives. These were all spontaneous, pluralist, autonomous movements largely concerned with addressing general problems such as hunger, unemployment, human rights, housing, democratic elections and inflation. Following a women's march in January 1984, the Plenario de Mujeres del Uruguay (Plenary of Uruguayan Women) was formed with the aim of coordinating women's participation in the struggles against the dictatorship. At the same time a quite new women's consciousness was beginning to develop. The participation of women in neighbourhood groups brought to light certain problems and inspired us to start reflecting about ourselves as women. For instance, where could we leave our children during meetings? Who would prepare the meals when we weren't there? 'I'm late because I had to do the washing.' 'He says the best way I can help is to stay at home and look after the children and cook'. The approach of elections, scheduled for early 1985, and consequent opening up of democracy led to a restructuring of traditional forms of participation and a resurgence of the trade union movement, but for women it wasn't a time of great change. All political parties included in their programmes proposals for improving the condition of women, formulated by women's groups from each party. However, this was chiefly an electoral gambit, the best proof being the lack of women at any decision-making levels, not to mention our total absence from the lists of candidates.[63]

Women were conspicuously absent in the newly elected parliament and government, which consisted entirely of men except for the Ministry of Education. Women were also absent from the leadership of the political parties, the national workers' organization and the student federation.[64]

Similarly in Chile, the grassroots mobilization of women was a significant part of the opposition to the Pinochet dictatorship and the movement for a return to democracy. The first to break the silence after the imposition of martial law in 1973 were the mothers and wives of disappeared prisoners who took to the streets to protest against the arrests, detention and disappearance of their husbands, sons and daughters. From the actions of these courageous women, the seeds of mass protest and the movement for democracy began to grow. Years of exile brought Chilean women into contact with the growing women's movement in other parts of the world and these experiences helped shape the struggle, particularly in the mid-1980s when the Chilean military junta began to permit Chileans in exile to return home. Women participated in the movement for democracy in different ways: in autonomous feminist groups and women's organizations, within political parties encompassing a wide range of political positions, in trade unions, and in movements of poor women. As the movement grew in anticipation of elections, women from all sectors and diverse political parties came together in an umbrella organization, Mujeres por La Vida (Women for Life). This organization made it possible to formulate women's demands for incorporation in the platforms of the various political parties. The need to work on several different levels at once was signalled in the slogan: 'For democracy in our country and in the home'.

Yet the 1989 elections resulted in a parliament and government overwhelmingly composed of men. A study reflecting on the reasons for this gave the following explanation:

- women face discrimination in the political parties;
- the style of political negotiation is alien to women;
- women have not given sufficient attention to the financial aspects of political campaigns;
- the women's movement lacks the internal cohesion needed to face these difficulties and raise up leaders from its ranks.[65]

Networking and alliance building in the women's movement and in community and political organizations, however, are opening new possibilities for women to move into the citadels of political power as candidates in national elections. In Chile, women who had for the past decade combined feminist and political activity within parties tested this strength in the campaign for the December 1993 elections.

*MORE WOMEN IN PARLIAMENT: CHILE**

In Chile women formed a political action group in October 1992 called Mas Mujeres al Parlamento (More Women in Parliament), for the purpose of promoting the empowerment and presence of women in politics and other leadership positions. Mas Mujeres seeks to bring greater numbers of women into public office and legislative seats, asserting that this will:

- make women's contribution to politics and in the decision-making process more adequately appreciated;
- increase recognition of the citizenship of women, inasmuch as they hold rights by themselves, independently of their family status;
- give vast sectors of the population more direct access to decision makers, inasmuch as the increased presence of

* Mas Mujeres al Parlamento, Santiago, Chile.

women in the public sphere will facilitate the transformation of social demands into public policies;

- strengthen democracy by closing the gap between the decision makers in government and the social movements where women prevail, adding to the transparency of the institutional process.

Mas Mujeres was joined by both women and men from political parties, as well as by independent workers, professionals, intellectuals and artists, 'all of whom seek to increase the political participation and the empowerment of women and to build bridges in the political sphere – where women have traditionally been excluded – and the sphere of social action where women have historically been active in large numbers in Chile.' The group launched a campaign in support of a woman candidate for parliament who had been a militant in both political movements and parties and in the women's movement. Her campaign platform contained distinctively pro-women and feminist statements around the fundamental concept of equity: 'Chile will only become a fully democratic country if real equality is reached for both men and women in every sphere of life.' The campaign focused on women's issues, gender relations, the state's response and solutions to basic needs and the quality of life, citizen safety, and the participation of men and women in private and public milieus. It called for:

- measures to insure legal equality for women by introducing reform to the constitution and to the civil, penal and labour legislation;
- the care of children as a function and responsibility of society as a whole and the state and not as a function exclusively female;
- creation of strategies to enable women's access to decision-making posts at different levels of the power structure;
- occupational training programmes geared towards women of low income groups;
- legislation related to divorce. ●

The candidate supported by Mas Mujeres al Parlamento won a seat in the lower house, along with several other women elected from a range of political parties. While still very much in the minority, the women consider their victory a breakthrough and as laying the groundwork for increased participation of women in politics.

Another significant development in Chile's transition to democracy was the creation of the Servicio Nacional de la Mujer (SERNAM), or National Women's Service. As a result of women's lobbying, the director of SERNAM was made a minister in the new cabinet. One of the major aims of SERNAM is to develop gender awareness in governmental bodies. This is part of a new approach which can be seen throughout Latin America. Women are no longer calling only for political parties to take up women's issues, they are calling for women to participate in the political process of social transformation. ●

The challenge is to build a different, pluralist, democratic and flexible civilization and how can this be built without us?[66]

Although there is still a long way to go to achieve a true democracy in which women participate on an equal basis with men, in many countries the foundations have been laid on which to build. The growing awareness – an essential step in empowerment – the increasing sharing of experiences and strategies, and the strengthening of networking and alliance building among women in politics give hope that women will take their rightful place in decision making in national and international policy making.

Table 4.4: WOMEN'S RIGHT TO VOTE, ELIGIBILITY AND ACCESS TO PARLIAMENT (AS OF 31 OCTOBER 1991)

COUNTRY	WOMEN'S RIGHT TO VOTE (YEAR)	WOMEN'S ELIGIBILITY TO PARLIAMENT (YEAR)	FIRST WOMAN IN NATIONAL PARLIAMENT (YEAR)
AFGHANISTAN	1965	1965	1965
ALBANIA	1945	1945	1945
ALGERIA	1962	1962	1962
ANGOLA	1975	1975	1980
ANTIGUA AND BARBUDA	1951	1951	1980
ARGENTINA	1947	1947	1952
AUSTRALIA	1901–1967	1901–1967	1943
AUSTRIA	1918	1918	1919
BAHAMAS	1962–1964	1962–1964	1977
BANGLADESH	1947	1947	1975
BARBADOS	1951	1951	1951
BELGIUM	1919–1948	1921–1948	1921
BELIZE	1945	1945	1984
BENIN	1956	1956	1979
BHUTAN	1953	1953	1975
BOLIVIA	1938–1952	1938–1952	1966
BOTSWANA	1965	1965	1979
BRAZIL	1934	1934	1934
BULGARIA	1944	1944	1945
CAMEROON	1946	1946	1962
CANADA	1917–1918–1950	1920–1960–1969	1921
CAPE VERDE	1975	1975	1975
CENT. AFRICAN REP.	1986	1986	1987
CHILE	1931–1949	1931–1949	1951
CHINA	1949	1949	1954
COLOMBIA	1957	1957	1958
COMOROS	1956	1956	no woman so far
CONGO	1963	1963	1970
COSTA RICA	1949	1949	1953
COTE D'IVOIRE	1952	1952	1965
CUBA	1934	1934	1940
CYPRUS	1960	1960	1963
CZECHOSLOVAKIA	1920	1920	1920
DEM. PEOPLE'S REP. OF KOREA	1946	1946	1948
DENMARK	1915	1915	1918
DJIBOUTI	1946	1986	no woman so far
DOMINICA	1951	1951	1940 nom.– 1980 ele.
DOMINICAN REPUBLIC	1942	1942	1946
ECUADOR	1946	1946	1957
EGYPT	1956	1956	1957
EL SALVADOR	1961	1961	?
EQUATORIAL GUINEA	1963	1963	1968
ESTONIA	–	–	–
ETHIOPIA	–	–	–
FINLAND	1906	1906	1906
FRANCE	1944	1944	1945
GABON	1956	1956	1961
GAMBIA	1960	1960	?
GERMANY	1918	1918	1919
GREECE	1952	1952	1952
GRENADA	1951	1951	1976

COUNTRY	WOMEN'S RIGHT TO VOTE (YEAR)	WOMEN'S ELIGIBILITY TO PARLIAMENT (YEAR)	FIRST WOMAN IN NATIONAL PARLIAMENT (YEAR)
GUATEMALA	1945	1945	1954
GUINEA-BISSAU	1977	1977	?
GUYANA	1953	1945–1953	1953
HAITI	1950	1950	?
HONDURAS	1957	1957	1967
HUNGARY	1945	1945	1945
ICELAND	1915	1915	?
INDIA	1950	1950	1952
INDONESIA	1945	1945	1949 app.–1955 ele.
IRAN (Isl. Rep. of)	1963	1963	1963
IRAQ	1980	1980	1980
IRELAND	1918	1918	?
ISRAEL	1948	1948	1948
ITALY	1945	1945	1946
JAMAICA	1944	1944	?
JAPAN	1945–1947	1945–1947	1946–1947
JORDAN	1974	1974	no woman so far
KENYA	1963	1963	1969
KIRIBATI	1971	1971	no woman so far
KUWAIT	not recognized	not recognized	no woman so far
LAO PEOPLE'S DEM. REP.	1958	1958	?
LATVIA	–	–	–
LEBANON	1926	1926	no woman so far
LIBERIA	1946	1946	1964
LIBYAN ARAB JAMAHIRIYA	1969	1969	?
LIECHTENSTEIN	1984	1984	1986
LITHUANIA	–	–	–
LUXEMBOURG	1919	1919	1919
MADAGASCAR	1959	1959	1965
MALAWI	1964	1964	1964
MALAYSIA	1957	1957	1959
MALDIVES	1932	1932	?
MALTA	1947	1947	1947
MAURITIUS	1956	1956	?
MEXICO	1947	1953	1952 nom.
MONACO	1962	1962	1963
MONGOLIA	1923–1924	1923–1924	1923–1924
MOROCCO	1963	1963	no woman so far
MOZAMBIQUE	1975	1975	1977
NAMIBIA	1989	1989	1989
NAURU	1968	1968	1986
NEPAL	1951	1951	?
NETHERLANDS	1919	1917	1918
NEW ZEALAND	1893	1919	1933
NICARAGUA	1955	1955	1958
NIGER	1948	1948	1989
NORWAY	1907–1913	1907–1913	1911–1921
PAKISTAN	1937	1937	1947
PANAMA	1941–1946	1941–1946	1946
PAPUA NEW GUINEA	1975	1975	1977
PARAGUAY	1961	1961	1963

Table 4.4: (CONTINUED)

COUNTRY	WOMEN'S RIGHT TO VOTE (YEAR)	WOMEN'S ELIGIBILITY TO PARLIAMENT (YEAR)	FIRST WOMAN IN NATIONAL PARLIAMENT (YEAR)
PERU	1950	1956	1956
PHILIPPINES	1937	1937	1941
POLAND	1918	1918	1919
PORTUGAL	1931–1976	1931–1976	1934
REPUBLIC OF KOREA	1948	1948	1948
ROMANIA	1929–1946	1929–1946	1946
RWANDA	1961	1961	1965
SAINT KITTS AND NEVIS	1951	1951	1984
SAINT LUCIA	1951	1951	1951 app.– 1979 ele.
SAINT VINCENT AND THE GRENADINES	1951	1951	1979
SAN MARINO	1960	1973	1974
SAO TOME AND PRINCIPE	1975	1975	1975
SENEGAL	1945	1945	1963
SEYCHELLES	1948	1948	1976
SIERRA LEONE	1951	1951	?
SINGAPORE	1948	1948	1984
SOLOMON ISLANDS	1945	1945	no woman so far
SOUTH AFRICA	1930–1984	1930–1984	1933
SPAIN	1931	1931	1931
SRI LANKA	1931	1931	1931
SURINAME	1953	1953	?
SWAZILAND	1968	1968	?
SWEDEN	1918–1921	1918–1921	1921
SWITZERLAND	1971	1971	1971
SYRIAN ARAB REP.	1949	1953	1958
THAILAND	1932	1932	1949
TOGO	1956	1956	?
TONGA	1960	1960	no woman so far
TRINIDAD AND TOBAGO	1945	1945	1971
TUNISIA	1959	1959	1959
TURKEY	1930–1934	1930–1934	1935
TUVALU	–	–	1989
UGANDA	1962	1962	1962 nom.
UNION OF SOVIET SOCIALIST REP.	1918	1918	1922
UNITED ARAB EMIRATES	not recognized?	not recognized?	no woman so far
UNITED KINGDOM	1918–1928	1918–1928	1919
UNITED REPUBLIC OF TANZANIA	1959	1959	?
UNITED STATES OF AMERICA	1920	1788	1924
URUGUAY	1932	1932	1942
VANUATU	1980	1980	1977
VENEZUELA	1947	1947	1948
VIET NAM	1946	1946	1946
WESTERN SAMOA	1990	1990	?
YEMEN	1967–1970	1970	1970
YUGOSLAVIA	1949	1949	1943
ZAIRE	1967	1970	1970
ZAMBIA	1962	1964	1964
ZIMBABWE	1957	1978	1924–1980

Source: Inter-Parliamentary Union

Table 4.5: WOMEN IN PARLIAMENT

COUNTRY OR AREA	% WOMEN HOLDING PARLIAMENTARY SEATS 1993
DEVELOPED REGIONS	
ALBANIA	5.7
AUSTRALIA	8.2
AUSTRIA	21.3
BELGIUM	9.4
BOSNIA AND HERZEGOVINA	?
BULGARIA	12.9
CANADA	13.2
CROATIA	4.3
CZECH REPUBLIC	10.0
DENMARK	33.3
FINLAND	39.0
FRANCE	6.1
GERMANY	20.5
GREECE	5.3
HUNGARY	7.3
ICELAND	21.8
IRELAND	12.1
ITALY	8.1
LIECHTENSTEIN	4.0
LUXEMBOURG	13.3
FORMER YUGOSLAV REP. OF MACEDONIA	4.2
MALTA	1.5
MONACO	5.6
NETHERLANDS	29.3
NEW ZEALAND	16.5
NORWAY	35.8
POLAND	9.6
PORTUGAL	8.7
ROMANIA	3.5
SAN MARINO	11.7
SLOVAK REPUBLIC	18.1
SLOVENIA	2.5
SPAIN	16.0
SWEDEN	33.5
SWITZERLAND	17.5
UNITED KINGDOM	9.2
UNITED STATES	10.8
YUGOSLAVIA (FED. REPUBLIC OF)	3.0
FORMER USSR	
ARMENIA	?
AZERBAIJAN	2.0
BELARUS	3.8
ESTONIA	12.7
GEORGIA	?
KAZAKHSTAN	6.7
KYRGYZSTAN	6.3
LATVIA	14.0
LITHUANIA	7.1
MOLDOVA	2.1
RUSSIAN FEDERATION	8.7
TAJIKISTAN	3.0
TURKMENISTAN	4.6
UKRAINE	?
UZBEKISTAN	9.6
AFRICA	
ALGERIA	10.0
ANGOLA	9.5
BENIN	6.3
BOTSWANA	5.0
BURKINA FASO	5.6
BURUNDI	9.9
CAMEROON	12.2
CAPE VERDE	7.6
COTE D'IVOIRE	4.6
DJIBOUTI	0.0
EGYPT	2.2
EQUATORIAL GUINEA	?
ETHIOPIA	?
GABON	5.8
GAMBIA	7.8
GHANA	7.5
GUINEA BISSAU	12.7
KENYA	3.0
LESOTHO	1.5
LIBERIA	6.1
LIBYAN ARAB JAMAHIRIYA	?
MADAGASCAR	?
MALAWI	11.6
MALI	2.3
MAURITANIA	0.0
MAURITIUS	3.0
MOROCCO	0.7
MOZAMBIQUE	15.7
NAMIBIA	6.9
NIGER	6.0
NIGERIA	2.2
RWANDA	17.1
SAO TOME AND PRINCIPE	10.9
SENEGAL	11.7
SEYCHELLES	45.8
SOUTH AFRICA	2.8

Table 4.5: (CONTINUED)

COUNTRY OR AREA	% WOMEN HOLDING PARLIAMENTARY SEATS 1993
AFRICA	
SUDAN	4.6
TOGO	6.3
TUNISIA	4.3
UGANDA	12.6
UNITED REPUBLIC OF TANZANIA	11.2
ZAMBIA	6.7
ZIMBABWE	12.0
LATIN AMERICA AND CARIBBEAN	
ANTIGUA AND BARBUDA	0.0
ARGENTINA	5.0
BAHAMAS	?
BARBADOS	3.6
BELIZE	0.0
BOLIVIA	?
BRAZIL	6.0
CHILE	5.8
COLOMBIA	4.3
COSTA RICA	12.3
CUBA	22.8
DOMINICA	12.9
DOMINICAN REPUBLIC	11.7
ECUADOR	5.2
EL SALVADOR	8.3
GRENADA	?
GUATEMALA	5.2
GUYANA	?
HAITI	3.6
HONDURAS	11.7
JAMAICA	11.7
MEXICO	7.6
NICARAGUA	16.3
PANAMA	7.5
PARAGUAY	2.5
PERU	6.3
SAINT KITTS AND NEVIS	6.7
SANTA LUCIA	0.0
SAINT VINCENT AND THE GRENADINES	9.5
SURINAME	5.9
TRINIDAD AND TOBAGO	13.5
URUGUAY	6.1
VENEZUELA	10.0

COUNTRY OR AREA	% WOMEN HOLDING PARLIAMENTARY SEATS 1993
ASIA AND PACIFIC	
BANGLADESH	10.3
BHUTAN	0.0
CAMBODIA	4.2
CHINA	21.0
CYPRUS	5.4
DEMOCRATIC PEOPLE'S REP. OF KOREA	20.1
FIJI	1.4
INDIA	7.3
INDONESIA	12.2
IRAN (ISLAMIC REP. OF)	3.4
IRAQ	10.8
ISRAEL	9.2
JAPAN	2.3
JORDAN	0.0
KIRIBATI	0.0
KUWAIT	0.0
LAO PEOPLE'S DEMOCRATIC REP.	9.4
LEBANON	2.3
MALAYSIA	5.0
MALDIVES	4.2
MARSHALL ISLANDS	3.0
MICRONESIA (FED. STATES OF)	0.0
MONGOLIA	3.9
NAURU	5.6
NEPAL	3.4
PAKISTAN	0.9
PAPUA NEW GUINEA	0.0
PHILIPPINES	10.6
REPUBLIC OF KOREA	1.0
SINGAPORE	3.7
SOLOMON ISLANDS	?
SRI LANKA	4.9
SYRIAN ARAB REP.	8.4
THAILAND	4.2
TONGA	3.3
TURKEY	1.8
TUVALU	7.7
UNITED ARAB EMIRATES	0.0
VANUATU	?
VIET NAM	18.5
WESTERN SAMOA	4.3
YEMEN	0.7

Sources: *The World's Women 1970–1990*, and Inter-Parliamentary Union.

1. Inter-Parliamentary Union (IPU), *Women and Political Power: Survey Carried Out Among the 150 National Parliaments Existing as of 31 October 1991*, Reports and Documents, No. 19, 1992. p. 1.
2. Ibid., pp. 5–19.
3. IPU, *Distribution of Seats Between Men and Women in the 170 Parliaments Existing at 30 June 1993*, IPU, Geneva, 1993.
4. United Nations Division for the Advancement of Women (DAW), 'Women in Government', statistical extracts from the DAW Data Base on Women in Decision-Making, DAW, Vienna, 1992, pp. 6–8.
5. Drude Dahlerup, 'From a small to a large majority: women in Scandinavian politics', quoted in Virginia Willis, 'Public life: women make a difference', paper for the Expert Group Meeting on the Role of Women in Public Life, DAW, Vienna, 1991, p. 10.
6. Drude Dahlerup, 'Women in political and public life', in *CEDAW Conference on the United Nations Convention on the Elimination of All Forms of Discrimination Against Women, 25–31 October 1991, Aarhus, Denmark*, International Alliance of Women and Danish Women's Society, Copenhagen, 1991, p. 46.
7. DAW, 'Public life: women make a difference', *Women 2000*, No. 2, 1992, p. 5.
8. Willis, 'Public life', pp. 8–18.
9. DAW, 'Public life', p. 5.
10. DAW, 'Women and decision-making', paper for Expert Group Meeting on Equality in Political Participation, DAW, Vienna, 1989, p. 11.
11. Ibid.
12. IPU, *Women and Political Power*, pp. 63–94.
13. Ibid.
14. Ibid., p. 80.
15. Ibid., pp. 80–83.
16. United Nations, *The World's Women 1970–1990: Trends and Statistics*, UN, New York, 1991, pp. 34–35.
17. Ibid., pp. 34.
18. Mira Janova and Mariette Sineau, 'Women's participation in political power in Europe, an essay in East-West comparison', *Women's Studies International Forum*, Vol. 15, No. 1, 1992, p. 119.
19. Ibid.
20. DAW, 'Expert Group Meeting on Equality in Political Participation and Decision-Making Report', DAW, Vienna, 1989, pp. 6–9.
21. INSTRAW, 'Women at the United Nations: struggling to be decision makers', *INSTRAW NEWS*, No. 17, 1992, p. 23.
22. Quoted in United Nations Non-Governmental Liaison Service (NGLS), *Go-Between*, No. 40, 1993.
23. United Nations, Administrative Instruction ST/AI/382*/, 3 March 1993.
24. DAW, 'Equality in Political Participation', p. 5.
25. Kathleen Staudt, 'Women in high-level political decision making', paper for the Expert Group Meeting on Equality in Political Participation and Decision-Making, DAW, Vienna, 1989.
26. DAW, 'Equality in Political Participation', p. 8.
27. Dahlerup, 'Women in political and public life', pp. 50–51.
28. Ibid., p. 50.
29. Ibid., p. 51.
30. IPU, *Women and Political Power*, pp. 95–101.
31. Margaret Alva, 'Women in public life', paper for the Expert Group Meeting on Equality in Political Participation, DAW, Vienna, 1989. pp. 14–15.
32. International Labour Organization (ILO), 'Affirmative action: a balance sheet', *World of Work*, No. 2, 1993, p. 11.
33. Ibid.
34. Ibid.
35. United Nations, Administrative Instruction ST/AI/382*/, 3 March 1993.
36. INSTRAW, p. 24.
37. IPU, *Women and Political Power*, p. 85.
38. Regina Rodriguez, 'America Latina: una nueva manera de hacer politicà', *Mujeres en Accion, No. 2*, 1993, pp. 28–30.
39. Staudt, p. 17.
40. Maria Nzomo, 'Women in politics and decision-making in Kenya', paper for the Expert Group Meeting on the Role of Women in Public Life, DAW, Vienna, 1991.
41. IPU, *Women and Political Power*, p. 84.
42. 'Women's Political Party Formed in the Philippines', *Women in Action*, No. 6, 1986, p. 12.
43. See Bella Abzug with Mim Kelber, *Gender Gap: Bella Abzug's Guide to Political Power for American Women*, Houghton Mifflin Co., Boston, 1984.
44. Willis, 'Public Life', p. 21.
45. Women in Nigeria, 'Women in Nigeria', *Women in Action*, No. 4, 1989, pp. 22–3.
46. Association for the Advancement of Feminism, *Women's News Digest*, September 1991.
47. Virginia Vargas, 'Women, vote for yourselves! Reflections on a feminist election campaign', in 'The Latin American Women's Movement', *Isis International Women's Journal*, No. 5, 1986.
48. Rodriguez, pp. 28–30.
49. *Speak*, No. 29, 1990, pp. 8–11.
50. Ibid.
51. Ibid.
52. *Speak*, No. 32, 1990, pp. 18–21.
53. *Speak*, No. 40, 1992, p. 6.
54. Women's Exchange Programme International, *News Bulletin*, Spring 1992.
55. *Women's Watch*, Vol. 6, No. 1, 1993, p. 9.
56. Helsinki Watch and Women's Rights Project, 'Hidden victims: women in post-Communist Poland', *News from Helsinki Watch*, Vol. IV, No. 5.
57. Janova and Sineau, pp. 124–5.
58. Sergei Shargorodsky, Associated Press, 'Women stand up to be counted as a political force', *Nation*, Thailand, 24 November 1993, p. A13.
59. *Le Monde*, Paris, 29 December 1993.
60. Janova and Sineau, p. 125.
61. *Women's Watch*, Vol. 6, No. 3, 1993, p. 9.
62. International Federation of University Women, *IFUW News*, January/February 1993, pp. 1–3.
63. Carmen Tornaria, 'Women's involvement in the democratic process in Uruguay' in 'The Latin American Women's Movement', *Isis International Women's Journal*, No. 5, 1986, pp. 24–7.
64. Ibid.
65. Alicia Frohmann, 'Democracia en Chile ¿ Donde estan las mujeres?', *Mujeres en Accion*, No. 2, 1993, p. 19.
66. Rodriguez, p. 30.

5 WOMEN AND DEVELOPMENT

The participation of women is a means to achieve the goals of development, through gender-aware, more efficient, economy-wide policies. It will contribute to achieving economic goals, such as economic growth, but it will also help identify the social goals the society is willing to pursue. Indeed, an idea which is gaining momentum is that increased participation of women in decision-making at all levels will help to 'adjust' the goals pursued through development.[1]

AS THE ABOVE STATEMENT by the Secretary-General of the United Nations indicates, women's participation is not only essential to economic development, it will also have a transformative effect on the goals of both economic and social development. Women's participation, thus, does not mean simply increasing women's numbers or integrating them into existing development models; rather, it is part of the process of empowerment and a way to make development policies and programmes more people-centred.

Before the United Nations Decade for Women (1976–1985), development policies and programmes were considered to be gender-neutral: that is, they did not distinguish between men and women but were assumed to benefit automatically all people, women as well as men. Attention was given to women primarily as mothers and carers, or as a particularly 'vulnerable' group. Consequently, programmes directed at women were related mainly to nutrition, child care, health and population, and aimed at improving family life and controlling women's fertility. Or programmes were welfare-oriented, designed to help women who were suffering from the worst ravages of poverty and malnutrition. Women's roles in agricultural and other forms of production went unperceived.

Beginning with Ester Boserup, whose ground-breaking book, *Women's Role in Economic Development*, was published in 1970, women researchers and activists began to make women visible as active participants in production, in the household and other sectors of the society. Studies revealed that women have often been victims of development programmes rather than beneficiaries, that many development programmes that were assumed to benefit everybody really benefited men only and often had negative effects not only on women but on the whole community. The high rate of failure of development policies, programmes and projects is attributable at least in part to the neglect or lack of knowledge of women's productive and reproductive roles.

In the analysis of why development programmes ignore women, a number of factors have been identified: (1) development planning that is geared to the economic growth model of development; (2) the elite-derived model which sees women as performing strictly domestic functions and men as performing all the economic and political roles; (3) the class background of national leaders, which alienates them from poverty; and (4) the 'general failure of the development process to provide all poor people, women or men, with power ...'[2] These underlying biases lead to the lumping together of the 'targets' of development into undifferentiated categories, such as the 'poor' or 'disadvantaged', without regard to different gender roles, needs and interests or to the effects of class and other socio-economic, cultural and political factors.

The expansion of women-and-

WHAT HAPPENS WHEN DEVELOPMENT PROGRAMMES NEGLECT WOMEN?

A project designed to bring a well to a remote Ethiopian village, where women had to walk five kilometres for water, enlisted the help of the men to build the well and trained them in maintaining it. Several months after the well had been completed, a mission to the village found that it had fallen into disrepair. It was discovered that in that culture it was the role of women to build and maintain the water supply and that, moreover, the task of fetching water had an important social function that had been ignored in siting the new well.[3]

In India, the introduction of dairies to improve the production and distribution of milk to urban areas had serious negative effects on rural women. Poor women who had traditionally milked buffalo, sold the butter in town and retained the milk for their families, were displaced by the dairies run by men. Since there was no alternative employment available, the women lost their cash earnings and their families lost the nutritional benefits of the milk.[4]

In Burkina Faso, the introduction of animal traction increased the amount of land the men could plough. As a consequence the amount of land that women had to weed by hand also increased, further burdening the overworked women.[5]

The expansion of the sugarcane industry in Belize in the early 1970s brought employment and income to men. With men no longer available to help clear the land, the women farmers produced less food and less fodder for poultry and small animals. Moreover, much of the money earned by the men flowed out for the purchase of trucks, liquor and imported prestige goods. As a consequence, there was a drop in both the nutritional status of the community and the status of women.[6]

In an area in Ghana, the introduction of cash crops left women with less time to cultivate food crops; to compensate, they substituted cassava for yams as it requires less work. Cassava, however, is less nutritious and cannot be intercropped with vegetables and legumes, as was the case with yams, because it depletes the soil too greatly. Kwashiorkor, a severe nutritional disease of children, began to appear for the first time.[7]

development studies opened the way for new areas of study and for the creation of new research methodologies. Researchers focused increasingly on the major roles that women play in both agriculture and the informal sector as well as on the complexity of their reproductive roles. Studies also showed that development research was gender-biased in technical fields as well as in sociological and economic studies. For instance, agricultural research institutes fail to study the production of subsistence crops, the primary responsibility of women, and the consequences of agricultural transition on women farmers. Gender-sensitive data is unavailable not only because data collection and statistical preparation fail to disaggregate statistics by sex, but also because data collection methodologies and questionnaires are biased against women. For instance, surveys and censuses often frame questions about labour in terms of the main or current work a person performs, or whether or not the person is earning an income. Since women are generally engaged in a wide variety of tasks, even simultaneously, and their income varies considerably from one season to another, such questions fail to capture the full range of women's work. Despite attempts of time-use surveys to account for women's

PHOTO: A. GRACIANO/UNICEF

Bolivia: Women carrying crops to market

unpaid work, many tasks performed by women for the well-being of the household and the community, and the allocation of their labour and resources, remain invisible.

WOMEN-IN-DEVELOPMENT APPROACHES ☐ By the mid-1970s and the International Year of Women (1975), a new policy to 'integrate women in development' gained a footing among development agencies. It was assumed that the neglect of women could be remedied and their situation improved by including them in development projects and programmes. The integration of women in development is a central element in what is variously known as the 'Integration', 'the women-in-development' or the WID approach, used by development agencies throughout the 1970s and 1980s. According to a framework drawn up by Caroline Moser, three WID policy approaches can be identified: equity, anti-poverty and efficiency, although, as she points out, there has never been a strict chronological development or separation of these approaches (see Table 5.1).[8] In examining how these approaches attempt to meet women's needs, this framework distinguishes practical gender needs and strategic gender needs, a concept developed by Maxine Molyneaux.[9] The term 'practical gender needs', refers to what women require in order to fulfil their roles and tasks; for example, training and access to childcare services. The term 'strategic gender needs', on the other hand, refers to what women require in order to overcome their subordination. The distinction is not always easy to make.

... What may seem practical gender needs for outsiders may have strategic potential as well for the women involved. For example, learning to ride a bicycle may be a practical improvement, but it also implies greater mobility and independence. Conversely, the tradition of 'dealing with practical problems first' may be reinforced by this distinction. 'First the practical needs, and then the strategic' is an idea which does not work, because they cannot be separated. A classical example is the use of improved woodstoves, which by itself solves neither environmental degradation nor women's own 'energy crisis' (their extra heavy workload caused by their problematic position).[10]

According to Moser, 'equity is the original "WID" approach' and is concerned with unequal relations between men and women in the family and in the marketplace and with integrating women into wage work: 'Hence it places considerable emphasis on economic independence as synonymous with equity.'[11] The equity approach attempts to meet women's practical gender needs for income and their strategic gender needs for equality with men through top-down legislative interventions by government and development agency programmes. However, according to Moser:

From the perspective of the aid agency, equity programmes necessitated unacceptable interference with the country's traditions ... [while] similar antipathy was felt by many Third World governments.[12]

In the face of this opposition, the equity approach was largely abandoned by most national and international development programmes and replaced with approaches that focused only on practical gender needs.

Anti-poverty is identified as a second WID approach, which differs from the equity approach in that it links the economic inequality of women to poverty rather than to female subordination. Directed to the 'poorest of the poor', it targets low-income women for economic

Table 5.1: DIFFERENT POLICY APPROACHES TO THIRD WORLD WOMEN

ISSUES	WELFARE	EQUITY
ORIGINS	Earliest approach: –residual model of social welfare under colonial administration – modernization/ accelerated growth economic development model	Original WID approach: – failure of modernization development policy – influence of Boserup and First World Feminists on Percy Amendment of UN Decade for Women
PERIOD MOST POPULAR	1950–70; but still widely used	1975–85: attempts to adopt it during the Women's Decade
PURPOSE	To bring women into development as better mothers: this is seen as their most important role in development	To gain equity for women in the development process: women seen as active participants in development
NEEDS OF WOMEN MET AND ROLES RECOGNIZED	To meet PGN in reproductive role, relating particularly to food aid, malnutrition and family planning	To meet SGN in terms of triple role – directly through state top-down intervention, giving political and economic autonomy by reducing inequality with men
COMMENT	Women seen as passive beneficiaries of development with focus on their reproductive role; non-challenging, therefore widely popular especially with government and traditional NGOs	In identifying subordinate position of women in terms of relationship to men, challenging, criticized as Western feminism, considered threatening and not popular with governments

PGN = Practical gender need
SGN = Strategic gender need

ANTI-POVERTY	EFFICIENCY	EMPOWERMENT
Second WID approach: – toned down equity because of criticism – linked to redistribution with growth and basic needs	Third and now predominant WID approach: – deterioration in the world economy – policies of economic stabilization and adjustment rely on women's economic contribution to development	Most recent approach: – arose out of failure of equity approach – Third World women's feminist writing and grassroots organization
1970s onward: still limited popularity	Post-1980s: now most popular approach	1975 onward: accelerated during 1980s, still limited popularity
To ensure poor women increase their productivity: women's poverty seen as a problem of underdevelopment, not of subordination	To ensure development is more efficient and more effective: women's economic participation seen as associated with equity	To empower women through greater self-reliance: women's subordination seen as problem not only of men but also of colonial and neo-colonial oppression
To meet PGN in productive role, to earn an income, particularly in small-scale, income-generating projects	To meet PGN in context of declining social services by relying on all three roles of women and elasticity of women's time	To reach SGN in terms of triple role – indirectly through bottom-up mobilization around PGN as a means to confront oppression
Poor women isolated as separate category with tendency only to recognize productive role; reluctance of government to give limited aid to women means popularity still at small-scale NGO level	Women seen entirely in terms of delivery capacity and ability to extend working day; most popular approach both with governments and multilateral agencies	Potentially challenging with emphasis on Third World and women's self-reliance; largely unsupported by governments and agencies; avoidance of Western feminism criticism means slow, significant growth of under-financed voluntary organizations

Source: Caroline O.N. Moser, *Gender Planning and Development: Theory, Practice and Training* (Routledge, London, 1993), pp. 56–57.

activity, usually small income-generating projects. The efficiency approach, which emerged in the late 1980s in the wake of the debt crisis, and is still widely used today, aims 'to ensure that development is more efficient and effective through women's economic contribution. Women's participation is equated with equity for women.'[13]

The efficiency approach assumes that women are an under-used labour force which can be exploited at low cost and that women's time is elastic and can be stretched to include tasks that fall upon them as a result of declining social services.

None of these WID approaches questions the model of development based on economic growth and determined by male policy makers and planners with little input from women. Consequently, criticism of the integration or WID approach emerged in the late 1970s and early 1980s, particularly among feminist researchers and activists, on the grounds of its failure to challenge the prevailing development model, its view of women as an untapped labour source which could be used to stimulate economic growth and industrialization, its focus on paid employment for women without taking into consideration the enormous amount of unpaid work women were already doing, its top-down interventions, and above all, its failure to include women's perspectives in planning and policy-making.[14] As Wanjiru Kihoro of the Africa Centre, London, states:

Many African women now see no point in being 'integrated' into the mainstream of Western-influenced development in which we have no choice in defining the kind of society we want.[15]

It is ironic that many of the attempts to integrate women in development resulted instead in their marginalization. Rather than really including women and their concerns in programmes, development agencies 'added women on' through special women's projects and women's components of projects. The fostering of small-scale, income-generating activities in handicrafts or fields of work considered to be women's traditional tasks, such as sewing and knitting, ignored the fact that the main activity of rural women was agricultural production. The effect was to further increase the workload of already overburdened women. Moreover, most of these projects were not economically viable. Too little attention was given to training in financial accounting, management and marketing. Introduction of new and appropriate technologies which might have alleviated women's work burden, and the provision of essential inputs and assets, were rare. Nevertheless some of these projects did provide women with opportunities to come together and develop organizing skills.

The initial attempts to promote the integration of women in development through the establishment of women's units within specialized agencies of the United Nations and women's bureaux or ministries at the national level were not, on the whole, very successful because of the limited financial and human resources allocated and their lack of power to change larger policies or to influence other ministries or agencies dealing with the economy and trade. Such units, frequently marginalized themselves, had the effect of marginalizing women's needs and concerns. Moreover, they led to the assumption that women's needs and issues were being taken care of by these marginal units and projects, and therefore did not have to be considered in the mainstream of development programmes.

NEW VISIONS OF DEVELOPMENT □

Parallel to the emergence of WID approaches, women began to develop new visions and strategies with a view to the construction of a more people-centred development model. A new framework for analysis began to emerge and to furnish a basis on which to challenge the mainstream development concept and planning.

In 1982, the Association of African Women for Research and Development (AAWORD) issued the Dakar Declaration on Another Development with Women in 1982 stating: 'We believe that the most fundamental and underlying principle of Another Development should be that of structural transformation.... Accordingly at international level, Another Development should replace the forms of dependent development and unequal terms of exchange with that of mutually beneficial and negotiated interdependence.... Nationally, models of development have to be based on the principle of self-reliance ... and the building of genuinely democratic institutions and practices. Such a model would ensure general participation – including that of women – in the definition and actual provision of the basic needs of all citizens, regardless of their race, creed, gender or age.'[16]

The DAWN (Development Alternatives with Women for a New Era) network of Third World researchers and activists challenged the belief that 'women's main problem in the Third World has been insufficient participation in an otherwise benevolent process of growth and development' and that 'increasing women's participation and improving their shares in resources, land, employment and income relative to men [are] both necessary and sufficient to effect dramatic changes in their economic and social position.'[17]

Articulating a vision of development in the book *Development, Crisis, and Alternative Visions: Third World Women's Perspectives*, DAWN affirmed the need for transformation of society, for all people to have opportunities to develop and for women's values and perspectives to have a central place in determining the kind of world we live in:

We want a world where inequality based on class, gender and race is absent from every country, and from the relationships among countries. We want a world where basic needs become basic rights and where poverty and all forms of violence are eliminated. Each person will have the opportunity to develop her or his full potential and creativity, and women's values of nurturance and solidarity will characterise human relationships.[18]

Very pragmatic and systematic short-term and long-term strategies are needed, DAWN stresses:

Improving women's opportunities requires long-term systematic strategies aimed at challenging prevailing structures and building accountability of governments to people for their decisions. Short-term, ameliorative approaches to improve women's employment opportunities are ineffective unless they are combined with long-term strategies to reestablish people's – especially women's – control over the economic decisions that shape their lives. Women's voices must enter the definition of development and the making of policy choices.[19]

Nevertheless, while envisioning more humane and just societies and emphasizing the need for long-term transformational strategies, women have not rejected the need for immediate strategies and reforms. As articulated by Kihoro:

Women, as the group most adversely affected by the existing development strategies, will have to be in the forefront of the definition of a new self-reliant and people-centered development.... This does not mean that the partial improvement of women's lives within the framework of the existing status quo is impossible. Each gain of the ordinary peasant and working-class women

represents a step leading human beings towards freedom and social equality.[20]

MAINSTREAMING WOMEN ☐ The unintended marginalization of women in development programmes, projects, and units led development agencies to rethink women-in-development approaches in the 1980s and to develop new arguments emphasizing the need to mainstream women: that is, to bring women from the margins into the centre of the main development programmes and of the institutions that deal with the economy.

While agreeing that women need to be central to development programmes, some women raised concerns about the consequences of mainstreaming. Does mainstreaming women mean that development agencies no longer need to give attention to the special concerns of women? Would mainstreaming cut off support to the growing number of women's groups, organizations and networks? And is mainstreaming just a new name for integrating women in development? There was also a fear that by jumping into the mainstream women would run the risk of drowning in a male-dominated and male-defined development agenda. Would the interest in women and the large body of research generated in the past two decades ensure women a permanent place on the agenda? In this view, mainstreaming must mean both increasing women's participation in development programmes and ensuring that women's perspectives, needs and concerns constitute the basis of the redefinition of development itself.

GENDER AND DEVELOPMENT ☐ The shift from the integration of women to mainstreaming since the mid-1980s has been accompanied by the shift in focus from women to gender. In contrast to the WID approach, this new approach is generally referred to as Gender-and-Development (GAD). Gender is here understood as the socially defined and constructed roles of men and women. Unlike sex, which is biologically determined, gender roles change from one place and culture to another and across time. For example, in nineteenth-century Europe it was considered that only men were suited for office work, whereas by the mid-twentieth century, secretarial work in offices was considered a female occupation. The twentieth century has seen rapid changes in many places in what are considered male and female roles. The focus on gender looks at the roles and needs of both women and men and at how these are interrelated, and thus lessens the risk of marginalizing women.

There are some who see the GAD approach as having the potential to bring in women's visions of development. The Canadian Council for International Cooperation states:

Gender and Development is emerging as a progressive approach to development from women's perspectives and experiences. It is part of the larger work of creating an alternative development model, for a world view which moves beyond an economistic analysis to include environmental, sustainable and qualitative (personal, ethical and cultural) aspects in its definition of development.[21]

The GAD approach, however, like that of WID, does not in itself question the prevailing development paradigm. Its potential to do so depends on how it is interpreted and applied.

MAINSTREAMING AND GENDER PLANNING STRATEGIES ☐ A

number of strategies have been developed to bring women into the mainstream and to make gender a central focus of development programmes. These include:

- strengthening women's units, groups and organizations to ensure gender awareness, to act as pressure groups and to monitor the implementation of main-streaming women;
- gender awareness and analysis training;
- building a critical mass of women inside development organizations;
- lobbying and pressuring development institutions.

Although sometimes regarded as contrasting with each other, the strategies are complementary and can be applied in mutually interactive combinations. A mass of women inside development institutions supporting and supported by strong women's non-governmental organizations and research groups can bring pressure to bear on policy makers and create a climate for gender awareness and analysis. The combination of strategies can enable women to participate in the mainstream and to empower themselves to determine the nature and goals of their participation. Openness to dialogue, collaboration, coalition building and co-ordination are the keys to success.

STRENGTHENING WOMEN'S UNITS AND PROGRAMMES The capacity of women's units, bureaux, programmes and organizations has been strengthened in many places to enable them to pressure governments and development agencies to mainstream women. Such units have assumed a major part of the responsibility for raising gender awareness, carrying out gender training and monitoring the implementation of mainstreaming throughout the institution.

FROM SMALL UNIT TO HIGH POLICY In the Netherlands, for example, the Women's Programme of the Development Cooperation section of the Netherlands Ministry of Foreign Affairs has been built up from a small women's unit to a programme with the capacity and the mandate to influence the mainstream of development projects, programmes and policy. The participation of women is mandated at the highest policy levels and since 1991 all projects and programmes have had to pass the scrutiny of the Women's Programme before being approved.

*ADVANCING TOWARDS AUTONOMY**

Jan Pronk

The age of the relaxed approach and simple directives has passed. Now for the first time, concrete women-and-development objectives are being laid down. We want to introduce both process criteria and impact criteria. As far as the process criteria are concerned, we have decided to use the well-known OECD/DAC [Organisation for Economic Co-operation and Development/Development Assistance Committee] women-and-development criteria ...:

- Women from the recipient countries who will be participating in the project, with priority given to women belonging to the target population, must be consulted about the design of the project [and] must be active participants during the implementation of the project.
- Barriers to female participation in the project must be identified in the project document and measures must be designed in order to overcome these barriers.

* Speech by the Netherlands Minister of Development Cooperation. *Informatie*, No. 16, 1991

- WID expertise must be used throughout the project cycle to ensure the full participation of women, and the project document should make it clear how this expertise and the WID factors will be applied....

In addition to the process criteria, impact criteria are being developed based upon two objectives: a negative one and a positive one. The negative one is: no programme financed by Netherlands Development funds may result in a deterioration in the position of women. The positive one is: a yet-to-be determined percentage of all project activities should result in a positive effect, that is an increase in the autonomy of women. Women's Impact Assessment will form a sort of methodological scenario of the entire project cycle with a set of instruments for checking whether the design, implementation and conclusion of the project meet the autonomy and DAC/WID criteria.

The early and systematic detection and exposure of the effects on the autonomy of women of a development co-operation programme can prevent negative consequences from occurring.

We distinguish four autonomy criteria to be applied per country, in accordance with local conditions:

- The economic position of women will be strengthened in terms of control over income and means of production without incommensurately heavy or additional burdens of work.

- The political and organisational position of women will be strengthened in respect of: participation in or control over independent organisational arrangements within the project structure; the same in organisations in the district, area or village; and the same at the regional or national level.

- The autonomy of women will be strengthened in respect of self-image; the image that others (men) in the project area have of women and dominant social preconceptions in regard to women.

- The physical autonomy of women will be strengthened; in other words, they will gain greater authority over their own bodies; control over their fertility, control over their own sexuality and recognition of or attention for women's health problems. ●

GENDER TRAINING Within development organizations and the United Nations agencies, gender training aims to provide planners with an awareness of women's and men's interrelated and changing reproductive and productive roles, and equips the planners with tools designed to ensure that women are fully part of their programmes and projects. The emphasis of the training is frequently on the gender analysis of projects and programmes.

Generally, gender analysis stresses the efficiency aspect of integrating women in development: production will be more efficient and projects will have a greater chance of succeeding if women are included. The efficiency approach to gender training is less threatening to male planners as it does not bring up questions of equity or empowerment. Gender training helps planners to identify the gender roles in a given place: namely, what men do and what women do and how their roles are inter-related, their respective access to and control over resources, the constraints facing them. One of the most striking revelations of gender analysis is almost always that women are performing many more tasks and working far more hours a day than men. This gender information can be used in planning appropriate project interventions and in allocation of project inputs, training and

THE YWCA GOING FROM STRENGTH TO STRENGTH

At the 1991 World YWCA Council, a Policy Statement on Development was drafted by a team of women representing 14 countries and adopted by the council.

The YWCA is one of the world's largest women's organisations, with 78 autonomous affiliated national associations in 91 countries, two-thirds of which are located in the developing world.

Founded in 1894, the World YWCA will be commemorating 100 years of work by and for women in 1994/5. An international network uniting 25 million grassroots women around the globe, its members work together to implement common social justice imperatives by increasing the participation of women at all levels of society. The aim of its programme is to liberate and empower women to achieve their full potential unfettered by gender stereotypes or artificial obstacles.

At YWCA workshops women learn the skills of leadership, advocacy, communications, lobbying, coalition building, and practical organizational management. Environmental degradation, sustainable development on small island states, violence against women, and structural adjustment policies have been the focal issues of recent workshops. The effectiveness of advocacy work is maximized through the coordination of local, national, and international levels.

At the grassroots level, much of the work is conducted by volunteer committees. Local women elect their governing boards and officers; they vote for representatives to the national boards who in turn elect national officers, appoint staff, and elect delegates to the World Council which meets every four years and is the movement's governing body. Delegates to the council are elected/selected by their national associations. All council delegates in turn elect the 20-member World Executive Committee and Officers from a list of women nominated by the national boards. The constitution requires that due regard is placed in the election process to achieve a broad spread of racial and national groupings. The task of the World Executive Committee is to implement the policy resolutions adopted by the World Council. It reports back to the council at the end of its four year term.

Through discussion, debate, and referendum, Council members formulate the policies and work priorities for the next four years.

The Councils have provided a first taste of democracy for women from many countries. Members of the World-Affiliated YWCA of South Africa shed tears of joy as they emerged from voting booths at the World Council in 1991, having had the first opportunity of their lives to cast ballots. And, although women are not represented at all levels in the political machinery of Bangladesh, members of the YWCA of Bangladesh have gained valuable skills in leadership and democracy. These skills were used in initiating a dialogue with the Muslim Women's League that led to the two groups setting up a Legal Advice Bureau for women in Dhaka.

The World Council in 1991 passed a Constitutional amendment legislating that the World YWCA Executive Committee be comprised of at least 25% *young* women, age 30 and under. The active involvement of young women in decision-making in the YWCA has challenged and invigorated the movement. All in all, the 1990's have provided World YWCA members with a broad education on the current state of development around the world.

Source: World YWCA, October 1994.

other benefits. While such interventions are still directed mainly to economic production, the information on women's time constraints may lead, for example, to the inclusion of labour-saving devices for household tasks in projects so that women will have more time and be more efficient in their market-related productive tasks.

A methodology of gender analysis known as the Harvard method, developed by the World Bank, has been widely used, with various adaptations, in agencies such as the United States Agency for International Development (USAID), the Canadian International Development Agency (CIDA), the United Nations Development Programme (UNDP) and the Food and Agriculture Organization of the United Nations (FAO). Various forms of gender analysis training are also in extensive use in governmental and non-governmental development agencies. Much of this analysis is based on case studies and project documents, does not question the dominant development model, and uses a top-down approach.[22] Some methods of gender training, while focusing on the different but interrelated roles of men and women, also examine questions of equity and empowerment. The gender planning methodology developed by Caroline Moser, for example, looks at both the practical and the strategic gender needs of women in its analysis of development projects and programmes.

Gender awareness or sensitivity training, on the other hand, is generally designed to build a wider consciousness of the inequalities and inequities in the relationships of men and women and of the structural and institutional discrimination that contributes to inequality, with the aim of changing attitudes and behaviour. Voluntary organizations and non-governmental organizations concerned with issues of justice and discrimination are more open to this type of gender training. Much grassroots gender awareness training is aimed at making women aware of their own situations and subordination as a first step in the process of empowerment, but it is also used to sensitize men.

Many women's non-governmental organizations have made gender training an important part of their work. For example, FEMNET, the African Women's Development and Communications Network based in Kenya, has trained hundreds of officers of the Ministry of Planning and National Development and community-level workers such as chiefs, councillors, researchers and journalists. The training team includes men who are convinced that men must change their attitudes, accept their responsibilities and work together with women to solve society's problems.[23] Another experience of training men comes from South Asia. Kamla Bhasin, one of the organizers of a series of gender workshops with men, reflects on the rationale:

Some of us women involved with training and keen to challenge patriarchy within development organisations also recognised the urgency to have a dialogue with senior male workers/decision-makers from voluntary organisations. Clarity and informed commitment at that level, we felt, was absolutely necessary for promoting women's development and a women's perspective of development. Although these days everyone can make some 'correct' statements on women, most NGO leaders have not yet critically examined their own behaviour, attitudes and assumptions towards and regarding women.[24]

While Bhasin acknowledges that training in the gender analysis of development projects is useful in making women and their contributions more visible to development planners, she is convinced that more far-

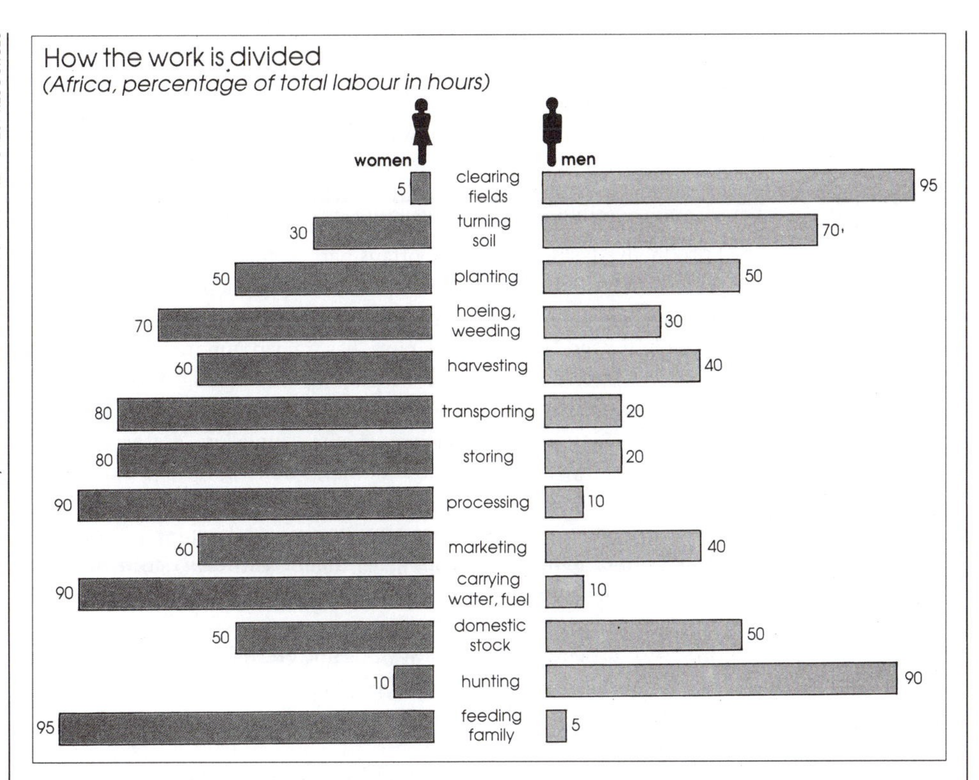

reaching gender sensitization is necessary: 'for a large number of NGOs who are seriously questioning the thinking, rationale and outcome of many development policies and programmes, who are interested not only to "invest" in women but also to empower them and to challenge patriarchy not only at the grass-root level but to challenge the patriarchal nature of development policies, programmes and development organisations'.[25]

GENDER WORKSHOPS WITH MEN*

Kamla Bhasin

During the last three years I have conducted six workshops with men – mostly senior men, in decision-making positions in NGOs. Two of these workshops were in India, two in Bangladesh and two in Nepal. All these workshops had 15 to 20 (men) participants, they were of 4-to-5 day duration, they were all residential, held in quiet and very simple places away from distracting cities. The following are the objectives of these workshops:

- to develop an understanding of gender and gender relations in the context of class, caste, north-south divide, etc.;
- to create an atmosphere that encourages the participants to critically reflect on their own understanding of gender relations and gender issues and on their own attitudes and behaviour;
- to help participants analyse the nature of development policies and programmes

* "Gender workshops with men: experiences and reflections", 1993.

in general and the policies and programmes of their own organizations in terms of their impact on women, ecological sustainability and equity;

- to evolve collectively a vision of an equitable and gender-just family, community and society and to develop a strategy to move towards their realization;
- to create a network of like-minded people and organizations.

In every workshop we try to make men talk about their personal lives and experiences, their personal relationships with women at home, at the place of work and in society at large, to make them realize that unlike other issues, gender cannot be dealt with merely as a subject of study, as an intellectual discourse. Changing gender relations, we emphasize, challenges each one of us to critically reflect on ourselves and to change, if necessary....

We begin every workshop with personal introductions where every one is asked to speak about his family background, present family status, his organization and his own work.... We begin by saying that we do not look at gender issues in isolation; we see them in the context of larger economic, political, social and cultural systems and we believe that changes in gender relations would require changes in other social systems and vice-versa....

Although the final list of issues discussed at these workshops is prepared in consultation with the participants, the issues tend to be more or less the same in every workshop:

- the situation and position of women and men in the society we live and work in;
- the concept of gender;
- patriarchy as a system and as ideology, and the origin of patriarchy;
- analysis of development policies and programmes in terms of their impact on ecology, on the poor (specially on women) and on the Third World;
- analysis of NGO structures, policies and programmes from the perspective of women;
- feminism and the women's movement in the country;
- a vision of a society without gender and other hierarchies;
- strategies for sustainable and gender-just development.

On every issue, our attempt is to move from social realities to generalizations and concepts. In order to get everyone to speak we encourage small-group discussion to thrash out most of the issues listed above. As resource persons, our task is to fill in the gaps in the discussions, add our views as and when necessary and provide conceptual/theoretical inputs. ●

EMPOWERMENT APPROACHES □ The concept of the empowerment of women as a goal of development projects and programmes has been gaining wider acceptance in the 1990s. According to Kate Young, the concept of empowerment, as used by development agencies, refers mainly to entrepreneurial self-reliance. Taking a critical view of the use of empowerment terminology by development agencies, Young states:

The term echoes the general emphasis within the mainstream on unleashing the capacity of individuals to be more entrepreneurial, more self-reliant. It is closely allied to the current emphasis on individualistic values: people 'empowering themselves' by pulling themselves up by their bootstraps.[26]

On the other hand, an empowerment approach to development can also mean people's participation in the policy making and planning processes. According to Young:

It is now recognised in development circles that economic growth and social betterment are best achieved when the mass of the population is informed about and involved in development aims and plans, and sees itself as a direct beneficiary of the expanded resources growth should bring. One of the ways to achieve this is structuring the decision-making process in such a way as to ensure widespread consultation at all levels of society about development goals, the processes by which those goals are to be reached and the resources needed to achieve them.... Empowerment can be a planning goal in the sense that government support is given to a range of interest groups and NGOs, by using them as consultative bodies or councils.[27]

A study entitled *Empowerment of Women in South Asia* identifies two approaches commonly used by development agencies: empowerment through economic interventions to increase women's economic status through employment, income generation and access to credit; and empowerment through integrated rural development programmes, in which strengthening women's economic status is only one component along with education, literacy, the provision of basic needs and services, and fertility control. These approaches are contrasted with that more generally used by women's organizations and other NGOs: empowerment through awareness building, capacity building and organizing women that leads to transformation of unequal relationships,

THE WOMEN'S EMPOWERMENT FRAMEWORK

The core of the Women's Empowerment Framework is its argument that women's development can be viewed in terms of five levels of equality, of which empowerment is an essential element at each level. The levels are: welfare, access, conscientisation, participation and control.

1. WELFARE, the first level, addresses only the basic needs of women, without recognising or attempting to solve the underlying structural causes, which necessitate provision of welfare services. At this point, women are merely passive beneficiaries of welfare benefits.

2. ACCESS, the second level, is essential for women to make meaningful progress. This involves equality of access to resources, such as education opportunities, land and credit. The path to empowerment is initiated when women recognize their lack of access to resources as a barrier to their growth and overall well-being, and take action to address this.

3. CONSCIENTIZATION is a crucial point in the Empowerment Framework. For women to take appropriate action to close gender gaps or gender inequalities, there must be recognition that their problems stem from inherent structural and institutional discrimination. They must also recognise the role they can often play in reinforcing the system that restricts their growth.

4. PARTICIPATION is the point where women are taking decisions alongside men equally. To reach this level, however, mobilisation is necessary. By organising themselves and working collectively, women will be empowered to gain increased representation, which will lead to increased empowerment and ultimately greater control.

5. CONTROL is the ultimate level of equality and empowerment. Here,the balance of power between men and women is equal and neither party has dominance over the other. At this stage in the Empowerment Framework, women are able to make decisions over their lives, and the lives of their children, and play an active role in the development process. Further, the contributions of women are fully recognised and rewarded.

Using the Empowerment Framework, development planners can determine whether a project or programme is at the welfare, access, conscientization, participation or control level, and determine the point of intervention, to move women to higher levels of equality and empowerment.

UNICEF, 'The Women's Empowerment Framework', *Women and Girls Advance*, Vol. 1, No. 1, 1993, p. 5.

increased decision-making power in the home and community, and greater participation in politics.[28]

Some of these ideas are also taking root in development programmes, and agencies are beginning to develop gender training frameworks that include the concept of empowerment. For instance, the United Nations Children's Fund (UNICEF) is using the Women's Empowerment Framework, developed by Sara Longwe of Zambia, as a 'tool to be used in its efforts to mainstream gender throughout UNICEF's programme planning process' and as a 'conceptual basis for gender-responsive assessment, evaluation and programming'.[29]

AT THE GRASSROOTS ☐ The evolution in policy on women and development reflects and is in turn reflected by what is happening at the grassroots. Many development agencies are gearing their programmes and projects to the empowerment of women through capacity building and through strengthening both women's organizations and women's participation in rural associations. Gender awareness activities for both men and women have also become an important part of some projects at the community level. Women's participation in grassroots organizations is increasingly recognized as crucial to their empowerment and as a way for them to help shape development policies. According to the Secretary-General of the United Nations, Mr Boutros Boutros-Ghali:

Given the importance of female leadership in community and grass-roots level organizations, non-governmental organizations have been identified as a key actor in empowering women, and in ensuring that an accurate knowledge of their true situation, of their actual and potential roles, and of obstacles to their economic participation, is reflected in the design of economy-wide policies.[30]

The Bangladesh Rural Advancement Committee (BRAC) is an example of an organization that has been instrumental in the empowerment of rural women and whose policies and practices are being changed by growing gender awareness and by women's collective strength. Founded in 1972, BRAC is one of the oldest NGOs in the country with a staff of 2,500, carrying out general development, education and health programmes and activities for both rural men and women. BRAC has organized over 2,500 groups in some 1,500 villages. Each village organization has a women's production subgroup. After initial failure in organizing vocational training in tailoring for women, on the mistaken assumption that it was traditional women's work and required few skills, over the years BRAC developed extensive non-handicraft employment training and programmes for rural women in horticulture, animal husbandry, poultry rearing, fish farming, rice processing, silk culture, veterinary services and other agricultural activities. Training in production skills is combined with attention to access to markets and credit and to the need to deal with conflicting interests of the rich and poor in a community.

In the villages, poor women have been gradually gaining confidence and learning how to handle conflicts of interests with their husbands and other males in the family and community as well as with landlords and rich and powerful people. Acceptance of changes in relationships and recognition of women's new roles is easier when the women are well organized and have collective strength. Women in the Bangladesh Rural Advancement Committee receive help from other members of their women's groups in family and community confrontations:

If another person does something bad to me, another member of the group will come forward to protest it ... I was alone, but now with me there are ten other members. They give me support.[31]

More women are joining the ranks of organizers and field workers, and BRAC has taken steps to address gender issues within the organization: it conducts gender awareness training of senior field staff so that they can identify and take steps to eliminate discriminatory practices and sexist attitudes; and it has established a Women's Advisory Committee to monitor and ensure that gender issues are given the priority they deserve and also that any gender discrimination is rooted out of the organization. The Women's Advisory Committee is dealing, for instance, with the issue of the different social behaviours that are expected of men and women organizers and with on-going discrimination against women in regard to restrictions on women's mobility after working hours, housing for women and maternity leave.[32]

Gender awareness training, as an instrument to change the attitudes of both men and women in communities, can be built in many different and culturally appropriate ways. For instance, the Baha'i International Community, in collaboration with the United Nations Development Fund for Women (UNIFEM), embarked on a project in the countries of Cameroon, Bolivia and Malaysia 'to encourage the empowerment of women by using traditional media – such as songs, dances and plays – to change the attitude of both women and men about the participation of women in community and family decision-making. Begun in 1991, the project is already showing dramatic signs of success. Increasing numbers of women are being consulted about community and family issues by men, and men are increasingly taking up tasks, such as farming, cooking and child-care, that were once viewed as the exclusive domain of women'.[33]

*TRADITIONAL MEDIA AS CHANGE AGENT – MEN AND WOMEN AS PARTNERS**

Entitled Traditional Media as Change Agent, the project is distinctive for its integration of well-respected ideas about development communication with the promotion of women's equality. Its most distinguishing characteristic is the degree to which it strives to involve both men and women in the process.

'What is groundbreaking about this project is that it is set up to involve men,' said Pamela Brooke, an independent development communications consultant who was contracted to provide the technical assistance to the project in Malaysia. 'Many projects for women involve just women, but it was the feeling ... that change could be better fostered through a consultative process between women and men,' said Ms Brooke. 'Because if you just end up with angry women sitting in the corner, it isn't going to change anything.'

In Cameroon, where the project has operated in seven villages, the men have begun to join women in the fields, they are consulting more with them about family finances, and they are allowing them a greater participation in community decision-making, according to surveys and outsiders who have visited the area. 'There is change,' said Madeline Eyidi ... [of] the United Nations Development Programme

* Baha'i International Community, *One Country*, Vol. 5., No. 3 (1993).

(UNDP) office in Yaounde, Cameroon.... 'The women have traditionally done the farming, but I saw the men starting to participate. They are helping the women'. ... According to Tiati à Zock, the national coordinator of the project in Cameroon, a survey done in early 1992 among some 45 families in each of the seven villages reported that the men made virtually all of the financial decisions alone. A follow-up survey, taken in 1993, indicated more than 80 percent of the families now make such decisions in consultation between husband and wife. Another telling statistic: in the village of Badan, the number of girls being sent to the village school has increased by 82 percent since the project started.

In Bolivia, the project is underway in eight villages in the southern central province of Chuquisaca. In the village of Poqonchi, where the project has been going the longest, comments made in focus group discussions indicate that women are now participating more in community decision-making, are more willing to express their desire for education, and are receiving from men more help with their daily chores. In addition, a woman was recently elected to the Poqonchi *sindicato*, a local political council. She is the first woman ever elected to the *sindicato* there and shortly after she was elected, the council passed a resolution urging greater attention to the concerns of women. In Malaysia, where the project has operated in two villages and an urban community, there are also concrete signs that women are becoming increasingly involved in community decision-making and organizations....

The biggest changes have come in Kampong Remun, a small and remote village in Sarawak, where the project has stimulated a variety of spin-offs. Using the project's methods for identifying community problems, the villagers have started a vegetable garden, built new latrines, and established adult literacy classes, which are designed primarily for the women but are open to men. Among the most significant aspects of the project is that its methodology is easily transferable to other countries and situations. The project essentially takes a three-step approach. It starts by training volunteers to act as community facilitators in helping to promote a grassroots analysis of the situation between men and women. It then focuses this analysis by emphasizing the equality of women as a basic moral and spiritual principle, drawing also on the techniques of Baha'i consultation to help build a consensus for action.

For example, one of the simple diagnostic tools used to help communities in their analysis was to ask participants to list all of the daily tasks of the average woman in the area. Participants were then asked to list the daily tasks of men. 'The difference in the work load was always so striking,' said Dr Richard Grieser, who served as trainer in Cameroon. 'In fact, the men often got very embarrassed, because the list was never even half as long as that of the women.'

In the final step, project participants then create and perform non-threatening media presentations to the community at large using traditional media, such as songs, dance, and plays. These general steps can be used almost anywhere in the developing world to promote the advancement of women.

'The project', said Ms Marjorie Thorpe, the deputy director of UNIFEM, 'starts with the premise that traditional media in non-literate societies – actors, dancers, puppeteers, ringmasters, singers – the message that they communicate is taken very seriously by the community and, therefore, if the message delivered could be one that enhances the status of women, then it will be an opportunity to begin a dialogue with the entire community – but in a manner that is non-threatening.'

Here is what some of the project participants say:

'The project is good because now my husband helps me with fire wood. I am now respected by my husband because I can say something and he listens to it and does it; before he would not. The song and theatre brought to me all these new ideas. There was a play about a wife and husband working hand in hand, a theatre on education of girls and another one on how to spend money' – Gbane Odette, 42, a farmer and mother of seven in the village of Yoko-Sire:

'My husband helps me more now with the housework that before he thought was the sole duty of woman. He carries the baby, cleans the dishes and clothes. I also learned the importance of children's education and that it is first my responsibility and now I try to take better care of them. I got those ideas through songs because through the songs I listened carefully to what was being said' – Zongayina Delphine, 36, a farmer and mother of six in Ndokayo village.

'Here in the village men and women were not used to working together but through the project I was surprised to see that they are working hand in hand. I personally have witnessed a change in my way of life. Concerning the equality of man and woman I see also that there is a change in the attitude of men. Now they consult with their wives. And I do the same. Before the project it was very difficult to know what women do with their money, but now my wife consults with me. I also work with my wife in the same farm, and I help with cleaning the house, for example; things I have never done before' – Dimessi Denis, 42, a male farmer in Ndokayo village. ●

The trend in projects designed to increase women's participation in wage labour is away from small income-generating projects in handicrafts to other types of economic ventures, such as dairying cooperatives or the production of goods and services that have relevance to the daily life of the community and are grounded in its existing resource base. In conjunction with such projects, training in financial management and marketing is often undertaken.

Greater attention is given to access to credit both because it is an essential element in the success of rural economic activities and because its lack is a major obstacle to women's emerging economic activities. For example, the well-known Grameen Bank in Bangladesh provides loans to thousands of landless farmers. Men and women are organized in separate credit groups, as is culturally expected in a Muslim society. The bank, which has a record 98 per cent repayment rate, relies on social collateral rather than on material collateral. The availability of loans to individual members of the group depends on the adherence of each member to rules and to repayment of loans, and peer pressure has proved very effective.[34] Other development programmes have responded to the need for credit by strengthening women's informal savings and credit groups, as in a rural project in Malawi where women expressed their preference for women-only credit clubs because women were better at repaying their loans than men.[35]

Extension services have found that strengthening women's organizations and their participation in other rural associations is an effective way of overcoming some of the difficulties that inhibit rural women's participation in extension activities: for example, cultural norms that prohibit male extension workers from having contact with individual women and the lack of transfer of information from men farmers to women. In some countries, women have expressed their preference for women-only groups because in such groups they could express themselves more freely. Moreover, women gain confidence from participating in women's groups; as well as skills in speaking, organizing and managing; a growing awareness of their needs and rights; and the ability and strength of numbers to take action. Such groups make it easier to arrange child care and organize mutual help.

Backed by the strength of their organizations, some women farmers have been able to demand that donors include their concerns in development programmes and projects. In Sierra Leone, for example, where wet lowland rice production was being proposed, a strong women farmers' organization in one village agreed to the introduction of the project on the condition that provision be made for the women's traditional crop, groundnuts. They threatened to refuse to cook unless their demand was accepted.[36]

Training women in organizational skills is another way to increase women's participation in rural organizations and their communities. An example is an FAO project in Honduras which trained women organizers chosen from the members of male-dominated peasant organizations with the twofold objective of increasing both women's influence in these organizations and their participation in agricultural extension activities through the formation of women's groups. Although the project met its goals, it encountered a number of difficulties. One problem was that the peasant organizations, which were expected to give financial support to the women organizers after the initial four-month subsidy provided by project funds, were reluctant to make resources available to women. Furthermore, the subsidy paid to the women, whose responsibilities were equivalent to those of full-time male organizers, was only half that of the men's remuneration. Other problems were related to women's efforts to combine full-time organizing work with household responsibilities, and the opposition women encountered at home.[37]

Nevertheless, the training increased women's involvement in agricultural extension activities and in decision making in the peasant organizations, as well as their self-confidence and ability to confront discriminatory practices and obstacles to their participation at the household and community level. At the end of the training, the women organizers committed themselves to form five to twenty groups of rural women each and, although they fell short of this goal, a significant number of groups were formed: 17 women organizers succeeded in creating 61 new groups comprising a total membership of 800 women within 18 months of completing their training:

The political impact of the women's training was felt in the household, the community and the peasant organizations. Women's involvement in organizations increased their responsibilities in the public sphere. Trained peasant women who belonged to predominantly male organizations began to demand increased decision-making power, and fought for recognition of their rights. The women of the National Peasants' Union (UNC – Union Nacional de Campesinos), for example, formed a bloc and in 1988 successfully demanded the right to vote within the organization. Female members of ANACH [Associacion Nacional de Campesinos de Honduras – the National Peasants' Association of Honduras) have pushed for greater representation at the regional level, demanding that at least one women be included in the hierarchy in each region.[38]

PHOTO: E. KENNEDY/WHO/FAO

Bangladesh: access to credit is essential to the success of women's economic activities

The improvement of women's status leads to changes in their relationships with men, and often brings problems and conflict which must be accepted as an inevitable phase in the empowerment process: 'Increased activity often caused personal problems for the women because they were taking on a non-traditional role. After a period of time, though, the positive results of the organizers'activities transformed village gossip into community respect. Women working as organizers universally agreed that they initially experienced rejection at home and in the community but that their struggle to work with women was worthwhile.... In the words of one woman, "I was a different person after the training. I had more confidence, and my husband didn't know what to do with me." After a period of personal struggle within the family, however, most husbands came to recognize the value of their wives' participation and allowed them to leave the house and travel to other villages.'[39]

Traditional handicraft and homemaking projects can also develop into successful rural production groups, and even lead the way in rural development. The Zvichanaka Farmer's Group in Zimbabwe is an example of such progress. Zvichanaka, which means 'everything is okay' in the local language, Shona, grew out of a women's sewing and knitting club. Saniso Mashayamombe, a member of the group, says that the problem with the sewing club was the low remuneration and its lack of relevance to their main activity, farming.[40]

The club was transformed into a farmers' group that used a demonstration plot to improve agricultural production techniques through advice, training and inputs such as fertilizer. Through the new approach, the women increased production of sunflowers and beans and learned to keep farm accounts. From member contributions and income from sale of produce, the group was able to save money and to tackle the persistent problem of transporting produce to the market. In addition to its economic outcome, the women's participation had a dramatic effect in building up their confidence and, consequently, in enabling them to assert themselves in the community. Rebecca Muvezwa, chairperson of Zvichanaka, says:

You can tell the difference between the members of our group and the others from the way they walk, their knowledge, their ability to reason or argue. They are not shy and withdrawn like others.[41]

Within the family, women are able to ask men to share household responsibilities to allow women to have time for other activities. This is reflected in the words of one member of the group:

These days, I can even tell my husband to stay at home and do the cooking while I go off to a training course.[42]

After the women of the Zvichanaka Farmers' Group had consolidated their strength, they decided to invite men to join the organization in order to take on certain tasks such as ploughing and fencing. To ensure that men do not come to dominate the organization, men's participation was restricted to 40 per cent of the membership. While half the leadership committee was composed of men, the chair was a woman. Significantly, men recognize that women are leading the way, as the husband of one of the members says:

In the past, it was always men who were the leaders. But now this government of ours has taught women how to take charge. So now we follow our wives to the groups.[43]

What of rural women who live in still more tradition-bound and conservative societies? The African Network for Integrated Development (RADI) which works among predominantly Islamic rural communities in Senegal, uses sensitization of both men and women as a crucial element in its efforts to empower rural women. RADI's particular experience shows that: 'realistically, the critical challenge is to find a culturally sensitive balance between change, progress and tradition. And with such a balanced approach to sensitization, local communities will perceive that this implies important changes in conservative attitudes and practices which continue to strengthen the roots of women's subordination and to obstruct the full participation of women in all spheres of society.'[44]

*MODEST BUT VITAL STEPS: CHANGING WOMEN'S LIVES IN RURAL SENEGAL**

Yeshica Weerasekera and Amie Diop

Created in Dakar in the mid-1980s to promote African and local solutions to development problems, RADI has been working in this Sahelian country to improve basic economic and social conditions in partnership with village-based community associations. Using a self-help and empowerment philosophy to counteract the hand-out mentality fostered by many mainstream development agencies, RADI promotes a pragmatic mix of subsistence agriculture and market gardening projects developed in concertation with these village associations....

At first, because of the 'community' and 'consensus-based' approach to problem-solving used by traditional village structures, the assumption was made that

* 'Modest But Vital Steps: Changing Women's Lives in Rural Senegal', African Network for Integrated Development (1993)

PHOTO: MAGGIE MURRAY-LEE/UNICEF

Farming is the main activity of most rural women in Africa

women would benefit from the resources generated on 'family plots' placed under the control of male heads of households and from communal-owned initiatives. Although RADI negotiated a special 'women's group plot' in each village to generate funds for women's specific needs, these turned out not to be very successful. Women's participation was poor on these special plots mainly because the resources generated were inadequate when shared out among the individual women group members, and the extra field work was an additional burden on their regular demanding routine of domestic and agricultural responsibilities. Even RADI literacy classes were poorly attended by women, despite the flexibility in their timing, because of the enormous demands made on women's time and energy....

When RADI was first invited to work with these village associations, women were constituted into small groups according to age group or extended family. RADI helped organise them together into larger women's associations with elected officials at the head of each association.

From the beginning, a major emphasis was put on sensitisation efforts.... However, in this milieu, change was not as easy as RADI agents had hoped it would be and they discovered that even simple changes can lead to major time-consuming complications and problems. For example, when organising village women's groups it is quite common for them to request labour-saving techniques and changes, first of all in order to alleviate their enormous work burdens and therefore participate in other organised activities. Thus when women predictably sought millet-grinding equipment to save them many hours of pounding and grinding millet by hand, it became necessary to ask men to contribute 'community funds' to existing women's resources for their purchase.

In one Serer village, Guelor, the men refused outright to help purchase these machines. They argued that the couscous made from millet ground by machines would 'taste like gasoline' and that the women would bring them bad luck due to their customary belief that millet ground outside of the hut during the rainy season would result in a bad harvest the following year. In this case, although discouraged, RADI agents continued their sensitisation efforts, resisting the urge to abandon the project. They reprogrammed meetings and had lengthy discussions with men in their community, in addition to providing educational campaigns, on the usefulness of millet-grinding machines and the overall social improvement they would bring through the increase in income for women. Even though the men in this particular village eventually agreed to contribute to the purchase of a millet-machine, there was still the problem of project management to resolve. Women were experiencing management difficulties and the men consequently complained that, because they had given funds for the purchase of the machine, they had the right to take over and manage it themselves if the women were unable to do so effectively.

It was from practical experiences like these that RADI agents have developed their work with women. From these cases they have learned the lesson that co-management of community goods is very difficult because it is usually the men who invest more financial resources, and consequently demand more control.... What is needed is very difficult to bring about in a sensitive and appropriate manner: deeper cultural and social shifts in certain traditional values which usually only evolve slowly over time.

Subsequent developments have brought important relative changes such as evidenced in the village of Nianar, where the development of a millet-grinding machine project remains under the exclusive control of women. Women decide everything and keep the income generated by fees levied on its use, and it is they who decide what to do with the profits. And as for men, if it interests them, they are invited to meetings, are asked about their point of view on the use of the money, or the profitability of the project. They make proposals but do not decide anything regarding the management of the project....

Amie Diop, the RADI women's programme officer ... speaks of the lack of awareness among some of her male colleagues. While some male programme officers have an understanding of the importance of promoting activities for women, very few of the field coordinators acknowledge the significance of the women's programme, having never directly worked with women before.... Amie attempts to overcome these constraints by promoting formal sensitisation sessions. In addition she always invites the field coordinators from each of the communities to sit in on the women's meetings, asks them to take minutes and learn from group dynamics, and most importantly to listen closely to the views, wishes, needs and demands of women. In some of the mixed meetings now it is possible to see women speaking out and even contradicting the field coordinator if they believe he has misrepresented the work of the women. A considerable change, and one that is not judged lightly by RADI agents who only a few years ago were holding meetings where women did not dare speak up or required the permission of their husbands to do so.

It has to be said that the sensitisation and consciousness-raising sessions of both men and women are a crucial element in making progress in this most conservative of milieux.... In this particular context, the burdens for women of health care, maternity, family responsibilities, community ceremonies, traditional customs and behaviour will not change rapidly or radically, especially if men do not understand the importance of alleviating the work burdens of women for social progress and well-being and are left unaware of the need to have women participate in more meaningful ways in community activities and decision-making. ●

1. United Nations, 'Development and international economic cooperation: effective mobilization and integration of women in development', Report of the Secretary-General, United Nations General Assembly, Forty-sixth session, Agenda Item 77(j), para. 42 (A/46/464).
2. Mary Racelis Hollnsteiner and Hoda Badran, 'Structures of inequality', *Assignment Children*, No. 49–50, Spring 1980, pp. 101–103.
3. A. Rani Parker, *Another Point of View: A Manual of Gender Analysis Training for Grassroots Workers*, UNIFEM, New York, 1993, p. 11.
4. Martha F. Loufti, *Rural Women: Unequal Partners in Development*, International Labour Organization, Geneva, 1980, p. 34.
5. David A Mitchnik, *The Role of Women in Rural Zaire and Upper Volta*, Oxfam, Oxford, 1977, p. 20.
6. Olga Stavrakis and Marion Louise Marshall, 'Women, agriculture and development in the Maya Lowlands: profit or progress', in Ann Bunzel Cowan (ed.), *Proceedings and Papers of the International Conference on Women and Food*, Consortium for International Development, Washington DC, 1978, pp. 157–74.
7. Bette Shertzer, 'The third world of women', *Food Monitor*, January–February 1979, p. 13.
8. See Caroline 0. N. Moser, *Gender Planning and Development: Theory, Practice and Training*, Routledge, London, 1993, pp. 55–79.
9. See Maxine Molyneaux, 'Mobilization without emancipation? Women's interests, the state, and revolution in Nicaragua', *Feminist Review* 11, No. 2, 1985, pp. 225–54.
10. Heleen van den Hombergh, *Gender, Environment and Development: A Guide to the Literature*, International Books, Utrecht, 1993, p. 41.
11. Moser, pp. 62–4.
12. Ibid., p. 65.
13. Ibid., p. 69.
14. For a summary of early feminist critiques, see Anita Anand, 'Rethinking women and development' and Marilee Karl, 'Women and rural development: an overview' in *Women in Development: A Resource Guide for Organization and Action*, ISIS, Rome and Geneva, 1983.
15. Wanjiru Kihoro, 'Why African women are still left behind', *Third World Network Features*, No. 967, 1992, p. 5.
16. *Development Dialogue*, 1982, pp. 13–14.
17. Gita Sen and Caren Grown, *Development, Crisis, and Alternative Visions: Third World Women's Perspectives*, A.S. Verbum, Stavanger, 1985, p. 11.
18. Ibid., p. 73.

19 Ibid., p. 75.
20. Kihoro, pp. 5–6.
21. Canadian Council for International Cooperation, citied in van den Hombergh, p. 41.
22. See, for instance, Aruna Rao, Mary B. Anderson and Catherine A. Overholt, *Gender Analysis in Development Planning*, Kumarian Press, West Hartford, 1991; Susan V. Poats and Sandra L. Russo, 'Training in Women in Development/gender analysis in agricultural development: a review of experiences and lessons learned', Food and Agriculture Organization (FAO), Rome, Working Paper No. 8, 1990; 'The FAO gender analysis training programme for professional staff', FAO, Rome, 1991.
23. Jacinta Sekoh, 'Attitude change is everyone's assignment', *FEMNET News*, Vol. 2, No. 3, 1993, p.21.
24. Kamla Bhasin, 'Gender workshops with men: experiences and reflections', unpublished paper, 1993, p. 2.
25. Ibid., p. 4.
26. Kate Young, *Planning Development With Women: Making a World of Difference*, Macmillan, 1993, p. 157.
27. Ibid., pp. 162–3.
28. Srilatha Batliwala, *Empowerment of Women in South Asia: Concepts and Practices*, FAO, FFHC/AD, New Delhi, 1993, pp. 23–38.
29. UNICEF, 'The women's empowerment framework', *Women and Girls Advance*, Vol. 1, No. 1, 1993, p. 5.
30. United Nations, 'Integration of women', para. 32.
31. Marty Chen, 'Developing non-craft employment for women in Bangladesh', in Ann Leonard (ed.), *Seeds: Supporting Women's Work in the Third World*, The Feminist Press, New York, 1989, pp. 91–3.
32. See *Access*, the newsletter of BRAC; and Chen, pp. 73–91.
33. 'Traditional media as change agent – Men and women as partners', *One Country*, Vol. 5, No. 3, 1993.
34. Andreas Fuglesang and Dale Chandler, *Participation as Process – What We Can Learn From Grameen Bank, Bangladesh*, Norwegian Ministry of Development Co-operation, Oslo, 1986.
35. Katrine A. Saito and Daphne Spurling, 'Developing agricultural extension for women farmers', *World Bank Discussion Papers*, No. 156, 1992, p. 59.
36. Charles Foubert, unpublished notes from an evaluation mission in Sierra Leone, 1987.
37. Susan Fleck, 'Extension "woman to woman" – training peasant women liaisons to reach peasant women', FAO, 1994, pp. 14–16.
38. Ibid., p.16.
39. Ibid., pp. 16, 18.
40. Colleen Lowe Morna, 'Women farmers lead the way', in Women's Feature Service, *The Power to Change*, Kali for Women, New Delhi, 1992, pp. 98–101.
41. Ibid., p. 101.
42. Ibid.
43. Ibid., p. 100.
44. Yeshica Weerasekera and Amie Diop, 'Modest but vital steps: changing women's lives in rural Senegal', African Network for Intergrated Development, 1993, p. 8.

6 INTERNATIONAL MOBILIZATION OF WOMEN IN AND AROUND THE UNITED NATIONS

In order to ensure that programmes and activities of concern to women are given the necessary attention and priority, it is essential that women should participate actively in the planning and formulation of policies and programmes and in decision-making and appraisal processes in the United Nations.[1]

THE CELEBRATION of the fiftieth anniversary of the United Nations (UN) in 1995 provides an occasion to review how women have worked in and around the UN to put women on its agenda, the interlinkages of the UN with the global women's movement, the mechanisms that the UN has established for the promotion of women, and how these mechanisms can be used in the struggle for gender equality as the twenty-first century approaches. Although women have become increasingly involved in UN conferences and parallel non-governmental activities since International Women's Year, 1975, women's participation in world bodies goes back to the times preceding the founding of the UN.

THE LEAGUE OF NATIONS □ Even before the birth of the UN, women mobilized to influence its predecessor, the League of Nations. As early as the Paris Peace Conference in 1919, international women's organizations lobbied to secure an article in the Covenant of the League of Nations that assured that posts in the League would be open to women as well as men.[2]

Throughout the history of the League, international women's organizations, with their headquarters based mainly in London and Geneva, were able to form consultative bodies to lobby the League on a wide range of causes including social reform, women's rights and peace. Very few women actually participated in the work of League itself because few women worked in international politics or the diplomatic service. When women did obtain posts in the League, these were mainly in the fields of humanitarian and social affairs, following the traditional gender division of labour. It is not minimizing women's work in these fields to acknowledge that their exclusion from other sectors prevented them from making a wider contribution. The concept that women have different values and concerns from men provided a framework for women's participation in the League: 'The identification of caring and co-operation as womanly values and women's long history of humanitarian work helped secure a place for them in connection with the League's social and humanitarian work.... At the same time, they fostered an awareness of women as a group with specific needs that deserved attention from the international community.'[3]

Drawing the attention of the League of Nations to women's civil and political rights was one of the main areas of work of the international women's organizations. On the invitation of the Secretary-General, women's organizations provided statements on the status of women to the League Assembly in 1935 in which they pointed out, in particular, the gap between legal guarantees of equality and the inequalities found in practice, including discrimination in employment.[4] The important contribution of women to the League of Nations set the stage for more concerted activities to advance the status of women through the United Nations.

WOMEN ON THE UNITED NATIONS AGENDA □ When the United Nations was formed in 1945, women representing national and international women's organizations helped to create the climate and support needed to include the principle of equality between women and men in the United Nations Charter.[5] The Charter states:

The Peoples of the United Nations determine to reaffirm faith in fundamental human rights, in the dignity and worth of the human person, in the equal rights of men and women ...

One of the prominent women signatories of the Charter who worked for the explicit mention of women in this document was Minerva Bernardino, delegate from the Dominican Republic. Another leading figure at the founding of the United Nations and in its early years was Eleanor Roosevelt, who presided over a commission established by the first General Assembly of the United Nations to draft the Universal Declaration of Human Rights. During the drafting of the Declaration, the Commission on the Status of Women successfully worked to ensure that the language of the document was inclusive of women. The Universal Declaration of Human Rights, adopted in 1948, affirms that: 'Everyone is entitled to all the rights set forth in this Declaration, without distinction of any kind, such as race, colour, sex ...'

An important mechanism for promoting the interests of women was established in 1946: the Commission on the Status of Women (CSW). There was a debate at the time about whether or not the establishment of a commission specifically for women might lead to their marginalization within the United Nations. On the other hand, it was felt that women risked being virtually ignored unless a body was mandated for their concerns. Composed of member states, the CSW has played an

COMMISSION ON THE STATUS OF WOMEN (CSW)
Established in 1946, the CSW is an intergovernmental body tasked to prepare reports and recommendations on women's rights in the political, economic, civil, social and educational fields. It reports to the Economic and Social Council (ECOSOC) of the United Nations. The CSW is the body that drafted the Convention on the Elimination of All Forms of Discrimination against Women as well as the documents for the United Nations World Conferences on Women, including the World Plan of Action for the Implementation of the Objectives of International Women's Year (1975), and the Nairobi Forward-Looking Strategies for the Advancement of Women (1985). Comprising forty-five member governments, with one third of its members changing annually, the commission meets once a year.

DIVISION FOR THE ADVANCEMENT OF WOMEN (DAW)
The Branch for the Advancement of Women established within the United Nations Centre for Social Development and Humanitarian Affairs (CSDHA) became the Division for the Advancement of Women (DAW) in 1988. In 1993, it moved from Vienna to New York; it is located in the United Nations Department for Policy Coordination and Sustainable Development (DPCSD). As the principal unit within the United Nations dealing with women, DAW serves as the Secretariat for the Commission on the Status of Women (CSW) and for the Committee on the Elimination of Discrimination Against Women (CEDAW). DAW is also an information and research centre as well as a contact point on women for national governments, intergovernmental bodies and institutions, NGOs and individuals. Its work includes planning policies and programmes on women, compiling reports on the monitoring of the implementation of international agreements on women, and organizing expert meetings and initiating research on key issues affecting the position of women.

important role throughout the history of the organization in the promotion of women's equality. A secretariat for women's issues and to service the CSW was also set up within the United Nations: the Branch for the Advancement of Women, which was transformed into the Division for the Advancement of Women (DAW) in 1988.

During the first decades of the United Nations, the Commission on the Status of Women focused on several major concerns of women: political and legal rights, access to education and training, work, and trafficking in women, an issue that international women's organizations had already urged the League of Nations to address. By this time, women in most countries had attained the vote and were eager to ensure their right to participate in political life. Their participation was also restricted in many countries by lack of rights in marriage and by lack of access to education. Moreover, women had entered the workforce in great numbers, and were also facing discrimination in employment and pay. The International Labour Organization (ILO) took up the issues of women workers, while the United Nations Educational, Scientific and Cultural Organization (UNESCO) addressed discrimination against women in education. As a result of these efforts, a number of international conventions were adopted.

EARLY CONVENTIONS CONCERNING THE STATUS OF WOMEN	Year Adopted
Convention for the Suppression of Traffic in Persons and the Exploitation of the Prostitution of Others	1949
Convention Concerning Equal Remuneration for Men and Women Workers for Work of Equal Value (ILO)	1951
Convention on the Political Rights of Women	1952
Convention Concerning Discrimination in Respect of Employment and Occupation (ILO)	1958
Convention against Discrimination in Education (UNESCO)	1962
Convention on Consent to Marriage, Minimum Age of Marriage, and Registration of Marriage	1964

The UN and its specialized bodies have a system-wide commitment to the advancement of women. UN bodies especially concerned with women include:

- Food and Agriculture Organization of the United Nations (FAO)
- International Fund for Agricultural Development (IFAD)
- International Labour Organization (ILO)
- International Research and Training Institute for the Advancement of Women (INSTRAW)
- United Nations High Commission for Refugees (UNHCR)
- United Nations Centre for Human Rights
- United Nations Children's Fund (UNICEF)
- United Nations Development Programme (UNDP)
- United Nations Educational, Scientific and Cultural Organization (UNESCO)
- United Nations Environment Programme (UNEP)
- United Nations Fund for Population (UNFPA)
- United Nations Fund for Women (UNIFEM)
- United Nations Industrial Development Organization (UNIDO)

- United Nations Non-Governmental Liaison Service (NGLS)
- United Nations Research Institute for Social Development (UNRISD)
- United Nations Volunteers (UNV)
- World Bank (WB)
- World Food Programme of the United Nations (WFP)
- World Health Organization (WHO)

The importance of non-governmental organizations (NGOs) was recognized by the United Nations from its inception and mechanisms were put in place to establish consultative relations between the Economic and Social Council of the United Nations (ECOSOC) and international NGOs which are concerned with economic, social, cultural, educational, scientific, technological and human rights matters. The work of NGOs in relation to the United Nations is facilitated by the Conference of Non-Governmental Organizations in Consultative Status with the United Nations Economic and Social Council (CONGO) which was established in 1948. It fosters co-operation among NGOs and helps strengthen the relationship between the United Nations and NGOs. The United Nations is currently reviewing its formal relations with NGOs in order to decide whether UN-NGO co-operation should be expanded and what forms it should receive in the future. An intergovernmental open-ended committee has been set up for this task, and it is expected to finalize its report in 1995.

Consultative status entitles NGOs to participate as observers at intergovernmental meetings and submit their views and proposals. Many of the international NGOs have permanent representatives in New York, Geneva, Vienna and other cities where United Nations offices and agencies are located in order to follow meetings and monitor the United Nations on a daily basis. CONGO has set up a number of bodies in Geneva, New York and Vienna on substantive issues including the Committees on the Status of Women in New York and Vienna and the Sub-Committee on the Status of Women in Geneva. These committees have established working groups on issues such as employment, peace, traditional practices, refugees, health, nutrition, the girl child and development education.

Because the United Nations is an organization of governments, it is crucial for women and NGOs to work also on the national level in order to monitor and assist in the implementation of international agreements and lobby governments to take up matters of concern in the international arena. NGOs can also demand augmentation of women in their country's delegations and preparatory bodies for international meetings. Another important task at the national and local level is that of building public awareness of existing international instruments and national plans of action for the advancement of women. Thus, for effectiveness, interlinking the local, national and international levels is crucial through three-way collaboration among committed women working in the United Nations, in government delegations and in non-governmental organizations.

While progress in advancing the rights of women in and through the United Nations was slow during the first twenty-five years of its existence, the groundwork in these years paved the way for an upsurge of activities in the 1970s, which was due to a combination of factors: more concerted efforts by international women's non-governmental organizations; the support of women professionals within the United Nations, government offices and delegations; research on the neglect of women in development policies and

PHOTO: ANNE WALKER/IWTC

Since the 1970s, women have increased their activities in and around the United Nations

programmes; and the stirring of the new wave of the women's movement.

INTERNATIONAL WOMEN'S YEAR □

The International Women's Year (IWY) 1975 and the United Nations Decade for Women 1976–1985 were landmarks in the action of the organization and constituted rallying points for the international mobilization of women. The events that led to the declaration of International Women's Year are described by Hilkka Pietilä and Jeanne Vickers in the book *Making Women Matter: The Role of the United Nations*, which gives an account of women's participation in the United Nations, especially during the Decade for Women:

An oral tradition in the UN family says that the seeds of IWY came from Finland. A non-governmental organization, the Women's International Democratic Federation, first proposed the declaration of a women's year, and WIDF's president then was a prominent Finnish parliamentarian, Hertta Kuusinen. Representing her organization as an observer at the 1972 session of the UN Commission on the Status of Women, Ms. Kuusinen, together with a number of other NGO observers, drafted a proposal which she convinced the Romanian representative on the Commission to present. The Finnish government representative at that time, Helvi Sipilä, seconded the proposal and ... the Commission decided to recommend to the General Assembly the declaration of 1975 as International Women's Year. Thus, IWY is one example of an NGO initiative taken up by the UN system – one which on this occasion exceeded all expectations, developing into a process with dimensions and repercussions such as the initiators had hardly dared to dream of.[6]

International Women's Year and the following Decade converged with the burst of energy and dynamism arising from both long-established and newly-formed women's groups and organizations around the world. The initiatives of the United Nations and those of the women's movement interacted with each other and had a transformative effect on the whole society. The IWY began to make an impact, even before it began: 'Preparations for the World Population Conference (1974) were already well underway when the decision on IWY was taken, and – hard though it is to believe – gave no recognition to women's role in population questions. This alarmed a number of NGOs and caught the attention of the new Assistant Secretary-General [Helvi Sipilä]. Early in 1974 these NGOs, together with Ms. Sipilä's Division for Social Development and Humanitarian Affairs, organized an unofficial preparatory meeting, the International Forum on the Role of Women in Population and Development...'[7]

As a result, the World Population Conference of 1974 did make the link between women and population. Similar efforts by NGOs and committed women in government and the United Nations led the World Food Conference, held in Rome the same year, to recognize women as major food producers.

WORLD PLAN OF ACTION FOR THE IMPLEMENTATION OF THE OBJECTIVES OF THE INTERNATIONAL WOMEN'S YEAR

Adopted in 1975, the plan proposed national action in the following areas:

- international co-operation and strengthening international peace;
- political participation;
- education and training;
- employment and related economic roles;
- health and nutrition;
- the family in modern society;
- population;
- housing and related facilities;
- social services.

Action on both the national and international levels was proposed in the areas of:

- research, data collection and analysis;
- mass media;
- participation of women in United Nations bodies;
- international exchange of information.

THE FIRST WORLD CONFERENCE ON WOMEN AND THE DECADE FOR WOMEN

□ The decision to hold a World Conference on Women in Mexico City during the 1975 IWY was made only one year in advance. Although there was in consequence little time to prepare, a World Plan of Action was drawn up and adopted at the Conference, which was attended by representatives of 133 countries. The World Plan of Action, emanating from an intergovernmental body, primarily addressed national governments and organizations within the United Nations system; it proposed actions and set targets for a ten-year period in a wide range of areas including political participation, education, health and employment.

The General Assembly of the United Nations approved the plan and declared 1976–1985 the United Nations Decade for Women, with the special sub-themes of Equality, Development and Peace. The Decade gave a renewed impetus to governments, NGOs and the United Nations to work actively for the implementation of the Plan of Action.

Parallel to the World Conference on Women, an NGO meeting was organized in Mexico City in 1975. Called the International Women's Year Tribune, it brought together 4,000 participants, a gathering of NGOs around United Nations conferences that was unprecedented up to that time. In hundreds of panel discussions and workshops, women debated the issues affecting their lives, and the excitement generated spun off in dozens of new initiatives such as MATCH International which links Canadian women's groups with women's groups in the South and assists them in organizational development and fund-raising, and the International Women's Tribune Centre (IWTC).

However, not all women's groups and organizations were represented there. Participation was largely limited to the long-established women's NGOs and to women from North and South America, whose participation was facilitated by proximity to Mexico. Very few of the new women's groups and organizations were able to participate because of their lack of access to information and finances. Moreover, some questioned the relevance of the conference and had doubts about achieving progress through intergovernmental recommendations and plans of action, while others prioritized the organizing and mobilizing of women on the local level.

Although the Conference was considered a success, its impact was not immediately evident and women's issues continued to be largely ignored in both national and international decision making. For example, the Conferences on Human Settlements and Economic Co-operation in 1976, the Water Conference and the Conference on Desertification in 1977, the Conference on Technical Co-operation Among Developing Countries and the Primary Health Care Conference in 1978 all failed to pay attention to women's roles, in spite of their obvious relevance to women. Towards the end of the 1970s, the World Conference on Agrarian Reform and Rural Development (WCARRD) in Rome was one of the first international conferences to acknowledge the importance of women. It declared that 'rural development based on growth with equity will require the full integration of women'. The meeting of NGOs parallel to WCARRD recognized women's role not only as the world's major food producers but also as knowledge-holders of traditional varieties of seeds, and thus as important actors in the preservation of plant genetic diversity.

THE UNITED NATIONS DEVELOPMENT FUND FOR WOMEN (UNIFEM)

Established in 1976 as the Voluntary Fund for the Decade for Women to fund innovative and catalytic projects, the Fund's name was changed to UNIFEM in 1985. It provides direct financial and technical support to low-income women in developing countries who are striving to raise their living standard. It also funds activities that bring women into mainstream development decision making. UNIFEM works in association with the United Nations Development Programme (UNDP).

THE UNITED NATIONS INTERNATIONAL RESEARCH AND TRAINING INSTITUTE FOR THE ADVANCEMENT OF WOMEN (INSTRAW)

The idea for a research and training institute for women grew out of the 1975 World Conference on Women and became a reality with the establishment of INSTRAW in 1982. INSTRAW carries out research and training with the aim of integrating women into the development process and promoting women's participation in politics and public life.

The Decade for Women gave birth to further UN bodies concerned with women: the United Nations Development Fund for Women (UNIFEM) was established in 1976 and the United Nations International Research and Training Institute for the Advancement of Women (INSTRAW) was set up 1982. Among the measures taken to strengthen the commitment of governments and intergovernmental bodies to improve the status of women at the national and international levels were: the establishment of women's units and focal points in UN agencies; the establishment of women's bureaux or ministries at the national level; and the setting up of monitoring mechanisms for the implementation of the World Plan of Action.

CONVENTION ON THE ELIMINATION OF ALL FORMS OF DISCRIMINATION AGAINST WOMEN □ The main instrument that emerged from the Decade for Women was the Convention on the Elimination of All Forms of Discrimination against Women, also known as the Women's Convention. Its origins can be traced to the Declaration on the Elimination of Discrimination against Women drawn up by the Commission on the Status of Women in 1963. Adopted by the General Assembly of the United Nations in 1967, the Declaration aimed to 'ensure the universal recognition in law and in fact of the principle of equality of men and women' and suggested that measures be taken to abolish discriminatory laws and customs and to change public opinion, recognizing the significant role of women's organizations in this regard. Following the Declaration, the Commission on the Status of Women began to draft the Convention on the Elimination of All Forms of Discrimination against Women. The World Plan of Action, adopted in 1975, urged that high priority be given to the preparation and adoption of the Convention. According to a report by the International Women's Rights Action Watch (IWRAW), 'It never would have been drafted and adopted without the dedication of a group of Commission delegates, many of whom were also active in women's organizations, who believed that the legal and human rights of women needed to be firmly defined and established internationally.... Adopted by the UN General Assembly in 1979, the Convention was signed by some fifty countries at the opening ceremony of the 1980 Mid-Decade UN World Conference on Women held in Copenhagen, Denmark.'[8]

The Convention, which came into force as a treaty on 3 September 1981, sets principles and standards to achieve equality between men and women, and to eliminate discrimination against women in all spheres of life. As of August 1993, 125 countries had become parties to the Convention, either ratifying or acceding to it. In addition, nine states had signed the Convention without yet ratifying it. While signing the document only obliges countries to do nothing that contravenes its principles, ratifying or acceding to the Convention obliges governments to pursue policies to eliminate discrimination against women as set forth in its specific articles. Governments that have ratified or acceded to the Convention are required to report on their progress in implementing it within one year after ratification and once every four years thereafter. However, a number of the parties to the Convention have ratified it with reservations.

The Committee on the Elimination of Discrimination Against Women (CEDAW) is the body to which the parties to the Convention must report. It comprises twenty-three members who are elected for four-year terms by the governments that have ratified the Convention. CEDAW members serve in their personal capacities and not as representatives of their governments. CEDAW meets annually to review the government reports on implementation of the Convention.

The Women's Convention is thus a major instrument to improve the situation of women at the national level and can be used by NGOs to promote greater gender equality. Women's organizations can also play a role in monitoring the implementation of the Convention, assist their governments in reporting on it, and submit

PHOTO: D. BUDD-GRAY/WHO/UNICEF

The 'Women's Convention' protects the rights of women and girls

independent reports to CEDAW. Annex II contains a summarized version of the Convention and further information on how it can be used by NGOs.

THE MID-DECADE CONFERENCE ON WOMEN □ In 1980, halfway through the Decade for Women, a second United Nations Conference on Women was held, this time in Copenhagen, to review the implementation of the World Plan of Action and to develop it further for the second half of the Decade. While the Conference accomplished this objective, it was also marked by debate that reflected the approaches of the traditional political blocs. Hilkka Pietilä and Jeanne Vickers explain:

> **Market economy countries stressed equality between men and women as the key factor in the struggle to improve the latter's status, while developing countries considered overall acceleration of economic and social development as the most important thing from the point of view of both women and men.... Socialist states held that equality between men and women was already a fact of life in those countries, and therefore emphasized the same political issues they stressed in all other UN fora.... General political issues came to the forefront ... those same issues (Palestine, Zionism, racial discrimination, etc.) which governments were disputing *ad infinitum* elsewhere. Big powers were playing their power game, developing countries fought for more equitable international trade and a new international economic order.[9]**

Because of this situation, some women complained that the women delegates (who comprised 73 per cent of participants) were simply expressing the same views as male representatives of the various political blocs and that the Conference was 'too politicized'. However, as the feminist activist and writer Charlotte Bunch stated:

> **The problem with the UN official conference in Copenhagen was not that it was 'politicized' but that it failed to consider issues from a feminist political perspective or even in terms of how they were specifically viewed or affected by women.[10]**

In this view, the Conference should have been an opportunity for women to bring forward their voices on major political questions and to give greater attention to specific concerns of women. Consequently, many women's groups accelerated their efforts on the national level to ensure that governments reflect women's concerns and views, while others that had prioritized work at the grassroots also became concerned with influencing national and international policy-making.

On the other hand, the parallel NGO Forum in Copenhagen, which brought together 7,000 women from North and South from both the long-established NGOs and newer feminist groups, provided the opportunity to discuss specific concerns (such as women and development, health and traditional practices) as well as to debate issues related to working with the United Nations. The questions raised included: How can women carry their struggle beyond that for greater equality in male-defined institutions and society to one for empowerment that will enable them to help define institutions and society? Will greater participation of women by itself be sufficient to bring about change or are other mechanisms needed?

Related to the nature of women's participation were questions about the integration of women in development: Could or should women be integrated into the present models of development or should these models not be radically transformed? A quote in the daily *Forum* newspaper that 'To talk feminism to a woman who has no water, no food and no home, is to talk nonsense' implied that priority must be given to providing women with basic needs. Many feminists, on the other hand, responded that the empowerment of women through awareness building and involvement in decision making were key elements in enabling women to gain access to water, food, shelter and other basic needs.

INTERNATIONAL WOMEN'S ORGANIZATIONS AND THE DECADE □ International women's organizations played a key role in organizing the parallel NGO meetings to the World Conferences on Women with the secretariats of the NGO Planning Committees based in New York. The NGO Committees on the Status of Women in New York and Vienna and the Sub-Committee on the Status of Women in Geneva also continued their day-to-day work with the United Nations.[11] For instance, the NGO Working Group on Traditional Practices was established in 1977 in Geneva under the umbrella of the NGO Sub-Committee on the Status of Women to take up the issue of female genital mutilation (FGM). Currently composed of twenty-eight NGOs with consultative status with ECOSOC, the group works on both the national and the international levels.

On the country level, an NGO representative and the Working Group Co-ordinator, who is an African woman, visit countries where FGM is practised to discuss educational and information programmes that take into consideration the culture of each country. Such programmes are designed and implemented by the national groups, while the NGO Working Group on Traditional Practices provides technical and material support. A landmark event for the working group was the organization of the first African NGO seminar on traditional practices in Dakar, Senegal, in 1984, in collaboration with the government of Senegal, WHO and UNICEF. According to the working group:

The seminar gave the appropriate African forum to discuss delicate issues such as FGM, early childhood marriage, nutritional taboos, etc. At the end of the seminar the Inter-African Committee (IAC) on Traditional Practices Affecting the Health of Women and Children was established. Since its creation, the IAC has endeavoured to set up viable national committees for implementing programmes. At present, the IAC has 24 national committees, which conduct programmes of research, education and information. IAC produces educational materials, information leaflets which are widely distributed. It organizes national and regional workshops, seminars and conferences. The NGO Working Group supports the IAC in fundraising and advocacy.[12]

On the international level, the NGO Working Group on Traditional Practices plays a strong and sustained advocacy role at international conferences and during the ongoing work of UN organizations and their commissions. At the UN Commission on Human Rights, for instance, the group brought up FGM as a human rights violation, called for governments to take action to stop it, proposed that a special UN working group be set up to study the problem, and collaborated in drawing up a report to the Commission. As a result, a Special Rapporteur was appointed to the UN Commission on Human Rights to follow up the matter of traditional practices. The group also works closely with WHO, UNICEF and the UN Commission on the Status of Women and has succeeded in raising international awareness of FGM as violence against women and as a serious health risk. In particular, the NGO Working Group on Traditional Practices played a key role in the drafting of Article 24.3 of the

PHOTO: LOUISE GUBB/UNICEF

Much of women's work is unrecognized and unpaid

Convention on the Rights of the Child, which states that 'States Parties shall take all effective and appropriate measures with a view to abolishing traditional practices prejudicial to the health of children'. The method of combined pressure and information campaigns at the national and international levels has brought the issue of FGM to the agenda of United Nations organizations which were initially reluctant to take it up, and the resolutions of organizations such as WHO and UNICEF now provide women's groups with support for their campaigns. However, the main strategy, education and awareness building, is a slow process, and pressure is still being brought on the UN and governments to take stronger measures.

The largely unrecognized work of women in maintaining the household and in the informal sector was taken up by the NGO Working Group on Employment of the NGO Sub-Committee on the Status of Women. The group lobbied the Commission on the Status of Women and submitted various statements on the economic value of women's unpaid work, building up interest. In 1989, the group participated in the preparation of a resolution which was passed by the Commission. These efforts have contributed to the awareness of the value of women's unpaid work and of the need for governments to assess its value and include it in their national accounts.

The International Working Group on Refugee Women of the NGO Sub-Committee on the Status of Women was established to: (1) monitor and advocate refugee women's issues with the office of the UN High Commissioner for Refugees, NGOs and other international organizations; (2) promote an exchange of information on refugee women; and (3) serve as a developmental network for refugee women. One of its first achievements was the publication *Working with Refugee Women – A Practical Guide.* After several years of advocacy for a senior position on women refugees with the United Nations High Commission for Refugees (UNHCR), such a position was established. Since then, the NGO Working Group has continued to advocate a strengthening of the role of the Senior Co-ordinator for Refugee Women, particularly in regard to implementation of Policy Guidelines on Refugee Women and the Protection of Refugee Women, calling on the UNHCR to take measures to examine the obstacles to protecting refugee women and children and to propose concrete action to overcome them. The NGO working group has also called upon the UNHCR to recognize women's claims to refugee status on the basis of gender and fear of persecution through sexual violence, and to ensure that women refugees have equal access to procedures for determining refugee status and to personal documentation. Further, the group has been pushing for the UNHCR to mainstream women's issues in all its programmes and to expand its People-Oriented Planning Training and ensure that all staff receive such training. Other major areas of advocacy have been: measures to prevent or remove threats to the personal security of refugee women, particularly violence of any kind, and prosecution of those responsible for such crimes; and measures to ensure the participation of refugee women in all stages of the planning and implementation of UNHCR programmes.

The methods that the NGO Working Group on Refugee Women uses for its work include:

- establishing a good working relationship with the Senior Co-ordinator for Refugee Women and co-operation with her to identify areas needing further work;
- meeting before the NGO and executive committee meetings of the UNHCR to discuss the issues and strategize its lobbying and advocacy work;
- preparing and distributing recommendations and resolutions at the executive committee meetings;
- lobbying government delegations to take up the Working Group's recommendations and resolutions;
- meeting with senior personnel of the UNHCR to discuss the Working Group's concerns and recommendations.

Following the 1993 meeting of the UNHCR executive committee, the Working Group identified areas that still need attention:

- under-representation of women in UNHCR staff and in key field positions;
- maternal and child health care and the inclusion of birth spacing information in health care services;
- implementation of policy requiring data collection on gender and age composition of the refugee population;
- cuts in programmes for refugee women and children due to financial constraints facing the UNHCR.

It is through such day-to-day work, mostly done on a voluntary basis, that NGOs are able to build up the trust that enables them to lobby effectively governments and international bodies.

THE END OF THE DECADE AND NEW BEGINNINGS □ The UN Conference on Women at the end of the Decade for Women, and the parallel NGO Forum were held in Nairobi in 1985. The UN conference had two major objectives:

- to critically review and appraise the progress achieved and obstacles encountered in attaining the goals and objectives of the UN Decade for Women;
- to adopt the Forward-looking Strategies for the Advancement of Women to the Year 2000.

In preparation for the 1985 Conference on Women, a World Survey on the Role of Women in Development was carried out by the UN which, however, was hampered by the lack of statistics, especially on women's unpaid work. This lack spurred the efforts to strengthen data collection and the disaggregation of data by sex at the international and national levels. A decision was taken to update the world survey every five years to provide comprehensive and regular data on women in all spheres of life.

The Nairobi Forward-looking Strategies for the Advancement of Women to the Year 2000 (FLS) was the result of a long process of preparation and government negotiation in the Commission on the Status of Women. Women's organizations contributed to it through collaboration and lobbying of their governments and through observer status at meetings of the Commission:

[Women] were also alert to the need to follow and lobby the preparations of their governments, having learned from previous experience that it is extremely difficult to influence intergovernmental decisions on the spot during a world conference. Preferably it must be done beforehand in each country, by women expressing their wishes and suggestions to the appropriate governmental bodies. And in order to make their efforts coherent it was necessary for women to coordinate their activities internationally as well, so that the same suggestions and pressures were applied in parallel in as many countries as possible. Links established at previous NGO conferences now helped groups and organizations wanting to act on specific issues to reach each other.[13]

THE NAIROBI FORWARD-LOOKING STRATEGIES (FLS)

The FLS was unanimously adopted at the Nairobi World Conference on Women. Under each of the major themes of the Women's Decade – Equality, Development and Peace – the FLS looked at the obstacles facing women, presented basic strategies to overcome these and identified measures for implementation. The comprehensive nature of the document can be seen in the list of the areas covered:

Equality

• Constitutional and legal • Equality in social participation • Equality in political participation and decision making

Development

• Employment • Health • Education • Food, water and agriculture • Industry • Trade and commercial services • Science and technology • Communications • Housing, settlement, community development and transport • Energy • Environment • Social services

Peace

• Women and children under apartheid • Palestinian women and children • Women in areas affected by armed conflicts, foreign intervention and threats to peace • Women's participation in efforts for peace • Peace education

Areas of Special Concern

• Women in areas affected by drought • Urban poor women • Elderly women • Young women • Abused women • Destitute women • Women victims of trafficking and involuntary prostitution • Women deprived of their traditional means of livelihood • Women who are the sole supporters of families • Women with physical and mental disabilities • Women in detention and subject to penal law • Refugee and displaced women and children • Migrant women • Minority and indigenous women

International and Regional Co-operation

• Monitoring • Technical co-operation, training and advisory services • Institutional co-ordination • Research and policy analysis • Participation of women in activities at the international and regional levels and in decision-making • Information dissemination.

Like the World Plan of Action, the FLS is an intergovernmental document. However, both these instruments urge governments and United Nations bodies to involve and collaborate with non-governmental organizations and grassroots women's groups in implementing the strategies, offering women many possibilities to increase their participation at the national and international levels to improve their situation. Moreover, following the Conference, mechanisms for monitoring the implementation of the Nairobi Forward-looking Strategies were established throughout the United Nations system.

The parallel 1985 NGO Forum in Nairobi, bringing together some 15,000 women from every corner of the world, was a demonstration and a celebration of the enormous growth and diversity of women's global participation:

[It was] a gathering of women from all over the world without equal in the past. It was also like a women's world fair in the richness of its arts and handicrafts, its inventions and inspirations, its research and achievements. Above all, it was a joyful union of sisterhood, experiencing the sense of power in working together hand-in-hand, seeing eye-to-eye. The strength and dignity of African women made an unforgettable impression.... Some 125 workshops and meetings were scheduled each day – about 1,200 altogether – and there was a constant flow of improvised gatherings, discussions, group meetings of all kinds and in all places, on the green lawns of the Nairobi University campus, under the trees here and there, in the Peace tent.[14]

In reflecting on the achievements of the NGO Forum in Nairobi, Dame Nita Barrow, the convenor, pointed out some of its lessons:

First and foremost, women learned more about the concerns of women around the world and in so doing many women lost some of the naivete and the complacency that allowed them to accept the status quo in their own countries. Sharing the experiences of other women stimulated them to think about things that needed doing in their own communities. In brief, we learned that there were universalities ... that women of all kinds found the ability to speak authoritatively about the issues really affecting them.[15]

The Decade for Women, however, had not achieved as much as many women had expected, and Dame Nita Barrow also raised some challenging questions for the future:

- How can we make sure that the NGO community will recognize that existing strategies have worked only up to a point, and that the time has come for newer, bolder endeavours?
- How can we encourage the involvement of a group of new, perhaps younger women to carry forward some of the concerns and strategies developed at Forum '85?
- How can we ensure the involvement of women from the South to bring their voices to the NGO community?
- How can NGOs make their voices heard in the United Nations so that women and women's affairs can be taken seriously?
- At the national level, how can the one or two women assigned to 'women's desks' have support as they go about sensitizing the largely male Ministries of Labour, Employment, Education, and so on, to the needs of women?
- What effect can Nairobi, the NGO Forum and the World Conference have

PHOTO: M. EUGENIA JELINCIC/ISIS INTERNATIONAL

The NGO Forum in Nairobi brought some 15,000 women together from all over the world on needed changes in law, economics and even tradition?

- Can we expect that Nairobi has strengthened individual and group action and therefore its cumulative effect?[16]

Women went home from Nairobi to take up these challenges at all levels: at the grassroots and in their communities, at the governmental level and at the UN.

NEW OPPORTUNITIES AND CHALLENGES IN THE 1990s ☐ The 1990s have presented new challenges and opportunities for women to build on the achievements and the lessons learned in the previous decades. While United Nations conferences represent only the tip of the iceberg, the visible culmination of years of hard work and preparatory activities, they are landmarks in the work of putting women on the UN agenda. Major UN conferences in the first half of the 1990s include: the United Nations Conference on Environment and Development, the World Conference on Human Rights, the World Conference on Population and Development, the World Summit on Social Development, and the Fourth World Conference on Women.

THE EARTH SUMMIT The United Nations Conference on Environment and Development (UNCED), or the Earth Summit, held in Rio de Janeiro in June 1992, was a major event in which women were able to put into practice their growing expertise. Networking among officials of the United Nations, government delegates, NGOs and local women's groups during the two-year preparatory process secured a victory for women, as recounted by Filomena Chioma Steady, the Special Adviser on Women for UNCED: 'The Earth Summit was an encouraging landmark event for women in that it achieved consensus on the important role of women in promoting sustainable development and recognized the need for strengthening women's expertise in the fields of environment and development as well as enhancing their legal and administrative capacities for decision making and managerial roles.'[17]

Lobbying tools and consensus emerged from the many preparatory activities and efforts. Notable among these was the World Women's Congress for a Healthy Planet in Miami in November 1991 which brought together 1,800 women activists and experts from all regions of the world. The *Women's Action Agenda '21* which was drawn up at this meeting provided critical input for UNCED. During the Earth Summit, the Planeta Femea, or Women's Planet, tent in the NGO Global Forum, organized by a coalition of Brazilian women's groups and the Women's Environment and Development Organization (WEDO), provided a place for women to deepen their discussions and plan for follow-up action. Throughout the preparatory period and during UNCED itself, women's NGOs also worked intensively, together with UN officials and government delegates, to influence the official conference documents.

Although scant attention was given to women in the initial preparations for UNCED, women's lobbying efforts resulted in an official decision to: 'ensure that women's crucial economic, social and environmental contributions to sustainable development be addressed ... as a cross-cutting issue, in addition to being mainstreamed in all the substantive work and documentation'.[18]

In fact, the official conference document, *Agenda 21*, contains a special chapter on women as well as specific reference to their roles throughout the text. How was this achieved? According to Anita Anand, Director of the Women's Feature Service, New Delhi:

The presence of a gender perspective in Agenda 21 testifies to the successful collaborative efforts and plain hard work of the many women's groups and agencies that took part in UNCED.... Women's advocacy supported the adviser [on women for UNCED] and influenced the discussions in UNCED's four preparatory committee meetings as well as at Rio. If the women's lobby at UNCED had not been effective, a weakened agenda for action would have emerged. The dialogue that women engaged in at their own pre-UNCED meetings enabled an international consensus to emerge on how they perceive environment and development. How did the groups lobby for a gender perspective? Women at UNCED met daily to be briefed by UN staff on current negotiations and to plan strategies on lobbying country delegates. No other group did this in such a sustained and coordinated manner. There was a committee of NGOs whose agenda was issue-based – forests, land reform, and such. But for the first time in an international conference, women were advancing a perspective, not an issue. The experience of women's advocacy at UNCED shows that an organized, articulate, persistent and representative group of people are needed to affect an issue or process. Style is also important; often women's advocacy groups resort to confrontation. Women need to become more adept at analyzing, talking about and negotiating with individuals and institutions that do not share their views.[19]

Agenda 21 provides a basis to give women's voices and concerns a central place in all further discussion and work on the environment and sustainable development. However, as Anita Anand says: '...to turn the policies in this document into action, we need the mechanisms.... All parties – the UN, governments, NGOs and individual citizens – have a part in making *Agenda 21* successful and enforceable.... Women need to become involved in local and national networks that are carrying the work of UNCED forward.... They need to rally and build a national consensus to strengthen international women's lobbies. Perhaps the most politically astute initiative is for women to negotiate a space for themselves in the home and the community.... Women's socialization often negates their participation outside the home, which is largely responsible for the lack of gender perspective in public policy. Unless sufficient numbers of women with a gender perspective enter mainstream activities – locally, nationally and internationally – little can or will be done to bring about change.'[20]

The connections between environmental issues and women's empowerment are increasingly being articulated by women within the mainstream of international development agencies. For instance, Elizabeth Dowdeswell, Under-Secretary General of the United Nations Environmental Programme (UNEP) and the United Nations Centre for Human Settlements (HABITAT), not only acknowledges women's significant role as environmental managers and the impact of the environment on women, she has also called for the organizations to explore the linkages between literacy, women's issues and the environment and to strengthen mechanisms to incorporate women's perspectives in both agencies.

THE GREENING OF THE EARTH CAN ONLY BEGIN WITH THE EMPOWERMENT OF WOMEN

ELIZABETH DOWDESWELL*

There are hundreds, thousands of depressing environmental statistics. The newspapers are full of them, television reports them, they are chronicled in our

* UN Under-Secretary General (UNEP-HABITAT)

PHOTO: S. SPRAGUE/WHO/UNICEF

Educated women are better able to protect their environment

workshops, conferences and meetings. Yet one statistic stands out as more distressing than any other: there are 600 million illiterate women in the world – more than twice as many illiterate women as illiterate men.

Why is this an environmental statistic?

Uneducated women are less able to help protect their environment. Uneducated women are more likely to bear greater numbers of children than their environment can fully support. Uneducated women are increasingly unable to become our partners in creating a sustainable future.

Women are vital to our vision of a sustainable future. They are the guardians of natural wisdom in their societies; they often are the principal ecosystem managers of their communities. They are the first educators, and can do the most to change the habits and beliefs of a new generation.

A recent special report in *People and the Planet* recites the litany of effects stemming from women's historical lack of access to education. Uneducated women tend to be less productive, and employed in less well-paid jobs, than educated women. They are less able to care for their children and keep them healthy. They marry younger and are less likely to use family planning. They are less likely to send their own children for schooling.

Illiteracy is an environmental problem because, in those parts of the world where environmental degradation has been greatest, the amount of time during the day that women must spend to eke out a bare existence from the land – gathering fuel, fodder, and firewood; working the fields; fetching water – rises in direct proportion to how bad the degradation has been. In such environments, girl children have no leisure for education; they are surrogate housekeepers.

Anil Agarwal, director of the Centre for

Science and Environment in New Delhi, writes, 'When the mother's work burden is made heavy by environmental degradation, it is practically impossible for the girl child to go to school.'

While Agarwal's research was carried out in a Himalayan village, its message is equally applicable to the poor across the world. Even when the family economy is not directly land-based, even in our urban centres where mothers supplement the household income through low-wage labour, a girl child is more likely to become a child-labour casualty than she is a schoolgirl.

Anyone who studies ecology soon comes to realize the cyclic nature of the world in which we live, the interconnectedness of seemingly unrelated phenomena. The cycle of despair that begins with unequal access to education and ends in environmental destruction is one of its most cogent examples.

That is why the single most important step towards sustainable living that governments can take – and that UNEP must support – is the education of women.

' "Think of the last man when you plan for your country" was the advice of Mahatma Gandhi,' Agarwal adds, 'but I have invariably found the last man to be a woman – struggling to survive, for the sake of her family, in a harsh environment, burdened with work and responsibilities but devoid of any power or control. The world's environment will never improve unless women can take control of their environment and become full and equal members of their communities. Greening of the earth ... can only begin with the empowerment of women.'

This is the kind of linkage that the United Nations Environmental Programme (UNEP) and the United Nations Centre for Human Settlements (HABITAT) were created to foster, and education must be part of the linkage. To us, the requisites for a sustainable future are best expressed in the UNEP mission statement: 'To provide leadership and encourage partnership in caring for the environment by inspiring, informing, and enabling nations and people to improve their quality of life without compromising that of future generations.'

This mission inextricably links education to sustainable living and a sustainable future.

We have just begun to explore at UNEP and HABITAT some of the linkages between literacy, women's issues, and the environment. We'd like to do more. And we plan to. The role of women in environmental issues cuts across the spectrum of UNEP and HABITAT activities, and we are looking at bolstering mechanisms to formally incorporate the unique perspectives of women in both agencies.

Every document on world development, from the Pearson Report of 1969 to the Brandt Report of 1987 and *Agenda 21*, has urged the case of universal literacy and an end to gender disparity in educational access.

Six hundred million women couldn't read these reports. A sustainable future – preserving our environmental heritage and fostering human development – requires that we do more than write about it. ●

WOMEN'S RIGHTS ARE HUMAN RIGHTS The success that women achieved at the World Conference on Human Rights, held in Vienna in June 1993, was even more striking. Like all world conferences, it was more of a beginning than an end: the declarations of such conferences remain empty words unless they are implemented. Women developed a comprehensive strategy for integrating women's rights into the World Conference on Human Rights and into the United Nations human rights mechanisms. They aimed at:

PHOTO: ANNE WALKER/IWTC

Delivering boxes full of the women's human rights petitions to the United Nations

- securing equitable participation of women and men in government delegations to the Conference and in all human rights bodies;

- including gender-specific information and analysis in both national and international documentation for the Conference;

- appointing a special rapporteur on violence against women for the United Nations Commission on Human Rights;

- strengthening the implementation procedures under the Convention on the Elimination of all Forms of Discrimination against Women;

- ensuring that all United Nations treaty bodies, thematic and country rapporteurs and working groups and specialized agencies address women's human rights by including gender-specific cases and information in the areas that fall within their mandates;

- giving attention to the vulnerability of women in world crisis situations such as the former Yugoslavia and Somalia and *vis-à-vis* religious and cultural intolerance that denies women's human rights and liberties;

- examining the issue of violence against women as one of the challenges to the full realization of human rights for all.[21]

The work for the inclusion of women in the World Conference on Human Rights and its documents began nearly two years before the meeting. Yet the groundwork was laid even earlier in the ongoing work of international women's NGOs, which for many years regularly made presentations on women's rights as human rights to the

United Nations Commission on Human Rights. Many factors contributed to women's success: the global mobilization of women; the international networking and information exchange including effective use of the media to arouse public opinion; and extensive accreditation of national and regional organizations to the Conference and its preparatory meetings.

A significant mechanism for organizing women's action and informing public opinion on women's human rights was launched in late 1991 during the sixteen Days of Activism Against Gender Violence organized by a coalition of women's groups and organizations: a worldwide petition drive asking the Preparatory Committee for the World Conference on Human Rights to 'comprehensively address women's rights at every level of the Conference proceedings' and demanding that 'gender violence, a universal phenomenon which takes many forms across culture, race and class, be recognized as a violation of human rights requiring immediate action'. Initiated by the Center for Women's Global Leadership and the International Women's Tribune Centre, this petition was sponsored by more than 900 organizations internationally. Women translated the petition into 23 languages and gathered close to half a million signatures in 124 countries. According to one of the initiators of the drive:

Women have used this petition to initiate discussion at the local and national level about why women's rights and gender violence are not already on the human rights agenda and what it would mean to include them. Women have also prepared for their regional conferences by developing agendas connecting women to existing human rights discussion in the region. In a number of countries hearings are being held where testimony is given on both individual complaints and group cases of violations of women's human rights. These are being documented and sent to the UN Commission on Human Rights as well as to the World Conference where there will be a Global Tribunal on the violations of women's human rights that have been highlighted from each region.[22]

Dozens of meetings on women's human rights were held on the regional and international levels, and whilst all of these contributed to developing an international consciousness of women's human rights, several were particularly significant in that women succeeded in bringing the results directly to the UN regional and international preparatory meetings. In Africa for instance, Women in Law and Development in Africa (WiLDAF), a network of groups working to promote and protect women's rights, organized a series of subregional meetings in order to involve more NGOs in the preparatory process. WiLDAF successfully applied to the Conference Secretariat before the preparatory Regional Meeting for Africa for inclusion of the meeting recommendations in the conference documentation. African women's groups also formed a committee to draft a common resolution on women's rights; several government delegates included their recommendations in their official positions.

Similarly, women in Latin America held a satellite meeting and produced a common sixteen-point advocacy position which was used in lobbying government delegates to the Regional Meeting for Latin America. In Asia, women were able to use the results of a conference on the trafficking in Asian women to influence the Conference. Meetings were also held in the Middle East, Europe and North America, and several international women's meetings brought together representatives of national and regional women's organizations and coalitions.

NGOs lobbied extensively for the resolution on women's rights as inalienable human rights which was passed by the Sub-Commission on Prevention of Discrimination and Protection of Minorities in 1992, and for the resolution calling for the integration of women's rights into all human rights activities and mechanisms, which was passed on 8 March 1993 by the Commission on Human Rights.

As in other conferences, women's achievements at the Vienna World Conference on Human Rights in 1993 were the result of an interactive process and collaboration between grassroots groups, activist women's organizations and international women's NGOs at the local, national, regional and international levels, as well as of lobbying governments and the building of links with government delegates. When women arrived at the World Conference on Human Rights, the bulk of their work had already been done, and during the Conference women maintained close contact with each other and with their supporters in the government delegations and UN staff through a daily caucus, lobbying in the corridors, sitting in on plenary and drafting sessions, and in the parallel NGO activities, especially in the Rights Place for Women. The final declaration reflected most of the recommendations that had been brought forward. Among the points that refer specifically to women are the following:

- The human rights of women and of the girl child are an inalienable, integral and indivisible part of universal human rights. The full and equal participation of women in political, civil, economic, social and cultural life, at national, regional and international levels, and the eradication of all forms of discrimination on grounds of sex are priority objectives of the international community.
- The equal status of women and human rights of women should be integrated into the mainstream of activity across the UN system.
- The World Conference on Human Rights stressed the importance of working towards the elimination of violence against women in public and private life, the elimination of all forms of sexual harassment, exploitation and trafficking in women, the elimination of gender bias in the administration of justice and the eradication of any conflicts which may arise between the rights of women and the harmful effects of certain traditional or customary practices, cultural prejudices and religious extremism.
- The United Nations should encourage the goal of universal ratification by all States by the year 2000 of the Convention on the Elimination of All Forms of Discrimination against Women.
- Treaty monitoring bodies should disseminate necessary information to enable women to make more effective use of existing implementation procedures in their pursuits of full and equal enjoyment of human rights and non-discrimination. New procedures should also be adopted to strengthen implementation of the commitment to women's equality and the human rights of women.
- The Commission on the Status of Women and the Committee on the Elimination of Discrimination against Women should quickly examine the possibility of introducing the right of petition through the preparation of an optional protocol to the Convention on the Elimination of All Forms of Discrimination against Women.
- The World Conference on Human Rights welcomes the decision of the Commission on Human Rights to consider the appointment of a special rapporteur on violence against women.

PHOTO: CENTER FOR WOMEN'S GLOBAL LEADERSHIP/DOUGLASS COLLEGE, RUTGERS UNIVERSITY

Speaking out on violations of women's human rights

- The World Conference on Human Rights recognizes the importance of the enjoyment by women of the highest standard of physical and mental health throughout their life-span [and] reaffirms, on the basis of equality between women and men, a woman's right to accessible and adequate health care and the widest range of family planning services, as well as equal access to education at all levels.
- Treaty monitoring bodies should include the status of women and the human rights of women in their deliberation and findings making use of gender-specific data. States should be encouraged to supply information on the situation of women *de jure* and *de facto* in their reports to treaty monitoring bodies.
- Steps should be taken by the Division for the Advancement of Women in co-operation with other United Nations bodies, specifically the Centre for Human Rights, to ensure that the human rights activities of the United Nations regularly address violations of women's human rights, including gender-specific abuses.
- Training for United Nations human rights and humanitarian relief personnel to assist them to recognize and deal with human rights abuses particular to women and to carry out their work without gender bias should be encouraged.
- The World Conference on Human Rights urges governments and regional and international organizations to facilitate the access of women to decision-making posts and their greater participation in the decision-making process. It encourages further steps within the United Nations Secretariat to appoint and promote women staff members.

At the NGO Forum that preceded the World Conference and at the NGO parallel activities during the Conference itself, the 'Rights Place for Women' provided a space for networking, exhibits, demonstrations, discussions, radio tapings, speak-outs and support groups, while workshops and panels focused on specific topics such as training in advocacy, and using the media, including radio, electronic mail and video. A major event that drew both the media and an audience of more than a thousand people was the day-long Global Tribunal on Women's Human Rights, in which thirty-three women from twenty-five countries testified to abuses of women's human rights in the family, war crimes against women, violations of women's bodily integrity, socio-economic violations of women's human rights, and political persecution and discrimination. The impressive amount of educational and informational materials produced by women around the world was also in evidence, including the book *Women and Human Rights* in this series, which gives a global overview of how women are confronting the problem of attaining recognition and enjoyment of their human rights.[23]

In a follow-up to the Conference, women's groups and organizations launched a new petition campaign calling upon the UN to fulfil the commitment to 'eliminate violence against women in public and private life' and to report on its efforts to promote and protect women's human rights at the Fourth World Conference on Women to be held in Beijing in September 1995. Continued pressure is needed to ensure that the conference recommendations are implemented and that sufficient funds and other resources are allocated for this purpose.

TOWARDS THE YEAR 2000 ☐ As we move towards the year 2000, the momentum built up since the 1970s continues to give impetus to the work in and around the UN on gender equality. Particular attention has been focused on the International Conference on Population and Development in 1994 and two major conferences scheduled for 1995, the fiftieth anniversary of the United Nations: the World Summit for Social Development and the Fourth World Conference on Women. The World Summit on Social Development will bring together heads of government to discuss social integration, the alleviation and reduction of poverty, and employment. This meeting is of great importance to women, for as DAWN says:

The Summit represents an ideal platform for drawing international attention to the close relationship between these issues and the condition and status of women. The active participation of women in the Social Development Summit should be seen as consistent with trends in women's organizing since the 1985 Nairobi Conference. Women are no longer limiting their organizing to women's conferences but have made their voice heard and their presence felt on all major international issues. Their organizing is now characterized by North – South alliances based on comprehensive analyses of the issues; analyses which explore links between social, cultural, economic and political factors, and link women's daily experiences to macro-economic policies at both national and international levels. Efforts to link research and analysis to activism underline the increased awareness of women's organizations of the political nature of their work.[24]

FOURTH WORLD CONFERENCE ON WOMEN Twenty years after the International Year of Women, the Fourth World Conference on Women: Action for Equality, Development and Peace, is to be held in Beijing, China in September 1995, during the 50th anniversary of the United Nations. According to the World Conference Secretariat:

[The United Nations World Conference on Women] will provide the opportunity to see how far the Organization has come with regard to gender issues. It will be the occasion to put forward a global vision of the 21st Century which fully reflects a gender perspective.[25]

The overall objectives of the Conference are:

- to create the impetus in society for women to move forward, well equipped to meet the challenges and demands of the 21st century for scientific, technological, economic and political development;
- to address the question of how women can be empowered by taking part more effectively in decision-making;
- to draw up a Platform for Action in order to ensure the completion of the unfinished work of implementing the Nairobi Forward-looking Strategies.

The World Conference on Women is the culmination of a process of broad-based preparatory activities at the national, regional and global levels in which the participation of NGOs has been encouraged and particular efforts have been made to involve women at the grassroots. The Secretary-General of the World Conference, Gertrude Mongella, has particularly stressed the need for non-governmental organizations to mobilize at the national and regional levels and to work together with governments for the common goal of focusing attention on a gender perspective of world development. Wide participation will also be needed in the follow-up phase to the Conference to ensure the implementation of the agreements. The documents expected to emerge from the preparatory process and the World Conference are: the report by the Secretary-General on the Second Review and Appraisal of the Implementation of the Nairobi Forward-looking Strategies, national reports, regional plans of action and the global Platform for Action. This document is intended to propose concrete, strategic measures to accelerate, through concerted and intensive action, the implementation of the Forward-looking Strategies. Crucial input to the Platform for Action will be given by the national reports from the Member States of the United Nations, regional plans of action developed at the regional preparatory meetings held by every UN Regional Commission in 1994, reports from United Nations agencies and expert group meetings organized by the Division for the Advancement of Women, and resolutions by the Commission on the Status of Women.

The Commission on the Status of Women (CSW), the preparatory body for the Conference, for which the Division for the Advancement of Women serves as secretariat, has highlighted the importance of involving NGOs in the preparations and follow-up to the conference:

Governments should take advantage of the considerable experience and commitment that exists among those NGOs who are active on gender issues and, therefore, should encourage and support NGO participation in the national, as well as the regional and international preparatory activities. NGO participation and cooperation is also needed to increase awareness about the Conference and, later, in the implementation of the results of Beijing. Governments should consider including some representatives of NGOs in their national delegations at regional preparatory conferences and at Beijing. Several regional preparatory conferences will be preceded by a regional NGO Forum. These conferences should take into account the input that will come from NGO meetings and activities.[26]

PHOTO: OLGA YOLANDA LOPEZ/ISIS INTERNATIONAL

At the Asia/Pacific NGO regional preparatory meeting for the Fourth World Conference on Women

As with past United Nations conferences on women, the Fourth World Conference will be accompanied by a parallel NGO Forum which will follow the pattern of past forums in giving women from around the world the opportunity to come together to discuss, exchange and develop ideas, perspectives, plans and strategies. Even more than with previous such events, women's organizations have mobilized extensively to prepare for the Beijing meetings and to participate in regional and national preparatory activities. This is significant because:

National preparations are crucial for successful regional conferences and for the Beijing Conference itself. They are the tool for rekindling the momentum for concrete and positive action for the advancement of women. They should galvanize society as such into bringing about change in the way women's role and status in society is perceived with the goal of achieving women's full equality, development and peace. National preparatory activities should be characterized by the involvement of society as a whole, women and men, and especially of women at the grassroots. They must lay the groundwork and sensitize society for the implementation of the Platform for Action after its adoption at Beijing. Preparations at the national level should be a device to strengthen national machinery for the advancement of women, to raise broad awareness at all levels of society, in public and private life, about gender issues and their impact on all aspects of society.[27]

The national reports are crucial, therefore, not only because they will be fed into the Platform for Action, but because they will help shape future action for gender equality in the country.

The 38th session of the Commission on the Status of Women, acting as the first Preparatory Committee meeting for the

Conference was held in New York in March 1994. It identified critical areas of concern to form the basis for the draft Platform for Action and strategies to achieve gender equality:

- The persistent and growing burden of poverty on women
- Inequality in access to education, health and related services and means of maximizing the use of women's capacities
- Violence against women
- Effects of armed conflict or other kinds of conflict on women
- Inequality in women's access to and participation in the definition of economic structures and politics and the productive process itself
- Inequality between men and women in the sharing of power and decision-making at all levels
- Insufficient mechanisms at all levels to promote the advancement of women
- Lack of awareness of, and commitment to, international and nationally recognized women's rights
- Insufficient use of mass media to promote women's positive contribution to society
- Lack of recognition and support for women's contribution to managing natural resources and safeguarding environment.

1. United Nations, *The Nairobi Forward-looking Strategies for the Advancement of Women*, UN, New York, 1985, para. 358.
2. See Carol Miller, 'Lobbying the League: women's international organizations and the League of Nations', unpublished PhD thesis, University of Oxford, 1992.
3. Ibid., pp. vi–vii.
4. Carol Miller, 'The interaction of national and transnational women's networks and the League of Nations Secretariat', paper for the British International Studies Association Conference, December 1991. Cited in Katerina Tomaševski, *Women and Human Rights*, Zed Books, London, 1993, p.95.
5. See especially Hilkka Pietilä and Jeanne Vickers, *Making Women Matter: The Role of the United Nations*, Zed Books, London, 1990.
6. Ibid., p. 73.
7. Ibid., p. 74.
8. Arvonne Fraser and Miranda Kazentsis, *CEDAW No. 11*, Report of the International Women's Rights Action Watch, August 1992, p.5.
9. Pietilä and Vickers, pp. 78–9.
10. Charlotte Bunch, 'Copenhagen and beyond: prospects for global feminism', *Quest: A Feminist Quarterly*, Vol. 5, No. 4, 1982.
11. Information on the NGO working groups comes from an interview held in Geneva on 12 January 1994 with representatives of international NGOs: Edith Ballantyne, Women's International League for Peace and Freedom; Leila Seigel, International Council of Jewish Women; and Anne Herdt, International Council on Social Welfare; and from an unpublished paper by Eva Craske, Soroptimist International; a report by Elsa Tesfay Musa on the International Working Group on Refugee Women; and a report from the Working Group on Traditional Practices, Geneva.
12. NGO Working Group on Traditional Practices, Geneva, unpublished paper, 1993.
13. Pietilä and Vickers, p.2.
14. Ibid., p. 3.
15. Nita Barrow, *Forum '85, NGO Planning Committee, Final Report: Nairobi, Kenya*, p. 11.
16. Ibid., pp. ii–iii.
17. Filomena Chioma Steady, 'Review of the implications for women of the recommendations of the 1992 Earth Summit', UNCED, 1992, p. 1.
18. Cited in Lezak Shallat, 'Getting women on the UNCED agenda', *Women's Health Journal*, No. 3, 1992, p. 56.
19. Anita Anand, 'The legacy of UNCED', *UNIFEM News*, Vol. 1, No. 1, 1993, p. 12.
20. Ibid., p. 13.
21. Charlotte Bunch, 'Human rights, development and violence against women', paper for the OECD – DAC WID Expert Group Seminar, May 1993.
22. Ibid.
23. Katerina Tomaševski. *Women and Human Rights*, Zed Books, London, 1993.
24. 'Social Development Summit: a significant event for women', *DAWN INFORMS*, No. 2, 1993, p. 6.
25. World Conference Secretariat, 'Guidelines for preparatory activities for the Fourth World Conference on Women: Action for Equality, Development and Peace', 1993.
26. Ibid
27. Ibid.

7 CONCLUSION: THE CHALLENGES AHEAD

The primary challenge facing women today is to maintain and increase the momentum of their participation and empowerment. On the one hand, there is reason to believe that the process of women's empowerment will continue to go forward: many conditions and mechanisms for women's empowerment have been established; greater emphasis on people's participation by policy-makers and growing gender awareness are creating a favourable climate for women to bring their concerns and perspectives onto the agenda; and the great strides forward that women have made in empowering themselves are opening up more opportunities for women's participation. All this can be seen in the increased numbers of women participating in their communities, in groups and organizations, in politics and public life, in development agencies and programmes; and in the transformative effect that this participation is having on structures and on redefining the local, national and international agendas.

ON THE POSITIVE SIDE, there has been an expansion of both basic and higher educational opportunities for women, greater recognition of women's unpaid work and social and economic roles, as well as wider representation of women in electoral politics. The greater recognition of women's contributions and roles in the development process has resulted in development policies for mainstreaming women. National and international legislation and mechanisms for the promotion of gender equality have also been established. Inheriting a rich history of activism, women's organizations are bringing new issues to the agenda and perspectives for the development of a more just and humane society that will be based on equal opportunities for participation and decision making for everyone, women and men.

On the other hand, universal gender discrimination persists and concrete measures are still needed to address the many obstacles that continue to stand in the way of women's access to participation and decision making. And whilst women are increasingly active in community organizations and non-governmental organizations and in social and political movements, they hold very few leadership and decision-making positions and constitute a small minority of those in elected and appointed political bodies and offices. New strategies must be developed for women to increase their access to such decision-making positions and bodies, to build a critical mass of women within political and social structures, and to create links between women working in public life and NGOs.

Gender awareness within governmental, intergovernmental and non-governmental bodies must be increased, and strategies and mechanisms for gender equity must be strengthened. Gender awareness must be translated into policy and action. Awareness building and skills building among women themselves is equally important so that more women gain confidence to participate in decision making and grasp their rights, and begin the process of empowerment.

The growing interest of governments and intergovernmental organizations in collaborating with NGOs presents women with the opportunity to strengthen their role and build the necessary interlinkages for ensuring that mechanisms for the advancement of women are established and maintained and that international and national instruments and legislation are implemented. NGOs, governments and inter-governmental organizations need to collaborate to find ways to achieve full representation of both women and men in decision making. Women's organizations need to increase their capacity for networking, lobbying and influencing policy.

There will be no democracy so long as women, who are half of the population, are excluded from decisions that determine their own future.

ANNEX I

A GUIDE TO EDUCATION AND ACTION

THIS BOOK IS INTENDED to be a tool that can be used for awareness building and promoting the process of empowerment. In giving a global overview of women's participation in politics and society, it is meant to stimulate thinking about particular situations and especially about how women, wherever they are, can increase and enrich their participation and decision-making power. Groups and organizations can use the book or parts of it as the basis of discussion in study groups, gender awareness workshops or other sessions. The following discussion topics are framed in a general way to allow users to select the topics most relevant to their own situation and to develop them further as appropriate.

CHAPTER 1

How do women participate in household management? In the economy? In politics? What social and cultural roles do women have in your community? How do women contribute to the family, community and country? What are the greatest inequalities between men and women? Are there statistics available to help you find out? In what areas are more statistics needed? What are the most significant factors that affect women's participation? Why? What are the greatest obstacles to women's wider participation?

CHAPTERS 2 AND 3

What do you know about the history of women's social and political participation in your country or area? In what kinds of organizations do women participate? What is the proportion of women members and are they found in the decision-making positions in these organizations? What issues and concerns are they dealing with? Have these organizations changed over the years? Have women been able to get their concerns on the agenda of these organizations? What kinds of strategies are women using to increase their participation and make it more visible within the organization? In the larger society? Which are the most effective strategies? Do these organizations network with others in your area, in other countries or regions? What would be the benefits of greater networking? In what areas would it be most necessary and useful? Are women trying to increase their access to information and media? How can information and media be used to increase women's participation and decision-making power? Do you think it is more effective to work in women's organizations or in organizations of both men and women? Is there gender discrimination or inequality in the organizations in which you participate? If so, how is this being dealt with?

CHAPTER 4

How are women participating in electoral politics in your country on the national level? On the local level? What is the proportion of women holding elected or appointed political office? In the civil service? At what levels? Why are there so few women in politics and in the higher levels of the civil service? What are the consequences of this? Are there women's political organizations? What kinds of activities do they carry out? Do they try to increase the number of women in politics? Do women politicians take up and promote women's concerns and perspectives? How can links be built or strengthened between women politicians and women's organizations? What do you think are the most effective strategies for promoting women's participation in politics?

CHAPTER 5

How would you define development? What are the negative effects of neglecting women in development programmes and projects? What are the most prevalent approaches to women and development in your area and how have these changed? How much gender awareness is there in the organizations and institutions in which you participate? What strategies are being used to mainstream women? To increase gender awareness? What still needs to be done? What is being done to increase women's participation in development efforts at the local level? How could these be more effective?

CHAPTER 6

How much do you know about the United Nations and its work for the advancement of women? Is your country party to the Convention on the Elimination of All Forms of Discrimination against Women? How is the implementation of the Convention being monitored? How have women influenced and participated in the UN conferences on environment, human rights, women, etc. on the national level? On the international level? What can be done to ensure that national and international instruments for the advancement of women are more effective and are implemented? What does participation mean to you? Why is women's participation important? What does empowerment mean to you? What strategies can women use to increase their participation and empowerment?

ORGANIZING A GENDER AWARENESS WORKSHOP

Many organizations now conduct workshops to raise the gender awareness of their members or staff. Gender awareness or sensitivity training aims to make men and women aware of the division of labour and the inequalities between men and women. Ways of overcoming the inequalities may require changes in organizational structures, work methods and personal behaviour.

There is no set formula for conducting a gender awareness workshop. Each gender awareness training must be designed with the particular needs and situations of the participants in mind. However, the following guidelines and suggestions may help in planning gender awareness workshops.

1. The need and purpose of the workshop should be clear. For instance, is it to help women become more aware of their own situation and of the obstacles to their participation? Is it to change attitudes and behaviour of men who discriminate against women? Or to help remove the barriers to women's participation in the decision-making of the organization? Or to create a favourable climate for the inclusion of women's concerns and perspectives in the work of the organization?

It helps to know what degree of gender awareness already exists among the participants.

Participants may be asked to set objectives and points for discussion either beforehand or at the beginning of the workshop. Participants should also be asked to give their expectations of the workshop and be given the opportunity at the end to review whether or not the objectives and expectations were met.

2. Gender training can last from a few hours to a week or more, depending on the

time and resources available and the objectives defined. Gender awareness is about changing the way people think, feel and act, and this takes time. However, participants may have time constraints that need to be taken into consideration. Training can be given in shorter sessions spread over a longer time. The venue should be easily reachable, and preferably away from distractions.

3. The number of participants should be small (about ten to twenty) to allow active participation of all. Depending on the organization, purpose of the training and situation, participants may be all men, or women, or a mixed group.

4. Building gender awareness requires a participatory methodology. This can include discussions, role playing, drama, singing, dancing, games and other appropriate exercises based on the participants' ways of self-expression. Breaking into smaller groups is a good way to encourage the active participation of everyone.

5. Facilitators and resource persons should be experienced in participatory methodologies. In workshops with men, it is useful to include men among the facilitators and resource persons, to avoid the development of male and female camps.

6. A relaxed, open and non-threatening atmosphere will promote active participation. Men, in particular, may feel threatened or even hostile, and it may be necessary to deal with and defuse tensions.

7. Personal introductions are important in a gender awareness workshop, even more than in other types of meeting. Time should be given for people to talk about themselves and their own situations and concerns in regard to the subject. Informal time for getting acquainted, singing, games or other activities can make breaking the ice easier.

8. Audiovisual materials such as flipcharts, black or white boards can be useful both for presenting and recording points that arise from the discussions and for involving participants through writing and drawing. Slides, videos, puppets, drawings and other audiovisuals are also useful for stimulating thinking and discussion.

9. It may be necessary for the facilitator or resource person to introduce the concept of gender, if the participants are not familiar with the term or its meaning. Participants can be involved by asking them, for instance, to list the roles that are expected of men and women, followed up by a discussion on whether or not these roles can be changed. Participants can also be asked to discuss how men's and women's roles have changed from those of their grandparents.

10. Simple exercises can help open people's eyes to gender discrimination and disparity. For instance, listing:

- all the tasks and responsibilities that women have outside the household;
- all the tasks and responsibilities that men have outside the household;
- all the tasks and responsibilities that women have in the household;
- all the tasks and responsibilities that men have in the household;
- the resources available to women;
- the resources available to men.

Comparing the lists and discussing them generally reveals the disparities between men and women in terms of the amount of work they do and the resources to which they have access.

Similarly, participants can be asked to list the discrimination, obstacles or oppression that men and women face in the family, society or organization, and these lists can be compared and discussed.

11. Dealing with misconceptions and fears, especially in workshops with men, may be necessary. For instance, in some workshops with men in South Asia, questions were raised about feminism being a Western phenomenon irrelevant to poor, rural women. The workshop facilitators asked the men to list the issues that the women's movement or feminists in South Asia had raised and to examine them one by one to see which of them were 'Western therefore not relevant to India, which were urban and not relevant to the rural women, which were elite women's issues and therefore not relevant to poor women.'[1] In the ensuing discussion, it became evident that all the issues raised were relevant to poor, rural women of the country.

12. Participatory evaluation and feedback exercises can be built into the workshop at the end of each phase as well as at the end of the workshop and after some months. Gender discrimination is deeply engrained and it is not easy to change. Men, especially, may be resistant to change, and gender awareness building usually requires both a great deal of patience and continuity. For maximum effectiveness, workshops require some kind of follow-up action, such as the formation of gender focal points and committees to monitor gender awareness and carry out further sessions.

1. Kamla Bhasin, 'Gender workshops with men: experiences and reflections', unpublished paper, 1993, p. 12.

ANNEX II

THE CONVENTION ON THE ELIMINATION OF ALL FORMS OF DISCRIMINATION AGAINST WOMEN

THE FOLLOWING IS A SUMMARY of the thirty articles of the Convention, and a discussion of the role of NGOs in monitoring the Convention, prepared by the International Women's Rights Action Watch (IWRAW) (from *CEDAW*, No. 11, August 1992).

ARTICLE 1: Definition of Discrimination

- any distinction, exclusion or restriction made on the basis of sex, which has the purpose or effect of denying equal exercise of human rights and fundamental freedoms in all fields of human endeavour

ARTICLE 2: Policy Measures to be Undertaken to Eliminate Discrimination

- embody the principle of equality in national constitutions, codes or other laws, and ensure its practical realization
- establish institutions to protect against discrimination
- ensure that public authorities and institutions refrain from discrimination
- abolish all existing laws, customs and regulations that discriminate against women

ARTICLE 3: Guarantees Basic Human Rights and Fundamental Freedoms on an Equal Basis with Men

ARTICLE 4: Temporary Special Measures to Achieve Equality

- temporary special measures may be adopted and must be discontinued when equality is achieved
- special measures to protect maternity are not considered discriminatory
- practices based on the inferiority or superiority of either sex shall be eliminated
- ensure that family education teaches that both men and women share a common role in raising children

ARTICLE 5: Sex Roles and Stereotyping

- social and cultural patterns must be modified to eliminate sex-role stereotypes and notions of the inferiority or superiority of either sex
- family education shall teach that men and women share a common responsibility in the raising of children

ARTICLE 6: Prostitution

- measures shall be taken to suppress all forms of traffic in women and exploitation of prostitution

ARTICLE 7: Political and Public Life

- the right to vote in all elections and be eligible for election to all elected bodies
- to participate in formulation of government policy and hold office at all levels of government
- to participate in non-governmental organizations

ARTICLE 8: Participation at the International Level

- the opportunity to represent their country at the international level and to participate in international organizations

ARTICLE 9: Nationality

- equal rights to acquire, change or retain their nationality
- equal rights to the nationality of their children

ARTICLE 10: Equal Rights in Education

- equal access to education and vocational guidance
- the same curricula, examinations, standards for teaching and equipment
- equal opportunity to scholarships and grants
- equal access to continuing education, including literacy programs
- for elimination of stereotyping in education and textbooks
- measures for reduction of female dropout rates
- equal participation in sports and physical education
- equal access to health and family planning information

ARTICLE 11: Employment

- the same employment rights as men
- free choice of profession, employment and training
- equal remuneration, and benefits, including equal treatment as to work of equal value
- social security
- occupational health and safety protection
- prohibition of dismissal on the basis of pregnancy or marital status
- maternity leave
- provision of social services encouraged, including child care
- special protection against harmful work during pregnancy

ARTICLE 12: Health Care and Family Planning

- equal access to appropriate pregnancy services

ARTICLE 13: Economic and Social Benefits

- equal access to family benefits, loans and credit
- equal right to participate in recreational activities, sports, cultural life

ARTICLE 14: Rural Women

- recognition of the particular problems of rural women, the special roles they play in economic survival of families and of their unpaid work
- ensure their equal participation in development
- right to participate in development planning and implementation
- access to health care and family planning services
- right to benefit directly from social security
- right to training and education
- right to organize self-help groups and cooperatives
- right to participate in all community activities
- right to access to credit, loans, marketing facilities, appropriate technology, and

equal treatment in land and agrarian reform and resettlement

- rights to adequate living conditions – housing, sanitation, electricity, water, transport, and communications

ARTICLE 15: Equality Before the Law

- guarantee of the same legal capacity as men – to contract, administer property, appear in court or before tribunals
- freedom of movement; right to choose residence and domicile
- contractual and other private restrictions on legal capacity of women shall be declared null and void

ARTICLE 16: Marriage and the Family

- equal rights and responsibilities with men in marriage and family relations
- the right to freely enter into marriage and choose a spouse
- equality during marriage and its dissolution
- the right to choose freely the number and spacing of children; access to information, education, and means to make that choice
- equal rights to guardianship and adoption of children
- the same personal rights as husband; right to choose family name, profession, or occupation
- equal rights and responsibilities regarding ownership, management, and disposition of property
- a minimum age and registration of marriage

ARTICLES 17–22: Detail the Establishment and Functioning of the Committee on the Elimination of Discrimination Against Women (CEDAW)

ARTICLES 23–30: Detail the Administration of the Convention.

THE ROLE OF NGOS IN CONVENTION MONITORING AND IMPLEMENTATION

Effective monitoring of Convention implementation and establishment of international standards of equality depend on deeper involvement of NGOs in the entire process... CEDAW members ... have consistently requested independent information from NGOs on the legal and practical situation of women, especially on the situation of poor women, in ratifying countries, and on changes in laws and policies that conform with Convention principles. This information is crucial to complete or round out the picture presented by governments... Information on the status of women and violations of their rights must be transmitted from local groups to national and international groups for presentation to CEDAW members and then the results of the CEDAW reviews, including their suggestions and recommendations, need to be transmitted back again, completing the circle...

Government reports ... are written within governments, by government officials, and they are often considered – and are – an extra burden for the government. However, the reports can serve multiple purposes. In addition to meeting the treaty obligation, they can also serve as needs assessments and guides for development planning and project design by the government, development aid donors and women's groups...

Simply helping the government find information sources becomes a useful entry point in the process. In [some] countries women's groups have put together coalitions to monitor and assist in government reporting. When a government knows it is being monitored by women's groups and others, it may put extra resources – staff, time or by hiring consultants – to meet the reporting requirements. After it is completed, the report ... can serve multiple purposes both for the government and for NGOs.

Another way NGOs in ratifying countries can evidence interest in the reporting process is to contact their national women's bureau or foreign ministry to inquire about the status of the government's current report or request a copy of the last report to CEDAW... This puts the government on notice that NGOs are aware of the reporting system and interested in what the government is reporting. If the report can be obtained from the government, it will serve as a useful tool for NGOs no matter what it says. If it is good, it will provide useful information. If it is incomplete or evasive, suggestions can be made for improving the next one. Such suggestions should be constructive, made with the understanding that governments can be analytical about obstacles to change or report progress, they can indicate that problems exist, but they will not criticize themselves in their own reports...

An even more important and effective way for NGOs to assist in the monitoring process is to put together a short independent NGO report on one or more of the major problems of women in the country and submit it to CEDAW directly or through IWRAW or another human rights groups. The Convention can either be looked at, article by article, from women citizens' point of view or groups interested in a particular issue covered by the Convention – education, health, employment, etc. – can document and describe the major problems for women pertaining to that issue or article. Because CEDAW members review numerous reports each year, and meet only once a year, they do not have time to read long, detailed NGO reports on each country. What CEDAW members need – and what NGOs can provide – is short, concise, factual information on the most important areas of discrimination against women, or a particular group of women, in a ratifying country. The process of providing independent information to CEDAW must be strengthened and continued if CEDAW's effectiveness is to be maintained and improved...

To be most effective, independent information should reach CEDAW's pre-session working group before they meet, but material presented at the time of the meeting is also effective. Material on countries coming up for review can also be sent to IWRAW or other organizations who are willing to submit it to CEDAW members. The source of the independent information does not need to be publicly stated but any group submitting information from a secondary source must be confident that the information has been documented.

IWRAW has produced a manual, *Assessing the Status of Women: A Guide to Reporting Using the Convention*. This manual is available from: IWRAW, c/o Women, Public Policy and Development Project, Humphrey Institute of Public Affairs, University of Minnesota, 301 19th Avenue South, Minneapolis, MN 55455, USA

ANNEX III

LIST OF ORGANIZATIONS

INTERGOVERNMENTAL

Asian and Pacific Development Centre, Pesiaran Duta, PO Box 12224, 50770, Kuala Lumpur, Malaysia

Food and Agriculture Organization of the United Nations (FAO), Via delle Terme di Caracalla, I-0-0100 Rome, Italy

International Fund for Agricultural Development (IFAD), Via del Serafico 107, I-00142 Rome, Italy

International Labour Organization (ILO), 4 route des Morillons, CH-1211, Geneva 20, Switzerland

International Research and Training Institute for the Advancement of Women (INSTRAW), Apartado Postal 21747, Santo Domingo, Dominican Republic

United Nations Centre for Human Rights, Palais des Nations, CH-1211, Geneva 10, Switzerland

United Nations Children's Fund (UNICEF), 3 United Nations Plaza, New York, NY 10017, USA; also Palais des Nations, CH-1211, Geneva 10, Switzerland

United Nations Development Fund for Women (UNIFEM), 304 East 45th Street, 6th Floor, New York, NY 10017, USA

United Nations Development Programme (UNDP), 1 United Nations Plaza, New York, NY 10017, USA

United Nations Division for the Advancement of Women (DAW), United Nations Department for Policy Co-ordination and Sustainable Development (DPCSD), DC-2, 2 United Nations Plaza, New York, NY 10017, USA

United Nations Economic and Social Commission for Asia and the Pacific (ESCAP), United Nations Building, Rajdamnern Avenue, Bangkok 10020, Thailand

United Nations Economic and Social Commission for Latin America and the Caribbean (ECLAC), Casilla 179-D-Depal, Santiago, Chile

United Nations Economic and Social Commission for Western Asia, P.O. Box 927115, Amman, Jordan

United Nations Economic Commission for Africa, African Training and Research Centre for Women, PO Box 3001, Addis Ababa, Ethiopia

United Nations Economic Commission for Europe (ECE), Palais des Nations, CH-1211, Geneva 10, Switzerland

United Nations Educational, Scientific and Cultural Organization (UNESCO), 7 place de Fontenoy, 75007 Paris, France

United Nations Environment Programme (UNEP), P.O. Box 30552, Nairobi, Kenya; also Palais des Nations, CH-1211, Geneva 10, Switzerland

United Nations High Commissioner for Refugees (UNHCR), Centre William Rappard, 154 rue de Lausanne, CH-1202, Geneva, Switzerland

United Nations Industrial Development Organization (UNIDO), PO Box 300, A-1400 Vienna, Austria

United Nations Non-Governmental Liaison Service (NGLS), Palais des Nations, CH-1211, Geneva 10, Switzerland; also 866 United Nations Plaza, New York, NY 10017, USA

United Nations Population Fund (UNFPA), 220 East 42nd Street, New York, NY 10017, USA; also Palais des Nations, CH-1211, Geneva 10, Switzerland

United Nations Research Institute for Social Development (UNRISD), Palais des Nations, CH-1211, Geneva 10, Switzerland

United Nations University (UNU), World Institute for Development Economic Research (WIDER), Katajanokanlaituri 6B, 00160 Helsinki, Finland

United Nations Volunteers (UNV), Palais des Nations, CH-1211, Geneva 20, Switzerland

World Bank, 1818 H Street NW, Washington DC 120433, USA

World Food Programme (WFP), Via Cristoforo Colombo 426, I-00145 Rome, Italy

World Health Organization (WHO), Avenue Appia, CH-1211, Geneva 27, Switzerland

NON-GOVERNMENTAL

Associated Country Women of the World (ACWW), Vincent House, Vincent Square, London SW1P 2NB, UK

Association of African Women for Research and Development (AAWORD), PO Box 3304, Dakar, Senegal

Baha'i International Community, 15 route des Morillons, CH-1211, Geneva 20, Switzerland

Caribbean Association for Feminist Research and Action (CAFRA), PO Box 442, Tunapuna, PO Tunapuna, Trinidad and Tobago

Center for Women's Global Leadership, Douglass College, 27 Clifton Avenue, New Brunswick, New Jersey 08903, USA

Change, PO Box 824, London SE24 9JS, UK

Committee for Asian Women (CAW), 57 Peking Road, 4/F, Kowloon, Hong Kong

Development Alternatives with Women for a New Era (DAWN), c/o Women and Development Unit (WAND), School of Continuing Studies, Pinelands, St Michael, Barbados

FEMNET, PO Box 54562, Nairobi, Kenya

Fempress, Casilla 16-637, Correo 9, Santiago, Chile

FIRE, PO Box 88, Santa Ana, Costa Rica

Flora Tristan Centre, Hernan Velarde 40, Lima 1, Peru

Inter-African Committee on Traditional Practices (IAC), 147 rue de Lausanne, CH-1202 Geneva, Switzerland

Inter-Parliamentary Union (IPU), Place du Petit-Saconnex, CH-1211, Geneva 19, Switzerland

International Baby Foods Action Network (IBFAN) PO Box 19, 10700 Penang, Malaysia

International Confederation of Free Trade Unions (ICFTU), 37–41 rue Montagne-aux-herbes-potagères, B-1000 Brussels, Belgium

International Council of Jewish Women (ICJW), 1110 Finch Avenue West, Suite 518, Downsview, M3J2T2 Canada

International Council on Social Welfare (ICSW), Koestlergasse 1/29, A-1060 Vienna, Austria

International Council on Women (ICW), 13 rue Caumartin, 75009 Paris, France

International Federation of University Women (IFUW) 37 Quai Wilson, CH-1201, Geneva, Switzerland

International Organization of Consumers Unions (IOCU), Regional Office for Asia and the Pacific, PO Box 1045, 10838 Penang, Malaysia

International Women's Rights Action Watch (IWRAW), c/o Women, Public Policy and Development Project, Humphrey Institute of Public Affairs, University of Minnesota, 301 19th Avenue South, Minneapolis, MN 55455, USA

International Women's Tribune Centre (IWTC), 777 United Nations Plaza, New York, NY 10017, USA

Isis International, PO Box 1837 Quezon City Main, Quezon City 1100, Philippines; and Casilla 2067, Correo Central, Santiago, Chile

Isis-Women's International Cross Cultural Exchange (Isis-WICCE), Box 4934, Kampala, Uganda

Kali for Women, A-36 Gulmohar Park, New Delhi, 100 049, India

La Leche League International, 9616 Minneapolis Avenue, PO Box 1209, Franklin Park, IL 60131, USA

Latin American and Caribbean Women's Health Network, Casilla 2067, Correo Central, Santiago, Chile

Lutheran World Federation/World Council of Churches, PO Box 2100, 150 route de Ferney, CH-1211, Geneva 20, Switzerland

Sister Namibia Collective, PO Box 40092, Windhoek, Namibia

Sistren Theatre Collective, 20 Kensington Crescent, Kingston 5, Jamaica

Soroptimist International, 19 Crofton Court, Heaten, Bradford BD9 5PG, West Yorkshire, UK

Speak Magazine, PO Box 261363, Excom, Johannesburg 2023, South Africa

Tanzanian Media Women's Association (TAMWA), Box 6143, Dar es Salaam, Tanzania

Women in Law and Development Africa (WiLDAF), PO Box UA 171, Union Avenue, Harare, Zimbabwe

Women Living Under Muslim Law, PO Box 23, 34790 Grabels, Montpellier, France

Women's Action Group, PO Box 135, Harare, Zimbabwe

Women's Environment and Development Organization (WEDO), 845 Third Avenue, 15th floor, New York, NY 10022, USA

Women's Feature Service, 49 Golf Links, New Delhi 110 003, India

Women's Global Network on Reproductive Rights, NZ Voorburgwaal 32, 1012 RZ, Amsterdam, The Netherlands

Women's International League for Peace and Freedom (WILPF), 1 rue de Varembé, CP 28, CH-1211, Geneva 10, Switzerland

WorldWIDE, Suite 903, 1331 H St., NW, Washington DC, USA

Young Women's Christian Association (YWCA), 37 Quai Wilson, CH-1201, Geneva, Switzerland

Zonta International, 557 West Randolph Street, Chicago, IL 60661–2206, USA

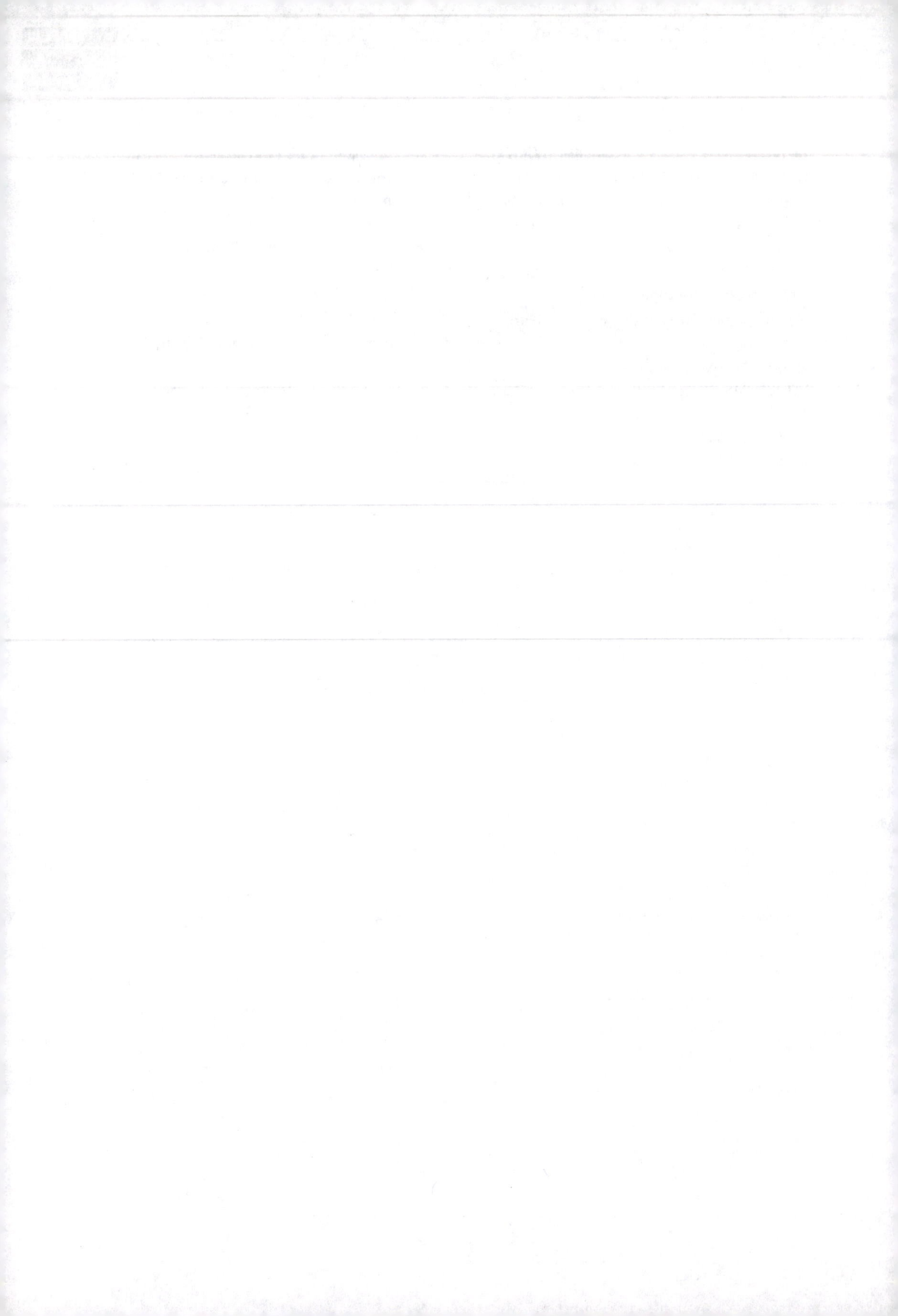

SELECTIVE BIBLIOGRAPHY

Abzug, Bella with Mim Kelber (1984) *Gender Gap: Bella Abzug's Guide to Political Power for American Women*, Houghton Mifflin Co., Boston.

Alatas, S. Masturah *True Picture on Rights of Muslim Women*, Sisters in Islam, Bangear Park, Malaysia.

Alva, Margaret (1989) 'Women in public life', paper for Expert Group Meeting on Equality in Political Participation, UN DAW, Vienna.

Anand, Anita (1993) 'The legacy of UNCED', *UNIFEM News*, Vol. 1, No. 1.

Baha'i International Community (1993) *One Country*, Vol. 5, No. 3.

Batliwala, Srilatha (1993) *Empowerment of Women in South Asia: Concepts and Practices*, FAO, FFHC/AD, New Delhi.

Beard, Mary R. (1973) *Women as a Force in History*, Collier Books, New York.

Bhasin, Kamla (1993), 'Gender workshops with men: experiences and reflections', unpublished paper.

Bhasin, Kamla and Nighat Said Khan (1993) *Some Questions on Feminism and its Relevance in South Asia*, Kali for Women, New Delhi.

Boulding, Elise (1976) *The Underside of History*, Westview Press, Colorado.

Bunch, Charlotte (1982) 'Copenhagen and beyond: prospects for global feminism', *Quest: A Feminist Quarterly*, Vol. 5, No. 4.

Bunch, Charlotte (1993) 'Human rights, development and violence against women', paper for the OECD-DAC, WID Expert Group Seminar, May.

Bussey, Gertrude and Margaret Tims (1980) *Pioneers for Peace: Women's International League for Peace and Freedom 1915–1965*, Alden Press, Oxford.

Carrillo, Roxanna (1992) *Battered Dreams*, UNIFEM, New York.

Chen, Marty (1989) 'Developing non-craft employment for women in Bangladesh', in Ann Leonard (ed.), *Seeds: Supporting Women's Work in the Third World*, Feminist Press, New York.

Chowdhury, Najma (1991) 'Role of women in public life in developing countries', paper for Expert Group Meeting on the Role of Women in Public Life, UN DAW, Vienna.

Committee for Asian Women and Korean Women Workers Association (1992) *When the Hen Crows … Korean Women Workers' Educational Programs*, CAW, Hong Kong.

Dahlerup, Drude (1991) 'Women in political and public life' in *CEDAW Conference on the United Nations Convention on the Elimination of All Forms of Discrimination Against Women, 25–31 October 1991, Aarhus, Denmark*, International Alliance of Women and Danish Women's Society, Copenhagen.

Duley, Margot I. and Mary I. Edwards (eds.) (1976) *The Cross-cultural Study of Women*, Feminist Press, New York.

FEMNET News (1993) Vol. 2, No. 3.

Fleck, Susan (1992) 'Extension "woman to woman" – training peasant women liaisons to reach peasant women', FAO.

Flexner, Eleanor (1972) *Century of Struggle*, Atheneum, New York.

Food and Agriculture Organization (FAO) (1991) 'The FAO Gender Analysis Training Programme for Professional Staff', FAO, Rome.

Food and Agriculture Organization, Freedom From Hunger Campaign (FAO/FFHC) (1989) *Pressing Against the Boundaries*, Report of an FAO-FFHC/AD South Asia Workshop on Women and Development, FAO, New Delhi.

Fraser, Arvonne (1993) *Women and Public Life*, IWRAW, Minneapolis.

Fraser, Arvonne and Miranda Kazentsis (1992) *CEDAW No. 11*, Report of the International Women's Rights Action Watch, August.

Fuglesang, Andreas and Dale Chandler

(1986) *Participation as Process – What We Can Learn from Grameen Bank, Bangladesh*, Norwegian Ministry of Development Co-operation, Oslo.

Griffen, Vanessa (ed.) (1987) *Women, Development and Empowerment: A Pacific Feminist Perspective*, Asian and Pacific Development Centre, Kuala Lumpur.

Helsinki Watch and Women's Rights Project, *News from Helsinki Watch*, Vol. IV, No. 5, 12 March 1992.

van den Hombergh, Heleen (1993) *Gender, Environment and Development: A Guide to the Literature*, International Books, Utrecht.

International Baby Food Action Network (IBFAN) *Fighting for Infant Survival: An Information Kit on the Promotion, Protection and Support of Breastfeeding*, IBFAN, Penang.

International Confederation of Free Trade Unions (ICFTU) (1992) *Equality: The Continuing Challenge – Strategies for Success*, ICFTU, Belgium.

International Federation of University Women (1993) *IFUW News*, January/February 1993.

International Labour Organization (ILO) (1993) *World of Work*, No. 2.

International Planned Parenthood Federation (IPPF), International Union for the Conservation of Nature (IUCN) and United Nations Population Fund (1993) *People and the Planet*, Vol. 2, No. 1.

International Research and Training Institute for the Advancement of Women (INSTRAW) (1992) *INSTRAW NEWS*, No. 17.

International Women's Tribune Centre (1993) *'95 Preview*, No. 2, October.

Inter-Parliamentary Union (IPU) (1992) 'Women and political power: survey carried out among the 150 national parliaments existing as of 31 October 1991', *Reports and Documents*, No. 19.

Inter-Parliamentary Union (IPU) (1993) *Distribution of Seats Between Men and Women in the 170 Parliaments Existing at 30 June 1993*, IPU, Geneva.

ISIS (1983) *Women in Development: A Resource Guide for Organization and Action*, ISIS, Rome and Geneva.

Isis International (1986) *Women, Struggles and Strategies*, Isis International, Rome.

Isis International (1991) *Directory of Third World Women's Publications*, Isis International, Manila and Santiago.

Isis International (1986) 'The Latin American Women's Movement', *Isis International Women's Journal*, No. 5.

Isis International (1992) *Women's Health Journal, No. 1.*

Isis International (1993) *Mujeres en Accion*, No. 2.

Isis International, *Women in Action*, Nos. 4 (1989), 6. (1986).

Isis Women's International Cross Cultural Exchange (ISIS-WICCE) (1991/92) *Women's World*, No. 26.

Janova, Mira and Mariette Sineau (1992) 'Women's participation in political power in Europe, an essay in East–West comparison', *Women's Studies International Forum*, Vol. 15, No. 1.

Jayawardena, Kumari (1986) *Feminism and Nationalism in the Third World*, Zed Books, London.

Kalima, Rose (1992) *Where Women Are Leaders: The SEWA Movement in India*, Zed Books, London.

Kihoro, Wanjiru (1992) 'Why African women are still left behind', *Third World Network Features*, No. 967.

Lutheran World Federation (1992) *A Clear Plan of Action*, LWF, Geneva.

Mabandla, Brigette (1992) 'Increased awareness by women of their rights', paper for Expert Group Meeting on Increased Awareness by Women of their Rights, including Legal Literacy, UN DAW, Vienna.

Manushi (1981) No. 8.

Miller, Carol (1992) 'Lobbying the League: women's organizations and the League of Nations', unpublished PhD thesis, University of Oxford.

Moghadam, Valentine M. (1993) *Modernizing Women: Gender and Social Change in the Middle East*, Lynne Reiner Publishers, Boulder.

Morna, Colleen Lowe (1992) 'Women farmers lead the way', in Women's Feature Service, *The Power to Change*, Kali for Women, New Delhi.

Moser, Caroline O.N. (1993) *Gender Planning and Development: Theory, Practice and Training*, Routledge, London.

Nzomo, Maria (1991) 'Women in politics and decision-making in Kenya', paper for Expert Group Meeting on the Role of Women in Public Life, UN DAW, Vienna.

Pietilä, Hilkka and Jeanne Vickers (1990) *Making Women Matter: The Role of the United Nations*, Zed Books, London; updated, and revised edition, Zed Books, London, 1994.

Poats, Susan V. and Sandra L. Russo (1990) 'Training in Women in Development/ Gender Analysis in agricultural development: a review of experiences and lessons learned', FAO, Rome, Working Paper Series No. 8.

Pronk, Jan (1991) 'Advancing towards autonomy', *Informatie*, No. 16.

Rau, Aruna, Mary B. Anderson and Catherine A. Overholt (1991) *Gender Analysis in Development Planning*, Kumarian Press, West Hartford.

Report of the International Workshop on Feminist Ideology and Structures in the First Half of the Decade for Women (1979) Asian and Pacific Centre for Development Women's Programme, Kuala Lumpur.

Rowbotham, Sheila (1974) *Women, Resistance and Revolution*, Vintage Books, New York.

Sen, Gita and Caren Grown (1987) *Development, Crisis, and Alternative Visions: Third World Women's Perspectives*, Monthly Review Press, New York.

Sister Namibia (1990) Vol. 2, No. 1.

Sivard, Ruth Leger (1993) *World Military Expenditures*, World Priorities, Washington, DC.

Speak, Nos. 29 (1990), 32 (1990), 34 (1991), 40 (1992).

Staudt, Kathleen (1989) 'Women in high-level political decision-making', paper for Expert Group Meeting on Equality in Political Participation and Decision-Making, UN DAW, Vienna.

Steady, Filomena Chioma (1992) 'Review of the implications for women of the recommendations of the 1992 Earth Summit', UNCED.

Stephens, Alexandra (1992a) 'Decolonising agricultural information', FAO Regional Office for Asia and the Pacific (FAO/RAPA), Bangkok.

Stephens, Alexandra (1992b) 'Women's participation in environmental management', paper for the Food and Agriculture Organization Regional Office for Asia and the Pacific (FAO/RAPA), September.

Tanzanian Media Women's Association (TAMWA) (1992) *Sauti ya Siti*, November.

United Nations (10 October 1991) 'Development and international economic co-operation – effective mobilization and integration of women in development', Report of the Secretary-General, United Nations General Assembly, Forty-sixth session, Agenda item 77(j), (A/46/464).

United Nations (1985) *The Nairobi Forward-looking Strategies for the Advancement of Women*, UN, New York.

United Nations (1991) *The World's Women 1970–1990, Trends and Statistics*, UN, New York.

United Nations Children's Fund (UNICEF) (1992) *Strategies to Promote Girls' Education*, UNICEF, New York.

United Nations Children's Fund (UNICEF) (1993) 'The women's empowerment framework', *Women and Girls Advance*, Vol. 1, No. 1.

United Nations Development Programme (UNDP) (1993) *Human Development Report 1993*, UNDP, New York.

United Nations Division for the Advancement of Women (UN DAW) (1989a) 'Expert group meeting on equality in political participation and decision-making report', UN DAW, Vienna.

United Nations Division for the Advancement of Women (UN DAW) (1989b) 'Women and decision-making', paper for Expert Group Meeting on Equality in Political Participation, UN DAW, Vienna.

United Nations Division for the Advancement of Women (UN DAW) (1992a) 'Public life: women make a difference', *Women 2000*, No. 2.

United Nations Division for the Advancement of Women (UN DAW) (1992b) 'Women in government', statistical extracts from the DAW Data Base on Women in Decision-Making, UN DAW, Vienna.

United Nations Economic Commission for Latin America and the Caribbean (ECLAC) (1989) *Women and Politics in Latin America and the Caribbean*, ECLAC, Santiago.

United Nations Library of Geneva (1993) *1843–1993 Bertha von Suttner and Other Women in Pursuit of Peace*, United Nations, Geneva.

United Nations Non-Governmental Liaison Service (NGLS) (1993) *Go-Between*, No. 40.

United Nations World Conference on Women Secretariat (1993) 'Guidelines for preparatory activities for the Fourth World Conference on Women: Action for Equality, Development and Peace'.

Vickers, Jeanne (1993) *Women and War*, Zed Books, London.

Weerasekera, Yeshica and Diop, Amie (1993) 'Modest but vital steps: changing women's lives in rural Senegal', African Network for Integrated Development.

Willis, Virginia (1991) 'Public life: women make a difference', paper for Expert Group Meeting on the Role of Women in Public Life, UN DAW, Vienna.

Women and Development Unit (WAND) (1990) *Womenspeak*, Nos. 26 and 27.

Woman's Action Group (1992) *Speak Out*, No. 19.

Women's International League for Peace and Freedom (WILPF) (1919) *Report of the International Congress of Women, Zurich, May 12 to 17, 1919*, WILPF, Geneva.

Women's Watch (1993) Vol. 6, No. 1.

Young, Kate (1993) *Planning Development With Women: Making a World of Difference*, Macmillan, London.

INDEX

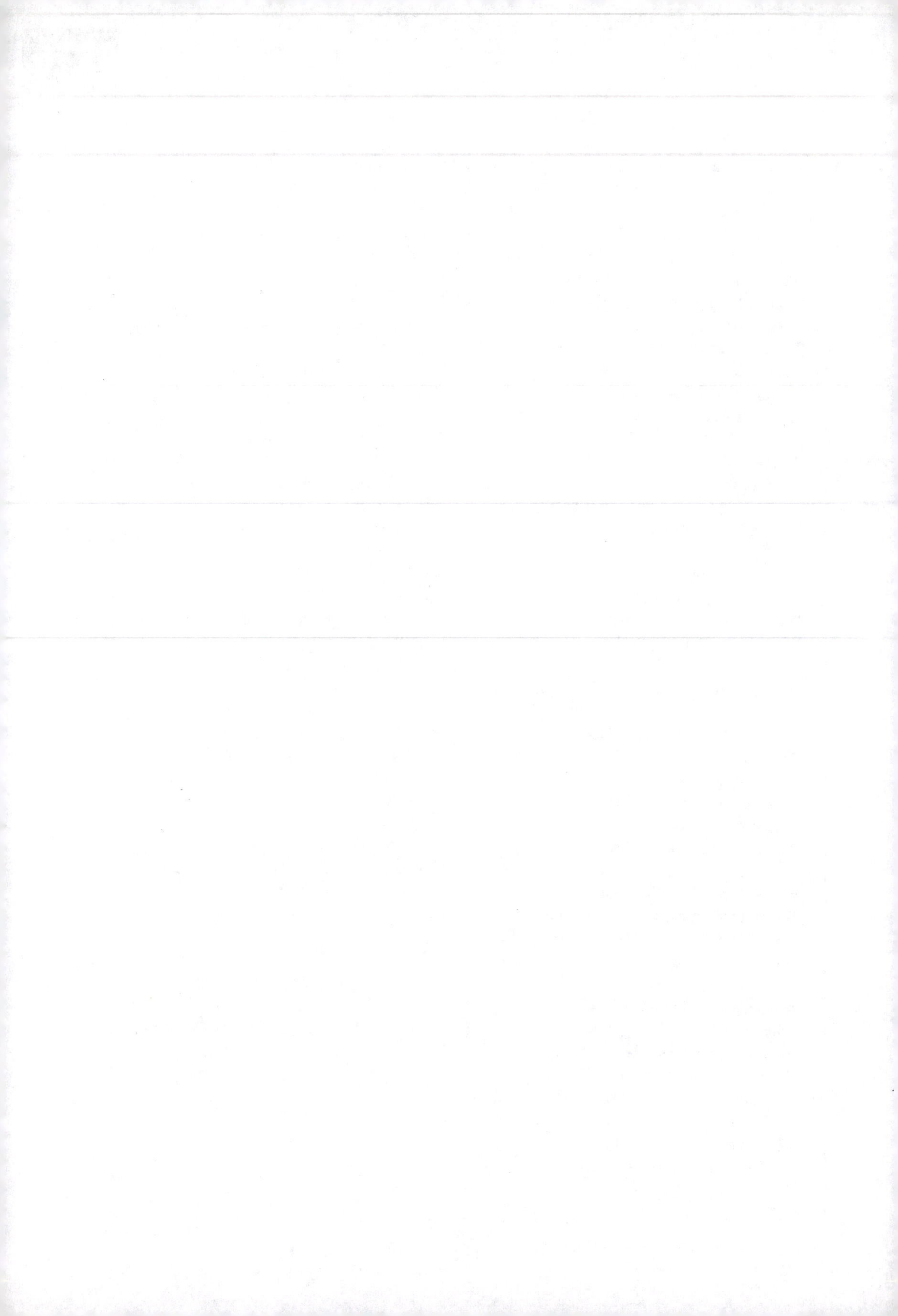

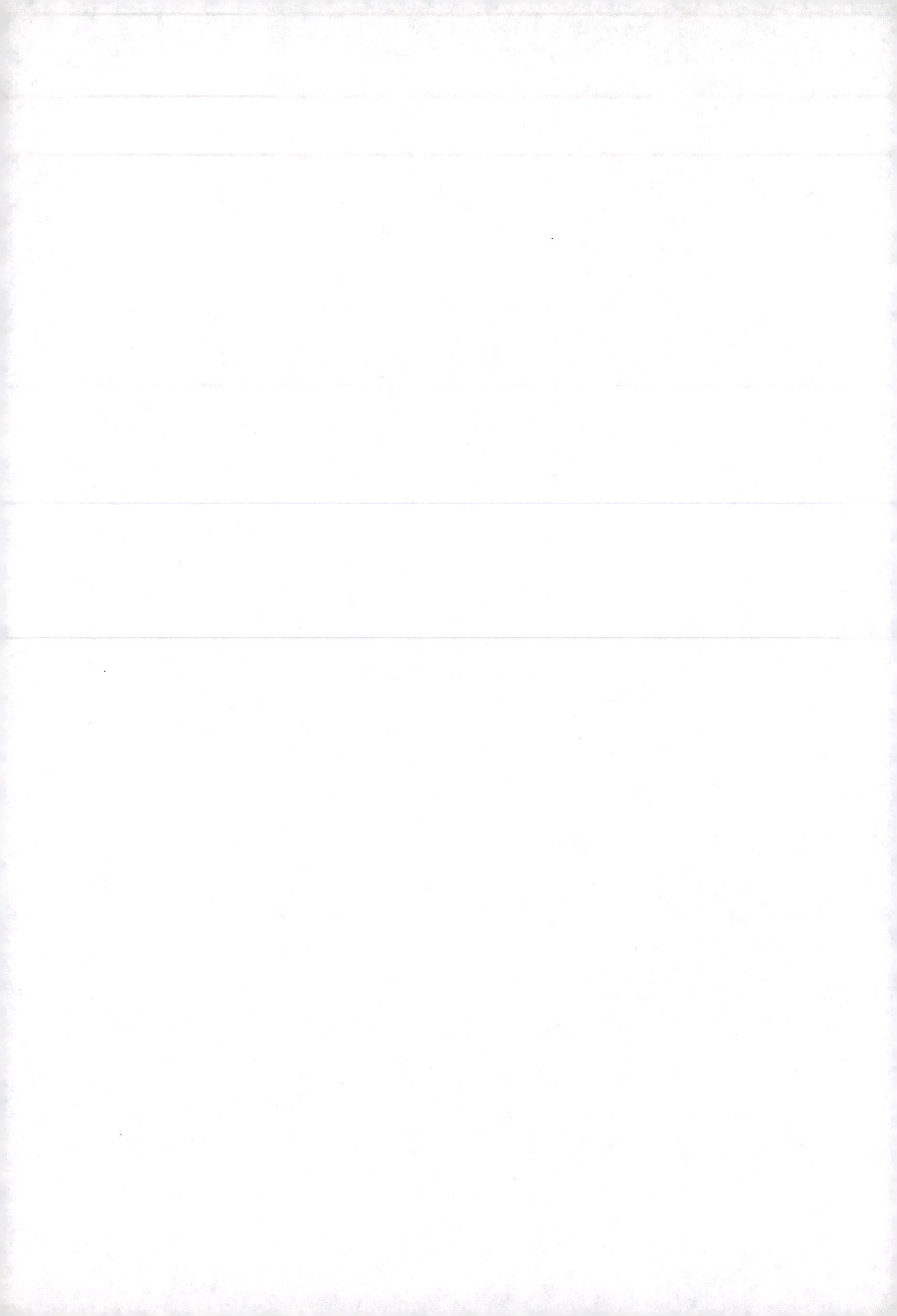

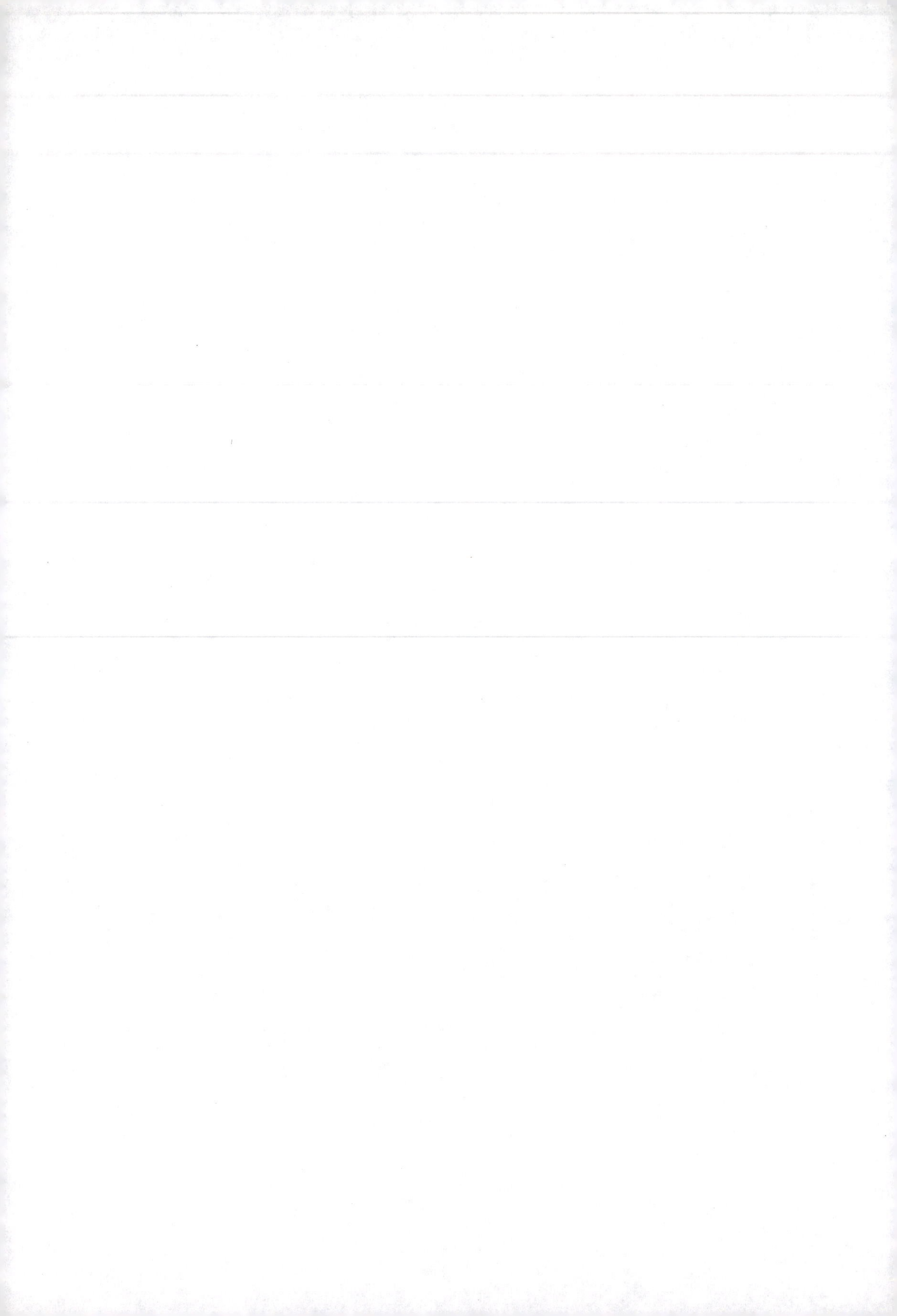

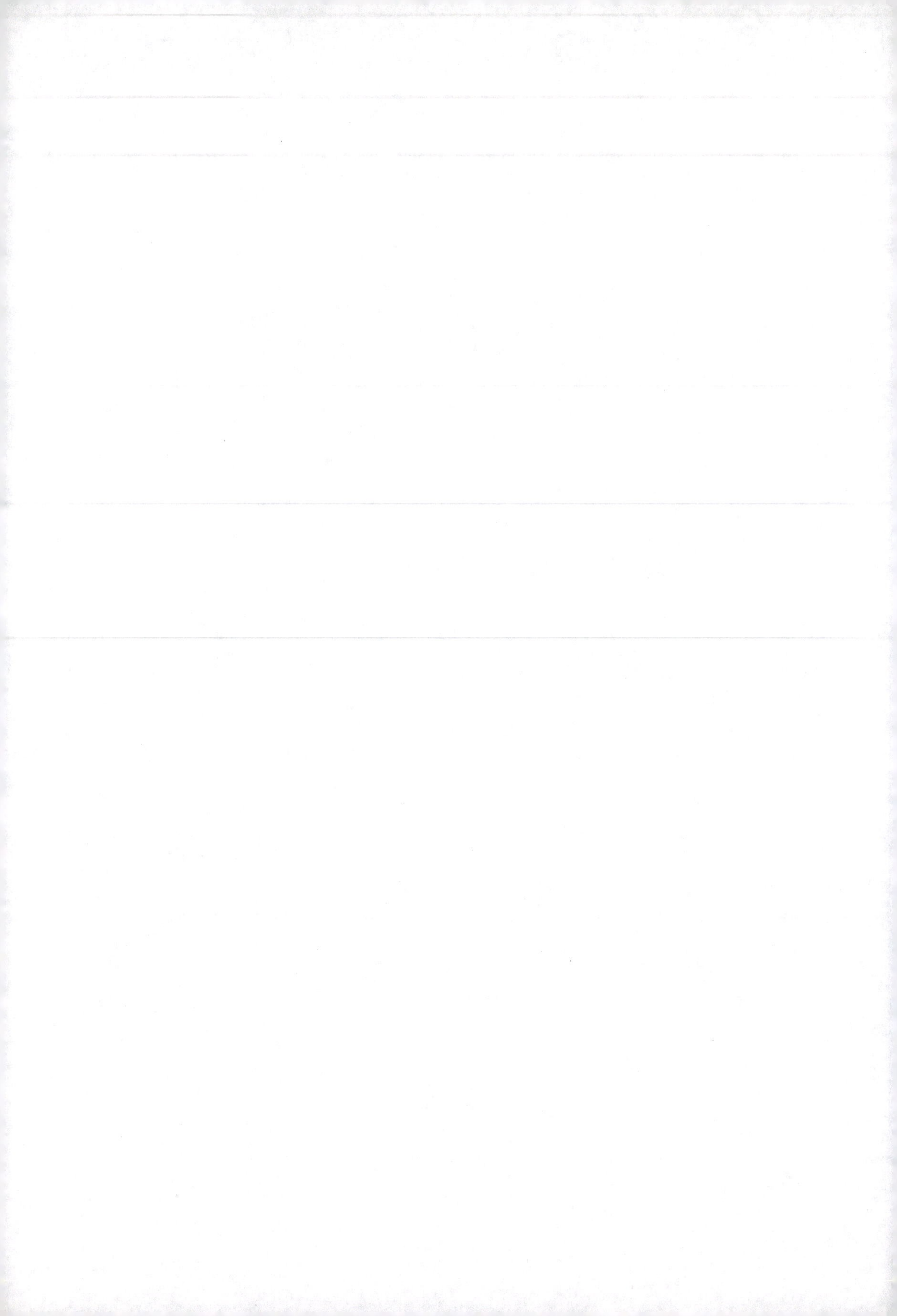

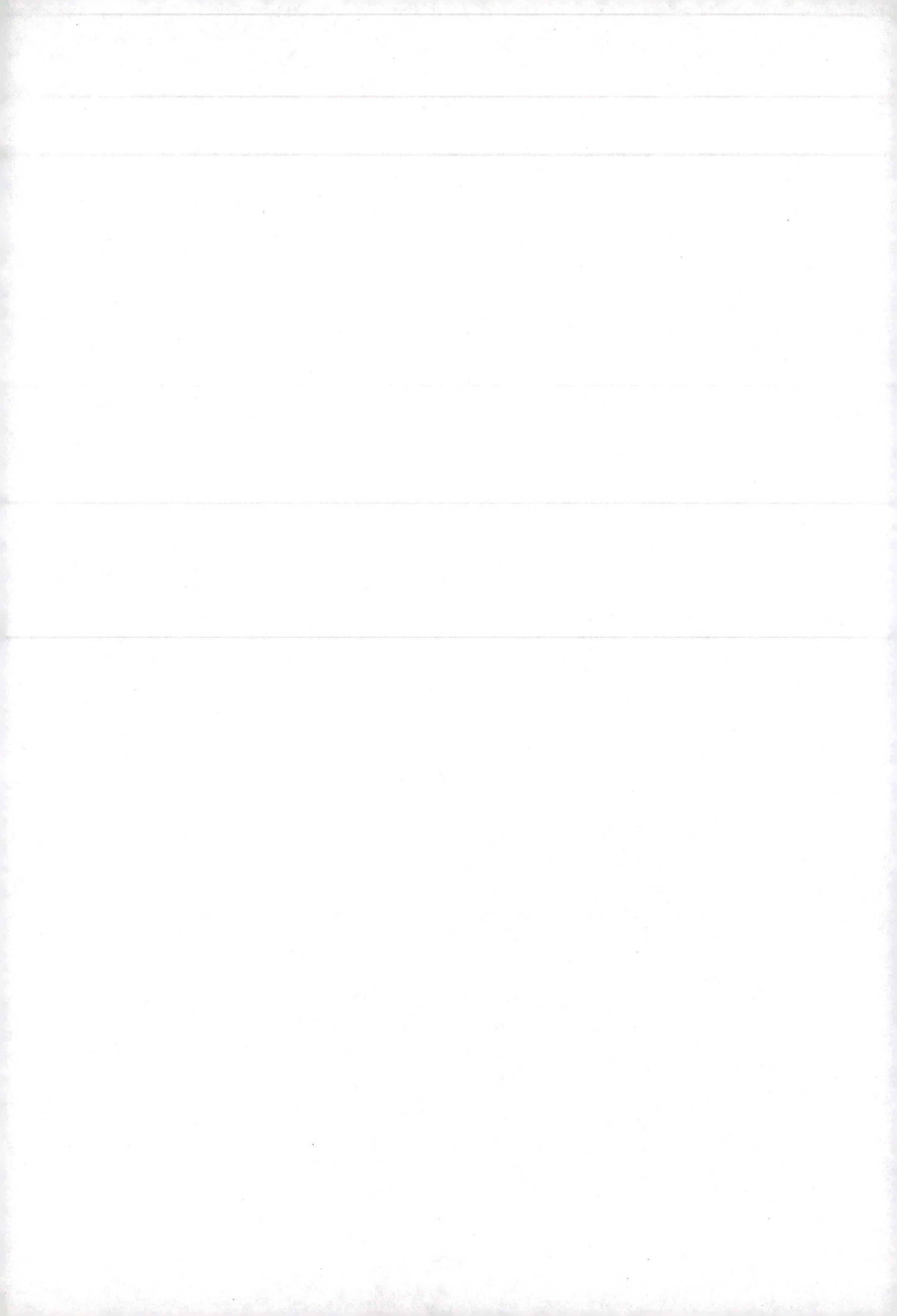